The Story of the Crusades

by the same author

★

The Story of the Crusades
1097–1291

by
ALFRED DUGGAN

With drawings by
C. WALTER HODGES

FABER AND FABER
24 Russell Square
London

First published in 1963
by Faber and Faber Limited
24 Russell Square London W.C.1
First published in this edition 1969
Printed in Great Britain by
The Bowering Press Plymouth
All rights reserved
© 1963 by Alfred Duggan

SBN 571 08990 9 (FPCE)
SBN 571 05619 9 (cloth)

Contents

Contents

Illustrations

PHOTOGRAPHS

1 BEAUFORT on the river Litani, belonged to the Lord of
Sidon. Besieged unsuccessfully by Saladin 1188. Captured
by Saladin 1190. Returned to the Christians by treaty 1240.
Garrisoned by Templars 1260. Fell to Bibars 1268.
> (*Photo courtesy Institut français d'archéologie de Beyrouth*)
>
> *facing page* 32

2 KRAK DES CHEVALIERS built in the reign of King Fulk,
1131–1143, to guard the fertile plain inland from Tripoli.
The Chevaliers are the Knights of the Hospital, who held it
because it was too exposed to be held by a lay lord. Besieged
unsuccessfully by Saladin 1188. Fell to Bibars 1271.
> (*Photo courtesy Institut français d'archéologie de Beyrouth*)
>
> *facing page* 33

3A KERAK IN MOAB built 1142 by Pain, Butler to King Fulk,
as the chief fortress of Outrejordan. In 1183 Saladin came to
the famous wedding feast held there. Later the headquarters
of Reynald of Chatillon. Captured by Saladin, after a long
and desperate siege, in 1188.
> (*Photo courtesy Cambridge University Press*)
>
> *facing page* 64

3B SIDON: The Castle of the Sea. Captured by King Baldwin I,
with naval assistance from Norway and Venice, in 1100.
The lordship of Sidon became one of the four great fiefs of
the Kingdom of Jerusalem. Fell to Saladin 1187. Recaptured
by Christians 1197. Fortified by St Louis 1253. Garrisoned
by Templars 1260. Evacuated 1291.
> (*Photo courtesy Institut français d'archéologie de Beyrouth*)
>
> *facing page* 64

7

Illustrations

4   MASIAF in the Nosairi mountains west of the upper
Orontes was never a Christian castle, though the army of the
First Crusade marched by it in 1099. From 1176 until *c.* 1250
it belonged to the Old Man of the Mountains, the chief of
the Assassins. But his famous enchanted garden was at the
castle of Alamut in Persia.

(Photo courtesy Institut français d'archéologie de Beyrouth)

facing page 65

DRAWINGS

MAPS

Note on Sources

For many of my facts I am indebted to Sir Steven Runciman, whose *History of the Crusades*, 3 volumes, Cambridge University Press, 1951–1954, will long remain the standard authority in English on this subject.

Other books which have greatly helped me are:

Sir Charles Oman: *A History of the Art of War in the Middle Ages*, 2 volumes, Methuen, 1924.

R. C. Smail: *Crusading Warfare*, Cambridge University Press, 1956.

R. Ewart Oakeshott: *The Archaeology of Weapons*, Lutterworth Press, 1960.

CHAPTER I

The Holy Places

Ever since the Church was founded at the first Pentecost there have been Christians in Jerusalem; though sometimes they took refuge in the countryside while the Holy City was attacked by hostile armies. In particular two Jewish revolts against Rome brought terrible retribution. In A.D. 71 the Temple was destroyed after a bitter and destructive siege; in A.D. 135 the Emperor Hadrian rebuilt captured Jerusalem as a normal Roman town, with temples in which the usual Roman gods were worshipped. But the Church endured. There has always been a Bishop, successor to St James; and a congregation, however small, for him to rule.

Therefore when the Emperor Constantine recognised Christianity as the official religion of the Roman Empire, some 300 years after the Passion, the sites of the main Holy Places were still remembered; just as we can still identify the sites burned in the Great Fire of London, 300 years ago. Constantine's mother, St Helena, could go straight to Calvary, where she dug up the True Cross. The well-remembered tomb where the Body of God had lain for three days is so near the place of Crucifixion that she was able to include both under the roof of a mighty Roman basilica, the Church of the Holy Sepulchre. A new city-wall was built out to the north to include this great shrine; for Calvary, like most places of execution, was originally outside the city. About the same time the Church of the Nativity was built at Bethlehem; and other Holy Places, some of less certain authenticity, were worthily commemorated. Pilgrims came to Jerusalem from all parts of the Roman Empire, as they have come ever since to this day.

The Emperor Constantine also founded a new capital at the city of Byzantium, renamed Constantinople in his honour. But by about the year 400 it was recognised that the troubles of the time were too grave to be dealt with by one sovereign, and the Empire was divided. The lands west of the Adriatic were ruled by an Emperor whose capital was nominally Rome, though in fact he lived at Ravenna; the Balkans and Asia Minor were ruled by the Emperor in Constantinople.

The western Empire was overrun by warlike barbarians, our ancestors. But the eastern Empire flourished until by the year 600 Constantinople ruled all the Greek lands of Europe and Asia, and in addition southern Italy and the north African coast right up to Morocco. The Emperor of Constantinople was by far the most powerful monarch in the known world; his only rival was the Emperor of pagan Persia, on his eastern frontier.

The east-Romans were devout Christians; though in Egypt and Syria the natives supported heretical sects because they disliked being ruled by Bishops sent from Constantinople. But the organisation of the eastern Church, whose liturgy was said in Greek, differed greatly from that of the west, whose Mass was said in Latin. In the west all Christians obeyed the Pope, who represented among other things the vanished civilisation of Rome; in Constantinople the unquestioned head of the

Church was the Emperor, who bore among his official titles that of Isapostolos, Equal to the Apostles. He appointed the Patriarchs of Jerusalem, Antioch, Alexandria and Constantinople, and might dismiss them at his whim. The Greeks agreed that the Pope was the senior Patriarch, but they would not take orders from him alone. They held that doctrine should be settled by a General Council, or at least by an agreement of the five Patriarchs; and that in matters of discipline their Emperor was supreme. Unfortunately the Empire was not hereditary. In theory the Emperor was elected by the people and the army; in practice he was often a successful soldier who had seized power by murdering his superior officer. Fear of rebellion might make him a cruel tyrant; and the more competent soldier-Emperors knew little of Church affairs.

In 610 the Persians invaded the Empire. In 614 they captured Jerusalem, with help from the large Jewish community within the city. Sixty-five thousand Christians were massacred, and the thirty-five thousand survivors sold into slavery. The Persians burned the Church of the Holy Sepulchre, and carried off the True Cross as a trophy of victory. In 630, after years of bitter fighting, the Emperor Heraclius defeated them and forced them to return the True Cross. A large part of it was sent back to Jerusalem; though to avoid another such disaster portions were sent to Constantinople and Rome. From these fragments many tiny splinters have been taken, the relics now venerated in churches all over the world.

For his liberation of Jerusalem Heraclius was reverenced by posterity as the first Crusader. But the war had continued for nineteen years, with appalling devastation from the Bosphorus right up to Mesopotamia. Both Persia and the Empire were greatly weakened.

Meanwhile, in 622, Mahomet began to preach among the Arabs. When he died ten years later Islam was supreme in Arabia. The Moslems appointed as the successor of Mahomet a Caliph, a supreme temporal and religious ruler, and under his guidance set out to conquer the world.

They met with amazing success. Both the east-Romans and

the Persians were too war-weary to undertake another long struggle. In 638 Jerusalem surrendered to the Caliph Omar. By 717 the Moslems had conquered the whole northern coastline of Africa, southern Spain, the Persian Empire and the eastern lands as far as India. But after the Moslem invasion had reached the very walls of Constantinople the east-Romans rallied; in Asia Minor the frontier of Christendom was fixed at the Taurus Mountains. Though the Caliph was now the most powerful ruler in the world the Emperor in Constantinople was still the most powerful Christian ruler.

In Jerusalem the Church survived. As well as a creed, Mahomet had laid down a code of laws for his followers, and in it he made provision for conquered peoples who would not accept Islam. For idolaters there was no mercy; conversion or death were the alternatives. But those who worshipped One God, the Peoples of the Book—Zoroastrians, Jews, and Christians—might live in peace under Moslem masters. Of course they must accept certain disabilities. They must pay an annual tax for the privilege of being left alive; they might never ride a horse nor carry a weapon; they might not convert a Moslem nor marry a Moslem girl, though Moslems might take Christian girls by force into their harems. Existing churches, including the Church of the Holy Sepulchre, remained Christian, but no new ones might be built. (This rule could be dodged by judicious bribery.) Disputes between Christians were judged by their own clergy, who were held responsible for the good behaviour of the laity and hanged if their flock rebelled. Such a life was not intolerable, and the Christians of Syria tolerated it; except for the mountaineers of Lebanon who became defiant Christian rebels. But these mountaineers had usually been in rebellion against the tax-collector from the plain.

The Christians of Syria and Palestine still regarded the Emperor in Constantinople as the head of their church. The Caliphs respected his military power, and heeded his protests on behalf of his fellow-Christians. Pilgrims continued to visit Jerusalem, welcomed by the Moslem rulers for the money they brought into the country.

In 800 the Pope crowned Charlemagne as Emperor. This new Empire naturally annoyed the Greeks, as we may now call the east-Romans. So Charlemagne negotiated directly with the Caliph Haroun al Raschid, who recognised him as protector of Latin pilgrims and allowed him to set up Latin hostels in Jerusalem for their convenience.

In the 10th century the Greeks grew stronger. They reconquered Cilicia and in 969 took the great city of Antioch. By this time there was no single Caliph ruling the whole Moslem world. A Caliph in Baghdad reigned over Mesopotamia and the east, while a Caliph in Cairo was obeyed by Africa; but both these Caliphs were spiritual figureheads whose power was wielded by the commanders of their armies.

In 1004 the Caliph of Cairo, Hakim, went mad. In an effort to extirpate Christianity he ordered the destruction of the Church of the Holy Sepulchre. But soon after he proclaimed himself to be God, and his Moslem subjects got rid of him. The Greek Emperor was permitted to rebuild the Holy Sepulchre and all went on as before; except that the Druze community among the mountains of Syria still worship Hakim and wait for him to come again.

By 1050 western pilgrims were visiting Jerusalem in large numbers. The journey was reasonably safe, by the standards of those days. The Hungarians and the Poles had been recently converted. A German had only to travel down the Danube, among Christians, until he entered the Greek Empire at Belgrade; then the Emperor's police would guard him until he reached Antioch. At the Syrian frontier he bought a safe-conduct from the officials of the Egyptian Caliph, who policed the road as far as the Holy Places. From France or England the normal route was by way of Rome to Bari, the capital of the Greek province of Italy, and then across the Adriatic to Durazzo at the head of the great road to Constantinople. Of course such a long journey had its hazards, and the expense was very great. A pilgrimage to Jerusalem, imposed as a penance, got rid of a disturber of the peace for at least a couple of years; and by the time he came back he would be too poor to make trouble. Sweyn Godwinsson, Harold's brother, was ordered to make the journey as a penance for his many crimes; in 1052, on his way back, he died of exposure among the mountains of Asia. But Nature was the most dangerous enemy; both Greeks and Moslems welcomed Latin pilgrims.

Two migrations broke up this peaceful arrangement. The Normans had a particular devotion to the warrior-angel St Michael, whose most famous shrine is on Monte Gargano in southern Italy. They went there in great numbers and presently intervened in the struggle between the Italian cities and their Greek governors. By 1059 the Pope had recognised the Norman leader Robert Guiscard as Duke of Apulia and Calabria, and Robert's brother Roger was campaigning against the Moslem rulers of Sicily.

Later the Normans crossed the Adriatic to pursue the war against the Emperor from whom they had conquered southern Italy. In Greece they won no permanent foothold, but they showed themselves to be dangerous neighbours. In Constantinople, where no one had hitherto bothered about barbarous Latins, the Normans were feared.

About the same time, the 1050s, the Turks appeared in Asia Minor. They were nomads from the steppe, moving south to pillage civilisation. They had recently become Moslems, though they were not yet strongly attached to their faith; they could sometimes be converted to Christianity, which could never be done with genuine Arab Moslems.

These uncouth Turks were awed by the superior culture of Baghdad. They could have overthrown the Caliph, but they preferred to be his servants; so long, of course, as the Caliph did what his servants told him. A Caliph who annoyed his Turkish advisers would be put away, and another Caliph chosen from the correct Arab family.

Turkish raids into the Greek Empire became more and more serious. All the raiders were mounted, usually driving a herd of spare horses, and the excellent Greek regular army seldom caught them before they had done grave damage. At last the Emperor Romanus Diogenes made up his mind that the only thing to do was to march east and fight a decisive battle with the Sultan of all the Turks wherever he might find him. In August 1071 the two armies met at Manzikert on the eastern frontier of the Empire near Lake Van.

The Emperor brought all the soldiers he could scrape together, perhaps as many as 100,000 horse. About half were drilled and disciplined heavy cavalry; the other half were the private retainers of noble families. The great weakness of the Empire was the lack of a true royal house, so that any famous general might snatch at the crown. Romanus, himself a famous general, had married the widow of the last Emperor; his young stepson Michael Ducas would share the throne when he came of age, unless in the meantime Romanus won such a great victory that his subjects begged him to reign alone. That was one reason why he wanted to fight a decisive battle. His second in command was Andronicus Ducas, a noble so powerful that the Emperor dared not leave him behind in Constantinople, and so well born that if he were present with the army he must hold a high command.

After a morning of hard fighting the Greeks began to give ground. They might have got away in good order, but Andronicus thought more of the interests of the house of Ducas than of the wellbeing of the Empire. He ordered the second line to retire, leaving the Emperor and his regular cavalry surrounded by the Turks. Romanus was wounded and captured.

The Empire never recovered from Manzikert. The regular army had been destroyed, and every surviving senior officer tried to win the throne for himself. Romanus bought his freedom, which made things worse by increasing the number of pretenders. Turkish bands roamed through Asia Minor, destroying the farms and killing the peasants until the richest and most populous part of the Empire had become a desert. For a time the great walled cities held out; but their garrisons no longer took orders from Constantinople, where rival Emperors continually rose and fell. The Turks entered Nicaea as mercenaries of a pretender; after he had been defeated they remained. Another Turkish chieftain gained possession of

Smyrna and began to build a pirate fleet. The great fortress of
Antioch was ruled by an Armenian general in the Greek army,
who to keep it paid tribute to the Turks. In 1085 his son sold
the city to the infidel. Other Armenian princes moved into the
mountains of Taurus and took over the fortresses of Cilicia.
The Armenians, a warlike race, were Christian heretics. The
King of Armenia had established Christianity in his realm a
few years before it became the religion of the Roman Empire,
and the Armenians have never forgotten that theirs was the
first Christian state. They would rather pay tribute to the infidel
and keep their ancient creed than obey the Greek Orthodox
Patriarch of Constantinople.

During all this chaos and destruction there occurred an odd
little incident. Before Manzikert Romanus had hired a band of
Norman mercenaries from Italy, led by a knight named Roussel
de Balliol. They escaped the battle because they were besieging
a nearby fortress. After the disaster Roussel established himself
as independent ruler of the city of Amasia in Pontus. His
government was so just, orderly and cheap that his Greek
subjects preferred him to their own Emperor. A young Greek
noble, Alexius Comnenus, was sent to suppress him. Alexius
had to give out that he had blinded his prisoner to stop the
Amasians continuing to fight for their Norman lord. Roussel
was not in fact blinded, because Alexius also admired and liked
him. It seemed that Latins, especially Normans, might be a
grave danger to the Empire. Given the choice, Greeks of the
Orthodox faith would rather be ruled by Latin Normans than
by their own extortionate governors.

In 1054 the Pope excommunicated the Patriarch of Constantinople, and the Orthodox Church has remained in schism
ever since. At the time it was seen as a personal quarrel between
two angry prelates, a quarrel that would soon be healed. It did
not affect the other Patriarchates, Jerusalem, Antioch and
Alexandria, whose subjects remained in communion with both
Rome and Constantinople.

Asia Minor was infested with Turkish bands. In Syria every
city was ruled by a different Arab or Turkish chieftain. The

mountains were held by Armenian nobles. Each of these rulers was at war with all the others. Jerusalem was fairly well governed by the officers of the Egyptian Caliph, but it was impossible for a pilgrim to get there from the west.

In 1081 Alexius Comnenus became Emperor of Constantinople. He had no soldiers except foreign mercenaries; in Asia Minor he held nothing but a few scattered seaports; the Normans of Italy menaced his European possessions. But he still had a great deal of money, and he was a very intelligent statesman. Above all, he was a patriot, who thought first of the welfare of his Empire. He was not interested in the fate of the Holy Places, save in so far as they might be useful to his own country.

CHAPTER II

The Preaching of the Crusade

In the spring of 1095 Pope Urban II held a council at Piacenza in northern Italy, principally to pass sentence on the western Emperor, Henry VI. The western Empire, set up by Charlemagne in the year 800, was now known as the Holy Roman Empire of the German Nation, a pretty accurate description. It included all the German-speaking peoples, with a shadowy suzerainty over Scandinavia, Poland and Bohemia, and a legal claim to dominion in northern Italy from the Alps down to Rome; though Italians only obeyed the Emperor when he was present at the head of a German army.

From the extent of his dominions the western Emperor ought to have been a great potentate, but two things limited his power. He could not begin his reign until he had been elected by the magnates of Germany; and though at this period they normally elected the eldest son of the late Emperor he had to promise them a certain amount of independence before they would do it. Secondly, he could not use the imperial title until the Pope in person had crowned him in Rome. Henry IV got over this second difficulty by setting up in Rome an opposition Pope of his own choosing, who duly crowned him. But this anti-Pope was not recognised outside the Empire; and now Urban II, French by birth, supported by France, England and the Spanish kingdoms, had won back Rome and north Italy from the Imperialists. The long feud between Papalists and Imperialists, Guelfs and Ghibellines, was already beginning to divide Italy.

At Piacenza envoys from Constantinople waited on the Pope. Now that the mighty Turkish horde had split up into numerous bands the Emperor Alexius hoped to go over to the offensive. But he lacked soldiers. The trained regular army which had been destroyed 25 years ago at Manzikert had never been replaced; because its recruits came from Asia Minor, now devastated by the Turks. Alexius, who had plenty of money, relied on foreign mercenaries, either heathen Patzinak horse-bowmen from the steppe, or the Varangian Guard of Scandinavians and English who fought on foot with two-handed axes. He had no heavy cavalry, and perhaps he remembered how formidable had been the Norman knights who followed Roussel de Balliol. He asked the Pope to proclaim to the council that knights would be serving God if they took service with the Greek army in defence of the oppressed Christians of Asia Minor. Alexius did not forget that he was the head of a church which had broken away from the Pope. He explained that he could not now heal the schism, for if he ordered his subjects to submit to Rome they would overthrow him. Of course after he had conquered the Turks he would be more powerful, able to compel even his bishops to do as he said. In the meantime his Latin mercenaries might bring their own priests ... Alexius was always quite willing to heal the schism if the Pope would meet him halfway. No Greek understood that the Pope cannot go halfway to compromise with error.

Urban promised to ask for recruits at a convenient opportunity. He was all the more willing because he feared that Constantinople was not so strong as its Emperor supposed. At any moment the Turks might break in; and then they would be on the borders of the Latin west, his own responsibility.

· By September the Pope was in Provence, where he met the Count and the local bishops. He summoned another council to meet at Clermont in November.

No important western king was represented at this council.

The Emperor Henry was the Pope's enemy. William Rufus of England was scarcely a Christian at all, except when he thought himself to be dying. One object of the council was to excommunicate King Philip of France for his treatment of his Queen. The Scandinavian kings were too far off, and the Spanish kings too busy fighting the Moors. When Pope Urban made his great speech, on 27 November 1095, no important layman was present.

The Pope spoke first of the danger which threatened the Christians of the East; let the warriors of the West march to their rescue. But then he went on to tell of the oppression of the Church in Jerusalem, and of the sufferings of pilgrims to the Holy Places. That was what really appealed to the crowd. The Bishop of Le Puy, in southern France, was the first to volunteer. Thousands followed his example. The meeting broke up in confusion.

Next day the assembled Bishops drew up rules for the projected expedition. Volunteers would wear a cross of coloured cloth sewn on their tunics; hence they were called in Latin *Crucesignati*, from which we get the word Crusader. The Bishop of every diocese was charged to look after the property of volunteers during their absence. If they fulfilled their vow, or died in the attempt, their sins would be forgiven. But if they turned back halfway they would suffer excommunication. The vow, it should be noted, bound them to drive the infidel from Jerusalem, and said nothing about the rescue of the oppressed Christians of the East.

The council also decreed that during the winter the Crusade should be preached throughout the west, to attract lords of greater standing than had attended at Clermont. The volunteers must be ready to start by the Feast of the Assumption, 15 August 1096, and they were to proceed in the first instance to a rendezvous at Constantinople. The legate appointed by the Pope to control the expedition was Adhemar, Bishop of Le Puy: the first man to volunteer and also an experienced pilgrim who had already travelled to Jerusalem and back.

An expedition of this kind was a complete novelty. In the

past men had fought to defend Christendom from the heathen, and been honoured for it; but never before had they proposed to march out to liberate a shrine which had been long in infidel hands. For the first time, Christendom was taking the offensive.

It seems possible that Pope Urban, carried away by his own eloquence and by the enthusiasm of his hearers, did not know what he was going to say until he had heard himself saying it. Certainly the result was nothing like what had been planned at Piacenza. Alexius had asked the Pope to stimulate recruiting for his mercenary army; he wanted soldiers to fight against the Turks in Asia Minor. But the Crusaders would march out perhaps as his allies, perhaps merely taking advantage of his benevolent neutrality, certainly not as his paid soldiers obeying his orders. They would concentrate in Constantinople, so that to begin with they must wage war on some Turkish bands. But their objective was Jerusalem, a city Alexius did not particularly wish to capture. The present ruler of Jerusalem was the Caliph of Egypt, who was on friendly terms with the Emperor; since both saw the Turks as dangerous enemies.

Alexius wanted above all things to recover the recruiting ground of Asia Minor; for more than 400 years the Greek Empire had got on very well without the Holy Places. As for the Crusaders, their aims were not clearly stated. They were to rescue the Christians of the east, and also to liberate Jerusalem. But which objective came first, and must both be achieved?

This ambiguity of aim runs through all the history of the Crusades, and does much to explain their ultimate failure.

Meanwhile Alexius made plans for the reception of his allies. He supposed he had plenty of time.

The great lords of the west also knew that it would be long before they could start. In winter many roads were impassable, and in spring the whole west was usually short of food. They must wait until next year's corn was ripe, which would be the middle of August at earliest.

They would also need an unprecedented amount of money. A lord's army was normally made up of his landholding knights, who fought for him instead of paying rent. But these knights were obliged to fight only for home defence. When William the Conqueror invaded England the knights of Normandy refused to follow him as a matter of duty; for a foreign expedition they must be promised wages or at least a share of the conquered land. No knight was bound in duty to follow his lord on Crusade. Many came eagerly, but until they reached the lands of the infidel, where they might live by plunder, they would expect rations and perhaps wages.

The lords also had to arrange the government of their lands while they were away, and a thousand other things. Nine months was a short time in which to get ready.

But meanwhile, as the Crusade was preached throughout the west, lesser men with lesser responsibilities were too excited to wait. Some preachers, also, had little foresight, in particular a holy man named Peter. He seems to have been a runaway French monk who had recently tried to visit Jerusalem and been turned back, after grave ill-treatment, by the Turks. From his ragged appearance he acquired the nickname of Peter the Hermit, though since he marched in the midst of 15,000 men he cannot have valued solitude. He went about France and the Rhineland urging his hearers to drop everything and set out at once for Jerusalem. By Easter, April 1096, he was in Cologne with a large band, made up mostly of unarmed peasants.

Peter had enlisted a few rather disreputable knights, of whom the chief was one Walter, known as the Penniless. When the pilgrims set out through southern Germany on their way to Constantinople Walter and the other mounted men rode on ahead. The Hungarians welcomed and fed them. By the end of May they had reached the Hungarian town of Semlin, facing the Greek town of Belgrade on the farther bank of the river Save.

The Greek officials were taken by surprise. They were not sure that they wanted quite so many allies, and anyway they had been told to expect them in the autumn. The harvest had not yet been reaped, and there was little food to spare for unexpected strangers.

Annoyed at the delay, Walter's men pillaged Semlin until the

The Emperor Alexius Comnenus

Hungarians drove them across the river; then they plundered the country round Belgrade. Alexius sent food, and soldiers to escort them to Constantinople. As soon as they were fed the pilgrims went peaceably; they were not a very warlike army. In July they reached Constantinople safely.

Peter's infantry, following behind, were less orderly. After a peaceful journey through Hungary they sacked Semlin. At the crossing of the Save they quarrelled with their Greek escort, and sacked Belgrade. The Greek soldiers were heathen Patzinaks; it was tactless of Alexius to send them to escort Crusaders, but they were the most trustworthy of his mercenaries. The Crusaders then pushed on to attack Nish, but failed to take it. By now more Greek soldiers were arriving, and the harvest was ripe. Under a strong escort and with enough to eat they travelled peacefully, until on 1 August they reached Constantinople. Alexius inspected them and was disappointed. These were not the kind of men who had followed Roussel de Balliol. They would never defeat Turks. In the meantime they were thieving about the city, so on 6 August the Emperor shipped them across the straits to Asia.

Peter's men and Walter's were now united in the fortress of Civetot on the south shore of the Gulf of Nicomedia, within striking distance of the Turks in Nicaea. Their supplies came from Europe by sea. Alexius advised them to halt where they were until the great lords joined them.

Of course these peasant Crusaders pillaged the countryside. Since they did not understand that their Turkish enemies were a conquering aristocracy they plundered chiefly the Christian villagers. The French would not cooperate with the Germans. Peter stayed in Constantinople, to beg from the Emperor.

Presently the French, raiding close to Nicaea, defeated a party of Turks and brought home a great herd of cattle. Determined to do better, the Germans attacked a castle beyond Nicaea. They took it, and found rich booty; but the Turks besieged them before they could leave and after eight days the Germans surrendered. Those who accepted Islam were enslaved, those who stood by their faith were slaughtered.

Marching out to avenge this disaster the French fell into an ambush. They fled back to Civetot with the Turks at their heels. The infidels galloped into the camp and massacred thousands of noncombatants. Only three thousand Crusaders got away to be taken back to Europe by ships of the Greek navy. By the end of October Peter's expedition had been destroyed, though he himself was still safe in Constantinople.

During the summer other petty adventurers had been gathering armies in Germany; no great German lords had volunteered for the Crusade, because their Emperor was at enmity with the Pope. This second wave of premature Crusaders contained more brigands than peasants. Before they set out they achieved a great massacre of Jews in the Rhineland, in spite of strenuous efforts by the clergy and imperial officials to keep the peace. It was well known that in a war between Christian and Moslem the Jews would back the Moslems; which may explain, though it does not excuse, this massacre.

Three separate contingents of these anti-Jewish Germans approached the Hungarian frontier. The Hungarians refused them entry because of their plundering habits. The Germans tried to fight their way through, and failed. Most of the survivors went home, though a few knights joined later, more orderly expeditions.

Peter the Hermit had recruited at least thirty thousand men, including noncombatants; the German expedition were also numerous, though we have no reliable figures. All had been destroyed, without in any way furthering the Holy War. By the autumn of 1096 the Crusade must have appeared a very doubtful enterprise.

CHAPTER III

The Great Lords Ride Out

B y August 1096 the greater lords were ready to start. The harvest would ripen as they travelled; they had saved or borrowed or otherwise gathered money; they had assembled well-armed followers. These followers might or might not be their feudal subjects. Since the Crusade was not a feudal obligation any pilgrim might enlist under the leader of his choice; who would usually be someone who spoke the same dialect and came from not too far away, but not necessarily the lord from whom he held land.

No kings rode on the pilgrimage. The leaders came from the next social grade, the nobles who ruled provinces directly under the crown. Perhaps the greatest man among them was Raymond, Count of both Toulouse and Provence. Since Toulouse was a fief of France and Provence a fief of the Empire he might play off one lord against the other and go his own way. He was an elderly veteran of campaigns against the Moors in Spain, married to a princess of Aragon; from his wealthy and cultured land he had collected a great sum of money. The Pope had stayed with him on his way to Clermont, and probably Raymond had advance knowledge of the Crusade before it was made public. Le Puy, whose Bishop was the Pope's legate with the expedition, lay within his dominions, so that in temporal affairs Bishop Adhemar was his subject. He had a con-

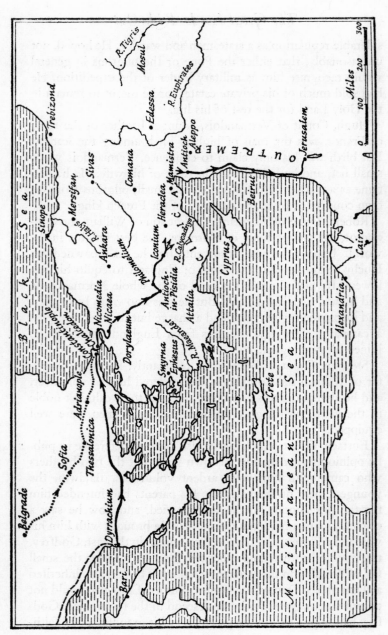

ROUTE OF THE FIRST CRUSADE

siderable reputation as a statesman and warrior. He hoped, not unreasonably, that either the Pope or the pilgrims in general would recognise him as military leader of the expedition. He had sold much of his private estate, for he meant to remain in the Holy Land for the rest of his life.

Hugh, Count of Vermandois, younger brother of the King of France, was the man of highest birth among the leaders. But birth was his only claim to eminence. Vermandois was a small fief, and he held it only in right of his wife. He had no fame as a warrior. His following was small, pilgrims from his own country or from the demesne of the French king.

Robert, Duke of Normandy, eldest son of William the Conqueror, led a large body of Normans, the best knights in the world. Usually he was insolvent, but he had pawned his Duchy to his brother the King of England to equip his followers. By birth he was the head of the whole Norman race, and he was a gallant knight. But he was known to be careless and incompetent; he could lead a charge but he could not plan a campaign. The few pilgrims from England and Scotland joined his contingent.

Stephen, Count of Blois, came reluctantly. His wife, daughter of William the Conqueror, had ordered him to volunteer, and he always did as she ordered. He was the wealthiest noble in the west, with a good business head; his men were well equipped.

Eustace, Count of Boulogne, also came in deference to public opinion rather than by his own wish; but the two brothers who came with him were ardent volunteers. Baldwin, the youngest, held no land because his parents had intended him for the priesthood; but he had married, and now he saw a chance to win a fief from the infidel. He brought with him his wife and children, and proposed to remain in the east. Godfrey, the middle brother, had inherited from his mother the small fief of Bouillon in the Ardennes; from her he had also inherited a claim on the Duchy of Lorraine, but the Emperor would not permit such a great Duchy to descend in the female line. Godfrey had hoped to win the great fief of his grandfather by faithful service to the Emperor, but all he got was the right to rule Lorraine as an appointed official, during the Emperor's pleasure; so his contemporaries called him Godfrey of Bouillon rather than Duke of Lorraine. He was the only important servant of the Emperor who volunteered for the Crusade. He also intended to remain in the east; before setting out he sold his land and resigned his appointment. He brought a strong following of Netherlanders and Lorrainers. It was so much stronger than his elder brother's that Count Eustace willingly served under him.

Robert, Count of Flanders, brought a strong contingent. Many of his men had served under his father, who as recently as 1090 had made the pilgrimage to Jerusalem and afterwards fought for a short time as a mercenary in the Greek army. The devout Flemings were enthusiastic pilgrims, and always important in Crusading affairs.

It was a little embarrassing that the Normans of Italy should also volunteer, since only a few years ago they had been at war with the Greek Empire. Bohemond of Taranto, a son of Robert Guiscard the conqueror, gathered a large contingent which included his nephew Tancred. With every excuse the Emperor Alexius doubted the good faith of these Normans and feared they were as likely to make war on his subjects as on the Turks.

The self-governing cities of northern Italy favoured the Crusade. They would be most valuable supporters, for they maintained efficient and warlike navies. But they wanted to make sure than an army would really reach Syria before they committed their ships, and in 1096 they did nothing. The western leaders had to plan their own journeys.

On the whole they did it efficiently. The recent invasion of England had shown that armies, with their warhorses, could be carried easily on shipboard. Most of the Crusaders preferred to go part of the way by sea, rather than march through the lands of the unsympathetic German Emperor and through Hungary where the rabble of German pilgrims had left a bad impression.

The Count of Vermandois started first. He went over the Alps and down to Bari, where he was joined by a number of

Italian Normans. But in the crossing to Durazzo he met a storm. Some of his ships were sunk, with heavy loss of life, and the survivors were in poor spirits when the Greek governor of Durazzo rescued them. Count Hugh, though received with great deference as the brother of the mighty King of France, was sent on to Constantinople under such a strong escort that his followers whispered that he seemed to be a prisoner.

Alexius was determined that so long as the Crusaders were within his dominions they would obey his orders. In particular they must travel only by the routes he had designated, and disembark only at the harbours where they were expected. When the Count of Alost tried to land at a port south of Durazzo his transports were attacked by Greek warships. The military police who made the Crusaders keep to the road were heathen Patzinaks, knowing no western language and quick to shoot their arrows. Thus Alexius preserved his country from pillage, but at the cost of great ill-feeling.

The next party to arrive was that of Godfrey and his brothers. Since they were on good terms with the German Emperor and on bad terms with the Pope they marched overland to Belgrade through Germany and Hungary. They proceeded peaceably under escort to Selymbria on the Sea of Marmora, which they reached in December. There they heard that the Count of Vermandois was held prisoner in Constantinople. That was true in a sense, though Hugh was quite content to remain at the luxurious Imperial court. In reprisal Godfrey's men began to pillage the countryside.

Count Hugh in person came out to Godfrey's camp to explain the situation. He also suggested that Godfrey might swear allegiance to Alexius. Godfrey refused, on the valid ground that he was already the man of the German Emperor, and could not serve two masters.

For the rest of the winter Godfrey and his men remained in camp. Alexius supplied them with excellent rations, but they could learn nothing of the progress of the other Crusaders. Understandably, they grew nervous.

Alexius also was nervous. He knew that by Easter all the

BEAUFORT CASTLE

KRAK DES CHEVALIERS

Crusaders would reach Constantinople, and that their united army would be strong enough to sack the city. Before then he must persuade Godfrey to cross over into Asia, and if possible get an oath from him. Godfrey sat tight in his camp, saying that before he took oath he must consult his colleagues on their arrival.

Towards the end of Lent Alexius stopped sending food, hoping to starve Godfrey into moving. The Lorrainers foraged for themselves until during Holy Week, April 1097, Godfrey led his forces in a formal attack on Constantinople. Alexius beat them off. At last Godfrey gave way. He would take oath, and cross to Asia.

Once Godfrey had yielded agreement was easily reached. On Easter Day he and his brothers swore that they would recognise the Emperor as lord of any portion of the Empire they might reconquer from the Turks. This was not homage as it was understood in the west; they did not swear to obey Alexius, or to accept his judgements. It was rather a treaty between two sovereign powers.

Alexius then feasted Godfrey and his comrades, and gave them splendid presents. Alexius was not really very rich, taking into consideration his obligations; all his soldiers and officials drew regular wages, while in the west public service was recompensed with land. By throwing money about Alexius hoped to convince the Crusaders of his power. He may also have thought that a western lord with money could keep order among his followers where a poor one would be disobeyed. But the bright idea did not produce the intended effect. When Crusaders saw his sacks of gold they did not think: 'What a mighty lord.' Instead they thought: 'This money should be spent on the Holy War.'

The Greeks never understood the motives of the Crusaders. They themselves disliked war as a vulgar, chancy operation; a civilised man ought to overcome his enemies by deceiving them, or by bribing some savage to do the fighting. They were not interested in the Holy Places. They wanted to save what was left of the Empire from the Turks, and if possible to win

back Asia Minor. Above all, they could not believe that anyone would fight the enemies of God just because they were
the enemies of God. In spite of their high-sounding speeches
these Latins must be out to make their fortunes; we must be
careful that they do not make their fortunes at our expense.

In addition, Alexius was genuinely shocked that Godfrey
had compelled him to fight on Good Friday; a thing he would
never have done willingly, even against a heathen enemy.

The Lorrainers were in an even worse fog of misunderstanding. They knew nothing of the fate of the other pilgrims; they
might all have been massacred as they entered the Empire, at
Belgrade or Durazzo. They did not understand the Greek way
of life, the custom of hiring heathen to defend the Christian
Empire, the absolute power of an Emperor who had fought
his way to the throne, the abject submission of his taxpaying
subjects, the complete lack of interest in the Holy War. Godfrey
was a gallant knight and a famous leader, but he never showed
himself a greater soldier than when he kept his men together in
the hostile suburbs of Constantinople.

As soon as Godfrey had taken his men over the straits to the
neighbourhood of Nicomedia another contingent of Crusaders
reached Constantinople. This was an unruly force, of mixed
origin, who had already skirmished with their Patzinak escort.
Since they had no one leader Alexius summoned a number of
them to his throne-room and asked them to take oath. During
the unseemly proceedings a knight sat down on the Emperor's
vacant throne; but in the end they all swore and went over the
straits to join Godfrey.

The next to arrive were the Normans of Italy, led by Bohemond of Taranto and Tancred his nephew. They were a tough
and efficient band, long used to campaigning abroad; not so
numerous as Godfrey's men, but even more dangerous to the
Greeks.

Bohemond knew his way about; a few years ago he had invaded Epirus. He crossed much of northern Greece unescorted,
without guides; though in Macedonia the Patzinaks caught up
with him. They began to shoot at stragglers, which brought

on a skirmish. But afterwards, perhaps because the Patzinaks were beaten, relations were on the whole friendly. By Easter Week the Crusaders were outside Constantinople, and Bohemond was received by Alexius.

Everyone knew that Bohemond, not a devout man, had come east to make his fortune. Alexius, remembering Roussel de Balliol, feared that he might carve out a fief from the remains of the Empire. He was eager to get an oath from Bohemond. For we all exaggerate the binding force of foreign customs and he supposed that no western knight would break an oath of fealty; just as some Christians of the present day suppose that no Moslem will ever touch alcohol.

But Bohemond aimed higher than a fief within the Empire. He hoped to be given military command of the whole Crusade; which had no one military leader, though Bishop Adhemar as papal legate was in general charge of policy. For this project he needed the support of Alexius.

Bohemond therefore swore all that was asked of him; and then suggested that the Emperor should appoint him Grand Domestic, imperial commander in chief. If he controlled the rations and funds which came from Constantinople he could impose his will on all the other Crusaders. Alexius saw the danger. As Grand Domestic Bohemond would rule the Empire, leaving no power to the Emperor. He did not refuse point-blank, but argued that the time was not yet ripe; later, perhaps. . . . So Bohemond gave his oath and got nothing in return. A Latin seldom got the better of a Greek in this kind of negotiation.

Tancred and some of the other Italian Normans would not swear anything. Instead they slipped over the straits by night. By the end of April all the Normans of Italy had joined their comrades in Asia.

Raymond of Toulouse was the next to arrive, after a very rough journey. That was his own fault, for choosing such an extraordinary route. Rather than undertake even a short voyage he went round the head of the Adriatic and down the Dalmatian coast. There was no decent road down that coast, where every sensible man travelled by ship. Lawless Slavs raided his baggage, and the moutains were even more dangerous than the raiders.

After forty days of alarm and hardship the Provençals reported to the Greek governor of Durazzo; who sent them off, under escort, by the great road to Constantinople. By this time provisions were scarce on a route already traversed by so many armies, and perhaps the Patzinaks were growing bored with escort duty. They were very quick to shoot at stragglers. In the numerous skirmishes there were casualties on both sides, and villages were sacked. The heathen wounded the papal legate, who was certainly no plunderer. Bishop Adhemar, a holy man, forgave his assailants; but the other pilgrims were deeply shocked at the sacrilege.

Count Raymond hurried on ahead of his men when he heard rumours that Bohemond might be appointed commander of the whole army. He would not take oath to the Emperor, for fear that he might be swearing to obey Bohemond. But after a week of haggling he swore not to harm the Empire, which satisfied Alexius. In his absence his men fought a pitched battle against imperial mercenaries, and were worsted. But by the end of April the Provençals also were in Asia.

Last to arrive were the Normans and Flemings, who had passed a pleasant winter in Italy; though during that winter they lost one eminent warrior, Bishop Odo of Bayeux, brother to the Conqueror. He had fought at Hastings, and later, as governor of England, had the courage to rebel against his brother. If he had lived to see Asia the Turks would have been the worse for it.

The Normans arrived by the usual route, by Durazzo to Constantinople, and had no trouble with their hosts. The Duke of Normandy, the Count of Flanders and the Count of Blois took oath to Alexius and then led their men into Asia, where their comrades had already formed the siege of Nicaea.

It seems probable that the Emperor Alexius expected the Turks to win. At one stage of his negotiation Count Raymond, who was something of a diplomatist, offered to serve under him if the imperial army would join the expedition. Alexius was forced to reply bluntly that he had no intention of taking part in the Holy War. In fact he was quite satisfied with the present state of affairs. These foreigners might risk their lives against the Turks, provided that any cities they won were returned to the Empire; and if they happened to be beaten the Empire would not be involved.

Alexius was not a coward, but he did not care for war; and he did not appreciate the fortitude of the Crusaders. Now that these enthusiastic western pilgrims had arrived in such numbers in his capital city his chief aim was to get them into infidel territory before they did any more damage to his peasants. The Turks would kill them, and the episode would be closed. The Turks had made short work of Peter's men; and these people, though better born, seemed to be no better disciplined. No Greek could understand the compulsions of chivalry.

CHAPTER IV

Across Asia Minor

In the Crusading camp there were more than a hundred thousand mouths to be fed. But these included many clergy, women and children; and the poorer ablebodied foot were untrained for war and inadequately armed. The strength of the army lay in its mailed knights.

A knight of *c.* 1100 wore much the same armour as his father had worn at Hastings—a long mailshirt of iron links on a leather foundation, reaching from his shoulders to his calves; a mail coif to protect his neck and throat; a conical steel cap with a vertical bar to protect his nose from sword-cuts. A few rich men wore mail breeches, which must have had cloth in the seat since no one would ride with mail between his bottom and the saddle. But most knights wore padded trousers, ending in low ankle-boots and long sharp spurs.

Slung from a strap over his right shoulder the knight carried a long kiteshaped shield, of leather reinforced with an iron rim and a central iron boss. His left arm fitted through the shield-straps, but the shield was too heavy to be moved easily and his left hand would be occupied with the reins. However, if the shield was held correctly it covered him from neck to left shin. A decorative design might be painted on the shield, but as yet there were no true heraldic charges.

On his left side hung a scabbard containing a double-edged

sword; this was used only for cutting, and the end was often blunt. His right hand carried the lance. When charging he tucked the butt of the lance under his right arm; but the point projected on the *near* side of his horse's head, so that his shield would cover him when he ran against the foe. At front and back of his saddle were high guard-boards, which protected his lower trunk where the mailshirt divided for ease in riding.

This did not make too great a weight for a horse of ordinary size. But a warhorse was expensive and hard to replace because it had been carefully trained. It would charge straight even though the reins were controlled only by the tips of the rider's fingers behind his shield, and in combat it would strike out with its ironshod forefeet. The warhorse was usually a stallion, which made it a nuisance in camp and an uncomfortable ride. On the march a knight would ride a hackney while a groom led his warhorse, of course on its near side; so the contemporary name for a warhorse was destrier, right-hand horse.

No troops in the world, Christian or Moslem, could withstand charging knights. But knightly tactics had certain limitations. The enemy must meet them fairly; knights quickly exhausted their horses against a foe who skirmished and gave ground. In a long charge they lost formation, for they were not accustomed to fighting in large squadrons or to obeying tactical orders. Every knight thought of himself as socially the equal of his leader, entitled to use his own judgement on the battlefield. Since he provided his own costly equipment he brought with him a number of servants and grooms to look after his arms and horses; these men were of little use in battle, but they must be fed.

It was very difficult to stop knights from charging as soon as they saw the enemy, and practically impossible to halt a charge once it had begun.

Crusaders of lower rank, who fought on foot, were not in general very formidable; though a solid clump of spears could guard an open flank or make a rallying-point for disordered knights. But the west had recently invented a weapon which impressed Greeks and infidels alike, the crossbow. This might be loaded with a windlass, or by a pull of the whole body; consequently it shot farther and more accurately than a hand-bow. A long bow needs a long arrow, and the archer cannot carry many of them. The missiles of a crossbow need not stretch from bow to string, and may be light and handy. The crossbowman rarely runs short of arrows.

To shoot with the crossbow is easy; great ladies shot deer with them, though of course the loading was done by an attendant. But they are intricate machines, which must be kept dry and constantly adjusted. Crossbowmen were craftsmen of some standing, lifelong professional soldiers who commanded high wages. There were never very many of them in a Crusading army.

The long bow of Crecy and Agincourt had not yet been invented. Any hand-bows carried by Crusaders would be meant for hunting rather than for war.

Turkish tactics were quite novel to western knights. The Turks were nomad horsemen, fighting at long range with the bow. Their bows must be short, to clear the withers of the horse; but they were stronger than they looked, often made from two antelope horns bent backwards in a double curve like 'Cupid's bow'. Every Turk had a string of horses, which his wives and children brought close to the front line; he could drop back to change mounts at intervals, so that a Turkish army was usually still full of running when western knights had exhausted their destriers. Every Turk carried a sabre for use at close quarters; but as a rule he had no armour and no shield. Turks would canter along an enemy line in open order, shooting their arrows; so that even if they did not outnumber the foe they would outflank him. When their arrows had shaken the hostile line they would charge all together; but they were never ashamed to give ground, and if the charge did not succeed they would retire and again begin skirmishing. They were accustomed to acting together in large bodies, when managing their huge herds of sheep; so that on the battlefield they obeyed orders more willingly than the many little con-

Turkish bowmen

tingents of Crusaders. These orders were made known by the
beating of kettle-drums, cooking pots covered in sheepskin
and carried on horseback. To Crusaders the noise was very
frightening, for drums were not used in the west and their own
trumpets were rather an encouragement than a means of passing signals.

In May 1097 the Crusaders sat down before Nicaea, where in
June the Duke of Normandy joined them. The Emperor sent
them engineers and guides, and supplied them with provisions.
Nicaea was a very strong fortress, but every western knight
was accustomed to besieging castles; they settled down happily
to build siege-engines and cast stones.

They had no supreme commander. A council of war issued
general orders and each leader administered his own contingent. But so far all the leaders were agreed. Whatever might be
their plans for the future it was obvious that they could not
advance farther until they had taken Nicaea.

They had been lucky in the time of their arrival; the Sultan of
Nicaea was far away to the eastward attacking a city of the
Armenians. Perhaps his agents in Constantinople had reported
the Greek opinion that the Crusade was doomed to failure.
Before the end of the month he came back to relieve his garrison. But for Turks this was the wrong kind of battle. To raise
a siege they must fight at close quarters. They were soundly
beaten, though the Christians lost some good knights including
the Count of Ghent, the first famous lord to fall in battle
against the infidel.

The Sultan of Nicaea was a good soldier. He saw that to
drive away a besieging army his men must charge, and that in
a stand-up fight armoured knights were sure to beat them; but
that if he met the Crusaders in open country his horsebowmen
could wear them down by shooting from a distance. He retired
to the eastward, after getting word to his men in Nicaea that
they must make what terms they could without further help
from him.

The Crusaders went on battering Nicaea. But its ancient
walls were stronger than any they had met in the west, and the

garrison could still draw supplies by boat across the lake which washes one side of the town. They had no boats of their own, so they asked Alexius to help them. He sent boats overland in great waggons, with skilled marines to man them. The general who led them had contacts among the Turks.

By 18 June the wall had been breached. An assault was planned for the next day. But Butumites, the Greek general, sent timely word to the Turkish garrison. During the night they came to terms with him. When the Crusaders formed up for the assault they saw the Emperor's banner flying on the wall and Greek soldiers guarding the gates.

Alexius gained an undamaged city. The Turks saved their lives and their property; they were detained in Constantinople until they paid ransom, and then released. The Sultan's Queen, a Turkish princess, was set free at once without ransom, to foster good relations between Greeks and Turks after these irrelevant Latins had left the neighbourhood. The Crusaders were spared casualties, but they were also cheated of the plunder of Nicaea. They felt angry and dismayed.

After crossing the straits with a great army Alexius ventured a few miles into Asia. Hoping to win forgiveness from the Crusaders, he sent for their leaders and gave them large sums in gold. In return they renewed their oaths; at last, after a stormy scene, even Tancred swore. But there was no longer any pretence that Greeks and Latins were allies in the Holy War. Alexius would feed the Crusaders, and pay them for any cities they conquered on his behalf. They were bound by oath to hand over these cities, and in the west oaths were taken seriously. But the Crusaders felt that they had been cheated into swearing. When they swore they had assumed that Alexius would march with them; now it was obvious that he would not fight the Turks.

A week later the Crusaders set off across Asia Minor. A Greek liaison officer, Taticius, went with them, bringing maps and guides. But it was 25 years since a Greek army had used the great military road to the east, and the maps were out of date. There was no cultivation, and the Turks had filled in the wells. Whenever Taticius promised water or forage which could not be found the Crusaders naturally saw it as another example of Greek treachery.

The great army marched in two columns, a day's journey apart. Ostensibly this was to make foraging easier. But in the first column were all the Normans of Normandy and Italy, the Flemings and the men of Blois; while in the second were the Provençals and the Lorrainers with the small following of the Count of Vermandois; which looks very like a division by mutual consent between Normans and their neighbours on the one hand, and the rest. Bohemond commanded the first column and Count Raymond the second; a convenient way of separating two bitter rivals for the supreme command.

At dawn on 1 July 1097 the first column lay encamped in a rolling plain near the ruins of the city of Dorylaeum, recently destroyed by the Turks. As they struck camp a great army of Turks rode over the low hills to the north.

The battle which followed was the crisis of the Crusade; if the Latins had been routed, which was what the Greeks expected, it is likely that the whole Crusading movement would have been abandoned.

The Sultan had brought on exactly the kind of battle he wanted. Other Turkish bands of Asia Minor had joined his standard; probably he outnumbered the great caravan of Crusaders, even with its many noncombatants. There was no point in the featureless plain which he must defend, no obstacle to hamper the movements of his horse. All day his men could shoot arrows into the Christian mass, keeping out of reach of the knightly lance. Knightly mail was arrow-proof, but the destriers wore no armour. After their horses had been shot the knights could do little damage. Then the Turks would charge home with the sabre. For Turkish warriors were not only skirmishers; their cautious evasive tactics were meant to culminate in a fight at close quarters.

Bohemond recognised the danger, and saw how to counter it. Bohemond was a selfseeking adventurer, who cared little for the liberation of the Holy Places; but he was a magnificent soldier, who brought a fresh mind to bear on a novel situation instead of doing out of habit what had been done last time. The other leaders deserve credit for following his instructions. That is especially true of Robert of Normandy, who must have felt that every Norman, even a Norman from Italy, ought to obey him.

Bohemond commanded the servants to pitch the tents again. The guy-ropes of the great pavilions made an entanglement which horsemen could not easily penetrate. Of course the camp lay beside a spring; women and servants could carry water to the fighting-men, an important advantage on a July day in Asia Minor. Crossbowmen could take cover among the tents; they needed protection for the slow loading of their weapons, but their arrows outranged the enemy's.

When the Turks appeared the knights were already leaving camp, so that with the army facing north the tents provided a strong anchor for the left wing. At Bohemond's command the knights turned left into line, and *stood still*. To avoid a premature charge Bohemond ranged a line of foot in front of them. Most of the better foot carried shields or at least wore some form of quilted or leather armour, which might keep out Turkish arrows; their bodies sheltered the vulnerable and precious destriers. This was a remarkable innovation, and it is equally remarkable that Bohemond got himself obeyed. Knights were normally reluctant to take shelter behind the despised infantry.

The coolness and commonsense of the Crusaders at Dorylaeum is really amazing. Every knight had been taught that the right thing to do as soon as he saw a mounted enemy was to charge and bowl him over. Here, in the greatest battle most of them had ever seen, they were ordered to stand still. We must remember that Bohemond, who led only the Normans of Italy, was of lower social and military rank than the Duke of Normandy or the Counts of Flanders and Blois; his comrades followed his advice because it seemed to them sensible.

Of course messages had been sent to the other column, the Provençals and Lorrainers. But the Turks seemed to be everywhere, and perhaps the messengers had not got through. Meanwhile Bohemond's formation saved the Christians from defeat, but did nothing to bring victory nearer. From sunrise to midday the Turks rode along the stationary Christian line, shooting their arrows. Horses and men fell continually.

After six hours of passive endurance the Christians were getting to the end of their courage. A sprinkling of knights left the front line to seek refuge among the tents, but a solid clump of pikemen drove them back to their duty. The Sultan saw that his foes were wavering, and gave the signal to charge with the sabre.

At that moment the knights of the second column arrived, having galloped a day's journey in a few hours. Most of them came into line on the right, ready to meet the Turkish charge with a counter-charge. That would have repulsed the Turks, without doing them very much harm; they were as well mounted as the Christians, and could shoot backwards at full gallop. But Bishop Adhemar, the papal legate, did more than come into line. He led a body of Provençals through the hills to come in on the Turkish rear. This is the only time he is mentioned as playing an active part in battle; but like most Bishops he came of knightly stock and could understand a battlefield. By good luck (why not say by God's help?) his charge coincided with the general Christian advance. Attacked in front and rear, the Turks broke in panic.

The Christians pressed the pursuit for as long as their horses could move. The Turks suffered heavily. The survivors were so frightened that they continued their flight after the danger was ended, so that for several days the Crusaders passed dead horses and abandoned baggage. Best of all, they captured the Turkish camp, with all the wealth of these nomads who carried their treasure in their tents. The booty was enormous.

The battle of Dorylaeum shows the Crusaders at their best. Everyone pulled his weight; there was no jealousy, no argument, no disobedience. It was a difficult situation, quite strange to every western knight. But Bohemond devised a plan, and all his comrades carried out his orders.

The Crusaders never found out how to defeat horsebowmen, unless they could attack some place which the horsebowmen must stand to defend. A battle against Turks was always a chancy affair.

But now the Turks were cowed. They withdrew northward instead of defending the cities they had captured after Manzikert. They were still nomads, whose homes were their tents.

Unfortunately it is difficult to cross any land which Turks have occupied for a generation, since they make a desert by their ordinary manner of life. As the Crusaders marched eastward they found the wells dry, the grass burned, and the fields uncultivated. August in Asia Minor was hotter than they had ever known. Heat and lack of water killed many destriers, so that knights had to march on foot in their mail. Sickness broke out, for men used to fighting in little feudal retinues did not observe the sanitary rules necessary in such a large host. At Iconium they halted for several days while Count Raymond recovered from a grave illness. They found the city deserted, but there was fruit and water in the suburbs.

At Heraclea another Turkish army awaited them, made up from more easterly bands who had not been present at Dorylaeum. But they had heard of the great defeat, and their morale was low. As soon as the Christians approached them Bohemond led a charge which persuaded them to withdraw northward.

It was now time to leave Asia Minor for Syria. Taticius, the Greek liaison officer, explained that there were two routes. The shorter led southeast through Cilicia to Antioch; but it crossed two ranges of mountains by two narrow and dangerous passes. The longer way, to the northward, avoided the worst of the mountains and would lead them through districts held by Christian Armenians.

By this time the Crusaders had been on the road for a year, since August 1096. They had shaken down into a veteran army, and they discussed the question in a sensible way. Most of them decided for the northern route; but Baldwin of Boulogne and Tancred, two adventurers seeking land for themselves, chose Cilicia.

Most of the towns hereabouts, from Cilicia as far as the Euphrates, were under Armenian rule. Thirty years earlier the ancient Kingdom of Armenia, near Lake Van, had been destroyed by the Turks; since then the warlike Armenian chieftains had been moving westward. In Cilicia they were a minority, but they became so prominent that in later days this angle where Asia Minor meets Syria was known as Lesser Armenia.

By the 11th century most Armenians had forgotten the doctrinal points which had led them into heresy, but they remembered that the Greeks used to persecute them when they had the power to do so. They hated the Emperor in Constantinople, but many of them were willing to submit to the Pope if he would allow them to use their native liturgy. The Crusaders got on very well with these warlike mountaineers.

Early in October the Christian army reached the flourishing town of Comana, inhabited by Armenians. They easily drove off the Turks who were then besieging it, and the citizens asked for a garrison to guard them. But Taticius pointed out that Comana lay within the old bounds of the Empire, and therefore must be given back to Alexius. The western leaders replied by asking him to nominate a governor; perhaps they wanted to remind the Greek officer that he had no troops at his command save a handful of guides. But Greeks can always get out of an awkward situation. Taticius named as governor of Comana one Peter de Alpibus, a Provençal mercenary employed by Alexius. So the town was governed by a Latin, and yet remained part of the Empire.

While the pilgrims were crossing the range of Anti-Taurus they heard a rumour that the Turks had evacuated Antioch. Everyone knew that Antioch was a very strong fortress, whose walls had been built by the great Justinian and kept in good repair until the place fell to the Turks less than twenty years before. But ever since Dorylaeum Turkish bands had been evacuating strong cities rather than face Crusaders, so the rumour sounded plausible. Raymond of Toulouse, hoping to score a point in his incessant campaign to be recognised as supreme military commander, sent forward five hundred of his knights to take over the city in his name.

The rumour proved false. The Turks of Syria, determined to hold Antioch, were in fact reinforcing the garrison. Raymond's knights, soon learning the truth, halted among the friendly Armenians of Anti-Taurus. But it so happened that when Raymond despatched them Bohemond was absent in pursuit of a band of Turks. It seemed to the whole army that Raymond had tried to steal Antioch for himself while his rival was away. Henceforth these two leaders, the best soldier in the army and its wisest and wealthiest statesman, watched one another with bitter jealousy.

The crossing of Anti-Taurus was the worst trial the Crusaders had endured since leaving Europe. Autumn had brought heavy rain; the excellent embanked roads marked on Greek maps had been neglected for more than thirty years even where the Turks had not deliberately destroyed them. Horses and baggage-mules fell over the cliffs. For miles the track was too dangerous for riding; the knights must walk in mail, leading their destriers. It was said that more Christians died on the mountain than had been killed at Dorylaeum.

Among those who died of sickness was the Norman wife of Baldwin of Boulogne; probably her three young children died about the same time. We know they came on the Crusade, and they are not mentioned later. During the whole march, from May to October, the fit must look after numbers of sick women and children; some died every day, though chroniclers note only the death of great personages.

On 20 October 1097 the Crusaders reached the plain of Antioch. They had advanced for more than four months through hostile country, all the time in touch with a dangerous enemy.

Meanwhile Baldwin and Tancred in Cilicia had been behaving rather badly. Baldwin had come east to win a lordship for himself, as well as to liberate the Holy Places. At Nicaea he had taken up with exiled Armenian politicians, who spoke of a warlike Christian population to the eastward, ready to rise against their Turkish oppressors. Perhaps even then he planned to set up an Armenian realm; he entered Cilicia at the head of five hundred knights and two thousand foot.

The more dashing Tancred, who knew nothing of local conditions but was willing to have a go anywhere, was three days ahead of him with the weak force of a hundred knights and two hundred foot. He was the first to reach Tarsus, where there was a Turkish garrison.

Instead of defending their wall the Turks rode out against Tancred, who defeated them. The Christian citizens took up arms and shut out the Turks from the citadel. Three days later, seeing Baldwin arrive with his larger force, the Turks slipped away under cover of night; and Baldwin rode up to find Tancred lord of Tarsus.

Baldwin threatened Tancred with open war unless he withdrew from the wealthy city. For the first time Crusader defied Crusader. But it did not come to blows, for Tancred moved on to the eastward.

As soon as Baldwin was inside Tarsus three hundred more Normans of Italy turned up, reinforcements who had heard of Tancred's success and had left the main army to join them. Baldwin would not allow them within the town. While they were camped outside the walls they were attacked by the Turks who had recently fled from the citadel; apparently the Turks galloped into the camp after dark, cutting down the sleeping Christians.

Baldwin's own followers were shocked. It was one thing to take a rich town from a fellow-Crusader, but quite another to expose Christian warriors to massacre. His men were talking of leaving him when suddenly his position was made secure. A fleet of western ships put into the river Cydnus, which flows through Tarsus.

The fleet was manned by pirates from the North Sea, Flemings and Danes; but they were at the same time genuine Crusaders, who had accomplished the long and dangerous voyage through the Straits of Gibraltar (with Moors lining both shores) to lend a hand in the Holy War. It was Baldwin's good luck that their leader was a native of Boulogne, one Guynemer, who was proud to take orders from the brother of his Count. A garrison of pirates was left to hold Tarsus, while Baldwin led his men back to the main army and the ships cruised eastward along the infidel coast.

Meanwhile Tancred had marched on to liberate Adana and Mamistra, Armenian cities whose small Turkish garrisons fled at his approach. At Mamistra Baldwin caught up with him; but now Tancred felt strong enough to shut the gates against the French. There was a little fighting between the two allied contingents; but then both sides felt ashamed of themselves, and the two leaders swore friendship in a solemn public ceremony. Baldwin hurried back to the main army to say goodbye to his dying wife. Tancred followed the coast to Alexandretta, which he liberated with the help of the pirate fleet. Then he also marched by way of the Syrian Gates to join the main army before Antioch.

Cilicia might have made a good Crusading lordship. It had strong natural boundaries, and its warlike Armenian population would rather be ruled by Latins than by Greeks. But the rivalry between Tancred and Baldwin ruined the chances of both. The net result was that weak Latin garrisons held Tarsus, Adana and Mamistra, while in the open country patriotic Armenian brigands jockeyed for position. But all the Turks had been chased away, and the army before Antioch could keep in touch with Europe through the convenient port of Alexandretta.

Baldwin was still determined to found an Armenian state. While the army marched down to Antioch he diverged to the east. For this second expedition he took a much smaller force, only eighty knights and their attendants; presumably because his brothers needed most of the Lorraine-Boulogne contingent for the stiff fighting expected before Antioch.

Baldwin found himself in a land which lacked a ruler. The open country was exposed to pillage by wandering Turks, but there was no important Turkish band nearer than Mosul. The towns were ruled by Armenian nobles who paid tribute either to the Greek Emperor or to some Turkish emir. They were glad to accept Latin protection, which was more effective than Greek and cheaper than Turkish.

During the winter Baldwin, at the head of an army of Armenians stiffened by his handful of knights, fought his way as far as Edessa, well beyond the Euphrates. The childless Armenian ruler of the city adopted him, and then was induced to abdicate. By March 1098 Baldwin, Count of Edessa, was lord of a fief on both banks of the Euphrates. As yet he had no feudal superior, though the Crusaders regarded his county as a detached command under the authority of the supreme council of war. By the terms of the oath sworn in Constantinople he should have given allegiance to Alexius, since his land lay within the Greek Empire as it had been in 1060. But most Crusaders held that oath to be void now that Alexius had withdrawn from the Holy War.

In the citadel of Edessa Baldwin discovered a great treasure, and he ruled as much by judicious outlay of money as by the sword. For example, a Turk named Balduk held the city of Samosate; the new Latin county cut him off from the other Turks, so he offered to sell his city for ten thousand gold bezants. Not only did Baldwin buy it, he enlisted Balduk and his Moslem freebooters as mercenaries. Then a neighbouring town, Saruj, revolted against its Turkish lord, who hired Count Baldwin to subdue it for him. In the confusion Balduk tried to grab Saruj for himself, but Baldwin cut off his head and dismissed his remaining Turkish mercenaries. When the dust settles Baldwin holds Saruj with a Christian garrison, but the mosque remains open for the convenience of the wholly Moslem population.

Presently the widowed Count Baldwin of Edessa married an Armenian heiress. Out of nothing he had built up a flourishing county. He played an important part in the tangled politics of the middle Euphrates, where Turks, Armenians and Greeks strove for mastery. But it was all done by a conjuring trick. He had very few western knights; his forces were composed of Armenians who preferred a Latin lord to a Greek, or of Greeks who preferred a Latin lord to an Armenian. So long as his money lasted he could also bribe the mercenaries of his rivals to betray their masters. Baldwin was clever enough to juggle all these different balls at once, but his county could only endure while it was ruled by a cunning and wealthy politician.

CHAPTER V

Antioch

A ntioch had once been the third city of the Roman Empire, surpassed only by Rome and Alexandria. Though its prosperity had decayed with the interruption of international trade it was still enclosed within the mighty fortifications of its prime, kept in repair until the Turks captured it in 1085. It was also important to the Crusade that Antioch was the seat of a Patriarch, senior to Constantinople. The Patriarch of Antioch had never quarrelled with the Pope, perhaps because he could seldom communicate with him. There was no schism to complicate relations with the local Christians, who followed the Greek rite.

The city lay below Mount Silpius, on the southern bank of the river Orontes twelve miles from its mouth. But the walls climbed to the summit of the mountain, where stood the citadel. The whole circuit of the defences, some ten miles round, was reinforced with four hundred towers. Within it the well-watered mountain afforded ample grazing for cattle.

In the winter of 1097 Antioch was held by a Turkish chieftain named Yaghi-Siyan. He owed allegiance to the Emir Ridwan of Aleppo; but he was notoriously unfaithful and two other Turkish potentates, Kerbogha of Mosul and Duqaq of Damascus, would be glad to establish a claim on his gratitude by rescuing him from the Crusaders.

As danger approached Yaghi-Siyan took routine precautions. He collected grain and live cattle, imprisoned the Patriarch, and converted the ancient cathedral of St Peter into a stable. He also asked help from his three Moslem neighbours.

On 20 October 1097 the Crusaders reached the Iron Bridge over the Orontes, a few miles east of Antioch. A Turkish garrison held the fortified bridge; but the Christians stormed it so quickly that they captured a convoy of cattle and grain destined for Antioch. Then they turned downstream to encamp before the northern face of the city. They built a bridge of boats to link their camps on both banks of the river, and settled down for a long siege.

There was now a change in the atmosphere of the Holy War. In Asia Minor there had been only one great army to beat, and at the outset of the campaign they had beaten it. Then they had advanced into the unknown, confident of victory. Small detachments had ridden aside to liberate Christian cities whose Turkish garrisons fled at the first assault. Since the surrender of Nicaea no city had been stubbornly held against them.

In Syria things were different. There were many more Turks, and they fought harder to defend towns which contained a considerable Moslem population. The army was smaller, since many pilgrims had died of hardship and many others had turned back. Nobody any longer expected help from Alexius. The land had been harried bare, so that they must expect to be cold and hungry while the war continued. From the outset every reasonable pilgrim had supposed that he personally might die before he could see Jerusalem, but no one had said in public that perhaps God's warriors would never get there. Now at every council responsible leaders discussed the possibility that the whole expedition might be massacred. Knights who had scrambled over the little stockaded castles of the west looked up at the sheer stone walls of Antioch, and could not imagine how to get inside them.

Perhaps Bohemond already hoped to get in by bribery; among his troops were Sicilians who spoke Arabic, and it was not hard to open communication with the townsmen. But the townsmen did not control the defences. Anyway, Bohemond kept his plans to himself; for if he got into Antioch he was determined to keep it. Other leaders might wish to return it to the Empire, in accordance with the terms of their oath.

In council Raymond opposed anything suggested by Bohemond. He was bitterly disappointed that no one had yet proposed that he should command the whole army. He had contributed the strongest and best-equipped contingent, he had been in the know even before the Pope preached the Crusade at Clermont, he was lord of Le Puy whose Bishop was papal legate. He had a moral right to the command. That his claims were ignored was all the fault of those plundering Normans who clung together against southern Frenchmen.

Besides, he had a plan for taking the city. Let them send for Alexius. If the Greek army arrived, with its excellent supply-train and its clever engineers, they would all eat well during the winter and knock a hole in the walls before spring.

The other leaders would not agree. What was the point of enduring hardship and hunger if every rich city they took was to be handed over to Alexius? Perhaps he would have to get Antioch in the end, but not before it had been thoroughly plundered by the gallant knights who had won it.

Until Christmas the army sat before the northern wall of Antioch, because no one could think of anything better to do.

During the autumn a Genoese fleet sailed into the harbour of St Simeon at the mouth of the Orontes, thus opening a good communication with the west. The exiled Patriarch of Jerusalem, who had taken refuge in the Greek island of Cyprus, organised convoys of provisions. Bohemond, with his customary skill in war, lured the Turkish garrison of Harenc to attack him in the open and destroyed them, which opened up another field for foraging. But after Christmas the army was hungry, and horses began to die of starvation. The leaders decided to send Bohemond and the Count of Flanders to plunder southward up the Orontes valley.

The Turks in Antioch learned that this large detachment had left the army, and on 29 December sallied out against the besiegers. There was a confused and bloody fight round the Bridge Gate to the north of the city. At one moment the Christians nearly fought their way in, but at the critical moment a loose horse disordered their ranks; in the end they withdrew to their camp with heavy loss.

Meanwhile on the 31st the Count of Flanders bumped into a large Turkish army; Duqaq of Damascus and the Emir of Homs were marching together to the relief of Antioch. Here again there was bloody fighting at close quarters, until Bohemond charged at just the right moment and the Turks fled. The foragers had lost so heavily that they returned at once with little plunder; but at least they had driven back a relieving force which might otherwise have raised the siege.

It is worth noting that in these two actions the Turks charged home without hesitation. In Asia Minor they had preferred to skirmish cautiously at long range, but now they felt they had the measure of their adversaries.

January was unusually cold, with incessant rain; and no firewood could be found. Common soldiers and camp-followers began to desert, slipping down to St Simeon to find a ship or setting out to retrace the dangerous road across the mountains. Nobody stopped them; they were almost certain to die of hardship, which was punishment enough, and every deserter meant one less mouth to be fed. But when Peter the Hermit ran off Bohemond had him fetched back. The flight of such a famous preacher would have discouraged all who remained. After Bohemond had threatened Peter in private he consented to stay at the front, and the affair was hushed up as much as possible.

In February Ridwan of Aleppo, with the Emirs of Hama and Diarbekir, recaptured Harenc and advanced on Antioch. The situation appeared so threatening that Taticius the Greek liaison officer fled by sea to Constantinople. The Crusaders assumed that he had run away in fear of the Turks; for home consumption he announced that the Latins, disgusted by the inaction of Alexius, had threatened to murder him. Whatever caused his fright, it is clear that this senior Greek officer made off because he was frightened. Every Crusader had good reason to be frightened.

In this tight place the council of war as usual took Bohemond's advice. The other leaders might distrust his selfish political aims but they recognised his supreme skill and daring on the battlefield. He assembled all the knights in the army who were still adequately mounted; there were only seven hundred of them. With this picked force he proposed to turn back an army of relief many thousands strong; while the Christian foot, stiffened by dismounted knights, defended the camp.

After dark on 8 February Bohemond led out his horsemen to the position he had chosen, a defile between a lake to the north and the river Orontes to the south; here was firm level ground for a charge, and no room for the Turks to skirmish and shoot arrows from a distance. At dawn the enemy approached, densely massed on the narrow tongue of land to form a solid target for the charge. At the first onset Ridwan's army broke in panic; the infidels fled all the way back to Aleppo without stopping. The knights pursued only as far as Harenc, where they captured the Turkish baggage-train, with ample provisions and many spare horses.

The Turks in Antioch had seen the knights ride out, even though Bohemond had waited for nightfall. In the morning they attacked the camp of the besiegers, and stern fighting continued until in the afternoon the knights rode back from their victory.

The whole competent and successful double operation bears the stamp of that great soldier, Bohemond. He understood the strength and weakness of Turkish tactics; and so had picked in advance the best place to meet an infidel army advancing down the Orontes. His control of his men is even more praiseworthy. In the heat of battle knights would often disobey their own lords, and Bohemond was not even their lord. But he persuaded them to lie quiet all night in ambush, to attack when he gave the word, to halt the pursuit at Harenc, and then to hurry straight back to the camp. If only Bohemond had fought more

Bohemond of Antioch

for the Holy Places and less for his own profit he would have been the greatest Crusader of them all.

In March an English fleet reached St Simeon, carrying Edgar Atheling, the Saxon claimant to the English throne. There is a puzzle here, for we know that late in 1097 Edgar was in Scotland, which does not leave him time to sail to Constantinople and then on to St Simeon. Sir Steven Runciman suggests that this fleet was manned by English Varangians from the Greek army, and that Edgar joined it in Constantinople. But the Varangians seldom left the Emperor's person. Perhaps a fleet of English Crusaders sailed in the summer of 1097, and Edgar came overland to join them later. That would fit in with the legend of St Godric of Finchale, an English sailor who had gone Crusading in the Holy Land before he settled down as a hermit at home. It is certain that Edgar was with the army before Antioch. Contemporaries noted that he became a close friend of Robert of Normandy; perhaps they found a bond in a common hatred of William Rufus, who had usurped the throne to which they both had a claim.

Raymond and Bohemond rode down together to St Simeon, to see what the ships had brought and to enlist recruits from their crews. This brought on another scrambling indecisive battle; for the Turks always sallied from Antioch when they saw their besiegers divided. Twice the convoy of stores changed hands. First the Turks captured it from Raymond, then Godfrey sallied from the camp and won it back. No one could be proud of this battle, but the Turks lost more men killed than the Christians.

That was the last sortie from Antioch. Reinforced from the fleet, and with working parties of handy sailors, the Crusaders built a fort opposite each gate of the city. Now the Turks began to be hungry, and in the Christian camp food became more plentiful since merchants could not sell to the infidels.

But in May came ominous news. The greatest Turkish ruler in those parts, Kerboga of Mosul, had gathered a mighty army of relief. Turks from as far off as Baghdad and Persia had joined his standard. Hitherto every Turkish chief had been pleased to see a rival crushed by these strangers; but now that the Crusade was proving a genuine danger to Islam the quarrelsome bands began to unite. Unless the Christians took Antioch soon they would have to retire; they could not fight Kerboga with a hostile city behind them.

By this time the two most important Christian leaders were completely at loggerheads. Bohemond, who had once offered to serve in the Greek army, now wished to treat liberated Antioch as Latin territory; and if Alexius made any objection he was ready to fight him.

Raymond, who had scrupled even to swear friendship with the Empire, now wished to restore all liberated territory to Alexius. He had come to the conclusion that only Greek wealth, organisation and administrative skill could keep the infidel at bay, and that the whole-hearted alliance of Alexius was worth any price.

It is the custom to reproach Bohemond for self-interest, but it was not really a question of morals. The object of the Crusade was to free Jerusalem, not to restore the Greek Empire to its frontiers of 1060. Christian Jerusalem might be more secure if backed by a friendly Empire, and so far Raymond was right. But a good many other people besides Bohemond believed that nothing would make Alexius into a genuine Crusader. The damage had been done when the Emperor, at the head of his well-found army, said goodbye to the Crusaders on the threshold of Asia Minor. If the Holy War was none of his business why should he reap its fruits?

But as a matter of practical politics it would be a great help if the Emperor would join them now, even at this late hour. He was said to be somewhere in Asia Minor, installing his governors in towns from which the Crusaders had driven the Turks. The council of war sent him a desperate appeal: if he would march at once, so that he joined them in time to fight Kerboga, his reward would be Antioch.

In the course of his slow advance Kerboga halted to mop up the little Crusading outpost of Edessa. It was sound strategy not to leave this nest of raiders on his lines of communications, and he knew that Baldwin had only a handful of knights. But the walls of Edessa were immensely strong. After besieging it during the last three weeks of May Kerboga began to worry lest Antioch should fall before he could reach it. So he broke up the siege and continued his march. That delay of three weeks proved to be a turning point in history, for during it Bohemond at last bought a way into Antioch.

From the start he had been looking for a traitor in the garrison, and at last he had found one: Firouz, an Armenian who had abandoned his faith to join what seemed to be the winning side, and now thought he might do even better for himself by changing sides again. We do not know how much he was paid, or what became of him after; but at that time he was in command of three towers on the western wall.

On 2 June Kerboga was very near, and the Crusaders were very frightened. The Count of Blois in particular was so frightened that he quite brazenly gathered his men and marched off to seek refuge with the Emperor. He had been chief quartermaster, in charge of the collection and issue of rations; so he knew as much as anyone about the prospects of the campaign. His desertion was likely to spread dismay throughout the army.

A few hours later Bohemond told the other leaders, in strict confidence, that the town would be betrayed to them that same night. The lesser men were not told, for fear the news should leak back to the Turks. As a pretext to get the troops under arms they were ordered to muster at sunset for a march against Kerboga. They must have felt very gloomy as they set out eastward to fight a hopeless battle; but they were very brave men, and they set out.

After the garrison had seen them leave they were turned about and led round Antioch to its western wall. At the head of sixty picked knights Bohemond climbed a ladder into the tower where Firouz awaited them. They walked downstairs into the city, and from the inside opened the great Bridge Gate to their waiting comrades.

Fighting continued until dawn, with Moslem and Christian

townsfolk helping their respective armies. In panic, Yaghi-Siyan tried to escape down the steep southern face of Mount Silpius; his horse fell with him, and a stray Armenian cut off his head while he lay stunned among the rocks. His son rallied the remnant of the garrison in the citadel. By morning Bohemond had cleared the long circuit of wall; but his assault on the citadel was beaten off, though he pressed it until he himself was wounded. On the evening of 3 June 1098 all Antioch except the citadel was in Christian hands—and Kerboga was only a few miles away.

There was no time to settle even the pressing question of the government of the city. Luckily the defences were undamaged, and the second thing to be done was to get the noncombatants and baggage safely behind them. The first thing, of course, was to release the Patriarch from his dungeon and reconsecrate the cathedral of St Peter. The Patriarch was a Greek, but the Crusaders liked him. In prison he had suffered for the Faith, being dangled in a cage before the wall when the Turks wished to hinder the battering of a weak spot; probably he would have been martyred if the city had not fallen by surprise. He was of course in communion with both Rome and Constantinople.

On 7 June Kerboga camped before the northern wall, on the site of the old Christian camp. He thought he could regain Antioch easily, and he wanted to be sure he would keep it afterwards; so he expelled the garrison from the citadel and replaced them with men of his own. Then he organised an assault from the citadel downhill into the streets.

The Crusaders had recognised the danger; every western knight was expert in siege warfare, though he might never have seen an army containing as many as a hundred mounted men. They had built a barricade, and lined it with their best men. After heavy fighting, in which the Duke of Normandy especially distinguished himself, the assault was beaten off.

Kerboga hoped to capture Antioch undamaged. Blockade was the obvious means. He knew that before the recent escalade both sides had been hungry, and that in the fighting of the 3rd the stores of the garrison had been scattered or pillaged. To send unarmoured Turks to fight at close quarters against mailed knights was a wasteful road to victory. On 10 June he extended his lines to enclose the whole city. At the last moment another group of deserters, including some noblemen of rank, broke through to St Simeon and took ship for Asia Minor. But the main army was trapped in the hungry city.

That same evening one Peter Bartholomew, a Provençal pilgrim of humble station, called on his lord Count Raymond and the papal legate, who shared the same quarters. He said that St Andrew had appeared to him in numerous visions, to tell him that the Lance which pierced Our Lord on the Cross was hidden under the floor of St Peter's Cathedral; Peter Bartholomew was to proclaim this to the whole army. He had not done so, because he feared that no one would believe him. Tonight, in this extremity, he had conquered his bashfulness.

Bishop Adhemar was not convinced. There seemed no good reason why the Holy Lance should have been buried under the floor of a church in Antioch, or why St Andrew should have chosen as his messenger Peter Bartholomew, rather a disreputable pilgrim. But they were all in a very tight place, and the story might be true. Count Raymond took Peter Bartholomew into his household, and a search of the cathedral was arranged for the 15th.

During the search workmen dug into the floor until they were ready to give up in despair. Then Peter Bartholomew got down into the hole and came up holding an iron lance-head. The morale of the whole army improved.

Even at the time many doubted the relic; nowadays it is completely discredited. But the idea was not absurd. A Roman soldier, St Longinus, pierced the side of Our Lord with his lance, and on the same day became a Christian; he would have treasured that Lance. Probably it is still in existence. But why Antioch? Why under the floor? Bishop Adhemar did right to feel puzzled.

Count Raymond appointed himself guardian of the precious relic which had been found by one of his men. Perhaps he hoped that this extra qualification would persuade the other

KERAK IN MOAB

THE CASTLE OF THE SEA

MASIAF, A STRONGHOLD OF THE ASSASSINS

leaders to recognise his right to supreme command. If so, he was disappointed.

It may have been his idea to send out Peter the Hermit to offer Kerboga a bribe to go away. This is Peter's last appearance in the limelight, though he lived until 1115; probably he was chosen only because the leaders feared that Kerboga would murder their envoy. Peter was considered expendable.

Kerboga had troubles of his own. His allies were quarrelling and threatening to go home; supplies were scarce in his stinking ravaged camp, occupied by one side or the other since October. But Raymond could not buy him off.

Then Raymond fell ill, and the chief influence in the council passed to his rival Bohemond. When in trouble Bohemond always fought. On 28 June the whole army marched across the river under his command. He had devised a sound plan of battle, which worked.

Nearly all the destriers had died of hunger. Most knights went on foot, some rode donkeys or oxen. Thus the columns of spearmen and crossbows, stiffened with dismounted knights, were more easily controlled than usual. As soon as the first contingent was over the bridge it halted and faced to the right. The second contingent marched behind it to take post on its left; and so on until the whole army was in line. This may have been done to satisfy the old rule of military etiquette that the right of the line, the post of honour, should be filled by the van. But it looks more like a piece of tricky close-order drill to make sure that the Turks did not seize the bridgehead before the crossing was complete and thus cut the Christian army in two.

Kerboga thought of trying a sudden pounce on the bridgehead; but his advisers persuaded him to allow all his enemies to cross the river, so that he could destroy them in one battle. Instead he posted a detachment far in advance of his right flank, to take the Christians in the rear.

Bohemond, manoeuvring his companies of foot almost in the style of Gustavus Adolphus, made some of his men face about to ward off the threat. No other battle of the middle ages shows such complicated movement in the face of the enemy. Bohemond was a great military genius.

At last the Christian line advanced on foot against the foe, the Holy Lance carried in the midst as a standard. Kerboga's horsebowmen, in loose order, met them with a shower of arrows.

But Kerboga had forgotten that his camp, with all the wealth of his nomad followers, lay just behind his line. They would not retire behind it, so they must meet the Christians where they stood.

The Crusaders advanced with unusual determination, partly under the inspiration of the Holy Lance, partly because they saw St George and other soldier saints charging with them. In the tension of battle warriors sometimes see more than is there; but if you believe in 'the communion of saints' you may also believe that these soldiers left Heaven for a few minutes to charge with their comrades in the Holy War.

Some of Kerboga's disloyal allies chose this moment to desert him. Soon all the Turks were fleeing. They ought to have escaped a dismounted pursuit, but a few miles to the east they must cross the Orontes; fugitives blocked the Iron Bridge until the Crusaders slew them by thousands. Kerboga got back to Mosul with a handful of followers, and never again did he menace the Christians.

The Turks in the citadel could see the battle; when their comrades fled they sent a message into the town, offering to surrender. The messenger was taken to Count Raymond, who from his sickbed commanded the rest of the sick with the duty of containing the citadel. (In the fantastic odds of the Holy War this was reckoned light duty suitable for the bedridden.) Raymond accepted the surrender, and sent up his banner to be displayed on the wall. The Turks sent it back again. They waited until Bohemond had returned from the battle and then surrendered to him in person. Afterwards they accepted baptism and took service in his following. They knew, if others did not, who led this Crusade.

The question then arose of the government of Antioch. The

leaders were bound by oath to return it to the Empire. But when those oaths were sworn it was assumed that Alexius would join in the Holy War. For two years the Crusaders had been away from home; for two bitter campaigns they had marched and starved and fought. Must they hand over to Alexius all they had won, just because long ago he had given them a few waggonloads of corn? If he saw them as his mercenaries, recruited for him by the Pope, then he had neglected to pay them.

The lesser men were determined that the skulking Greeks should have nothing. The more responsible leaders agreed with them on the merits of the case, but they saw that it would be hard to preserve Antioch for Christendom if a hostile Empire barred the land route to Europe. With great public spirit they offered Alexius one more chance to do his duty. Hearing that he was somewhere in Asia Minor, they sent him a message by Hugh of Vermandois: if the Emperor and his army reached Antioch by November he would have the city; but if he had not arrived by then the Crusaders would advance towards Jerusalem, leaving a Latin garrison in Antioch.

The Count of Vermandois was leading home a group of Crusaders who thought they had done enough. They had not fulfilled their vow to liberate Jerusalem; but probably they had not planned to be away for more than two years, and their fiefs in Europe could not get on indefinitely without them. It seems that their comrades in Antioch did not reproach them as deserters.

In Asia Minor Count Hugh was amazed to find no trace of the Greek army. On the contrary, the Turks were once more on the rampage. They attacked him on the march and inflicted heavy casualties. Among others the Count of Hainault was missing, believed killed; a great nuisance for his county, which would lack a settled government until it was known for certain whether he was alive or dead.

Count Hugh found the Emperor in his palace in Constantinople. Blandly Alexius explained that he had been at Philomelium when the Count of Blois arrived with news that Ker-

boga was before Antioch and must inevitably destroy the
Christian army. To keep clear of this disaster Alexius had
prudently scuttled home to Europe. When Count Hugh pressed
him to start for Antioch at once, and perhaps share in the glory
of liberating Jerusalem, Alexius replied that autumn was the
wrong season to open a campaign; perhaps he might do something in the spring. Obviously conditions would never be suitable for the Greek army to attack those dangerous Turks.

Meanwhile in Antioch the Crusaders quarrelled. Bohemond
held the citadel and most of the walls; he had also granted a
block of houses to the Genoese admiral, whose fleet gave him
safe communications with Europe. He had brought about the
capture of the town, which according to the laws of war gave
him a strong claim to govern it. Most of the other leaders were
content to leave him in possession.

Count Raymond was not. He hated Bohemond, and he hoped
that if Antioch were returned to the Empire, Alexius would
appoint him to rule it. His men held the fortified bridge over
the Orontes and the palace of the Turkish ruler. There was a
serious danger of civil war within the city.

The Crusaders had promised to wait for Alexius until
November, and they needed rest after the hardships of the
campaign. But food was scarce in the ravaged plain. Most of
the leaders went off to Cilicia, or to Edessa, or on further raids
into infidel territory. Robert of Normandy took over Latakia,
which had been the most southerly city of the old Greek
Empire. But he taxed his new subjects too heavily, so the Greek
townsfolk drove him out and fetched a Greek garrison from
Cyprus.

In crowded Antioch, where so many corpses had been hastily
buried, an epidemic raged. In August the Bishop of Le Puy
died of it. The leaders at once wrote to the Pope to suggest that
he come out himself to assume command of the victorious
army of Christendom; but if not he must send another papal
legate, for there were complicated ecclesiastical problems to be
solved.

There were indeed. Bishop Adhemar had always doubted the

68

Holy Lance, and while he lived Peter Bartholomew kept quiet. Now he broke out into fresh revelations. In a vision the dead legate confessed to him that he had been punished in Purgatory for his lack of faith in the relic, though now the prayers of the Crusaders had squeezed him into Heaven. Then St Andrew laid down what the army must do next. Bohemond should keep Antioch, Raymond should command the attack on Jerusalem, and—something quite new—all Greek bishops in liberated cities should be replaced by Latins.

So far the schism between Rome and Constantinople had not been imported into Antioch; the Patriarch John was obeyed by Latins as by Greeks. When in October Raymond captured the Moslem town of Albara he filled it with Christian settlers and gave them as Bishop a Provençal, Peter of Narbonne. This Peter was the first Latin to rule an oriental see; but then there was no Greek Bishop in Moslem Albara. He was consecrated by his Greek metropolitan, the Patriarch John. In any case the appointment mattered little except as a precedent; for Peter soon abandoned his cathedral to march with the army to Jerusalem.

This new revelation embarrassed Count Raymond. He was guardian of the Holy Lance, and believed in it; but he was also the chief advocate of friendship with the Greeks. The lesser Crusaders made up their minds without hesitation. They knew that Bishop Adhemar had been a holy man. If Peter Bartholomew said that he had been in Purgatory, and had barely escaped Hell, then Peter Bartholomew was a liar and this Lance of his a bogus relic.

It is not unfortunately so easy as that. Perhaps Peter Bartholomew was tempted into relating false visions, but this does not prove that his first vision was false. In this world we shall never know the truth about the Holy Lance.

As winter approached the pilgrims were eager to get away from Antioch, its hunger and its disease; and even more eager to fulfil their vow by liberating Jerusalem. Simple knights grumbled that they were kept hanging about while the leaders squabbled over the government of the city. Bohemond wanted it. He had captured it. He was warrior enough to defend it. Let him keep it. Count Raymond, the friend of the faint-hearted Emperor, was delaying the Holy War. By the end of the year the rank and file were threatening to march without their leaders unless the leaders moved quickly.

Therefore on 13 January 1099 Raymond led his men south. Robert of Normandy soon followed, with Tancred and a few of the Normans of Italy. Godfrey of Bouillon and the Count of Flanders marched independently. But Baldwin remained in his new County of Edessa and Bohemond in his new Principality of Antioch. The style of Prince was rare at that time, but in Italy a few Principalities were held directly from the Pope as suzerain. It meant that Bohemond did not regard himself as the vassal of any secular ruler, whether the Emperor of Constantinople or a future Christian King of Jerusalem; but that he might perhaps acknowledge an ecclesiastical overlord.

At last the Crusaders had broken the back of their enormous task. Dorylaeum had frightened the Turks; though it had been won largely by accident, because the enemy lost touch with the second column of the army. At Antioch Kerboga had been beaten fair and square, by better men and the superior leadership of Bohemond. Crusaders, fighting in God's cause, could beat anybody. All were certain of victory.

CHAPTER VI

Jerusalem Liberated

There was no powerful enemy between Antioch and Jerusalem. The Crusaders had fought their way clean through the Turkish dominions and out at the other side. The cities of Syria were in the hands of various Arab rulers, some of whom employed small numbers of Turkish mercenaries. Jerusalem, and all Palestine south of Beirut, was held by the Caliph of Egypt.

Arabs did not fight after the Turkish fashion; they were lancers, who charged at speed on their beautiful horses. But these swift horses were smaller than western destriers, and their riders wore lighter armour. Each Arab chief led only a small band of warriors; rival chiefs were often glad to see him defeated, even by Christians.

The Caliph of Egypt, a bitter enemy of the Caliph of Baghdad, ruled wide lands in Africa; his vizier, who governed on behalf of the sacred monarch, was absolute master of his subjects and therefore had plenty of money. His army was very numerous, but his light horsemen could not joust against heavyweight knights. There were also infantry in the Egyptian forces. Since the days of the Pharaohs no one has bothered to bring Egyptian peasants to the battlefield; they are a feeble race, easily put to flight. But Egyptians are also natural engineers, who spend their lives managing irrigation ditches.

In sieges these fellaheen were clever at digging mines and entrenchments. For battle the vizier used black Sudanese foot, gallant archers who would face charging cavalry.

In general, Egyptian armies were not dangerous in the open field. But they were large, and well equipped for passing through desert country; if they besieged a fortress they must be quickly driven off before they undermined its walls.

During January and February Raymond led his men up the Orontes valley and then turned west to besiege the town of Arqa near Tripoli. The infidels of Hama and Homs made no effort to delay him; but before Arqa he stuck. By March Godfrey and the other leaders, save Bohemond, had reached Arqa by the coastal road from St Simeon. They refused to recognise Raymond as leader of the whole Crusade, which he had been calling himself for the last two months, and the council of war was seldom agreed on any question. Tancred, the best professional soldier present now that Bohemond had decided to stay in Antioch, gave it as his opinion that the army was fought out. They should advance no farther until reinforcements reached them from Europe.

But Alexius sent a message saying that he would be in Syria by the end of June, and that if they waited for him he would march with them to Jerusalem. That decided them to go on. No Latin believed that the Greek army would fight the infidel; if Alexius was not lying he would come only to take Antioch from Bohemond.

The Caliph of Egypt sent envoys, with an offer to recognise all the present conquests of the Crusaders if they would advance no farther; he would also open the pilgrim route to Jerusalem. These were not the first overtures from Egypt, whose Caliph hated the rival Caliph of Baghdad more than he hated the Christians; at that moment an embassy from the Crusading army was in Cairo. But the Crusaders' proposal was that the Egyptians should withdraw from the Holy Places and fix their frontier in Sinai—a reasonable basis for peace that would have saved much bloodshed; the Egyptian Caliph could get on very well without Christian Holy Places. Neither side would give way and the negotiations broke down.

Alexius also was negotiating with Cairo; hoping to form a common front against the Turks, and perhaps a common front against the Crusaders. When the Latins learned of these negotiations they were more than ever convinced of Greek treachery and double dealing.

In the meantime, what was to be done about Arqa? Raymond refused to abandon the siege; but all the others were eager to march on Jerusalem at once. During Holy Week Peter Bartholomew produced a string of unconvincing revelations, obviously designed to support the view of his lord Count Raymond. Tancred called him a liar. Peter Bartholomew offered to prove by miracle that the Holy Lance was a genuine relic. On Good Friday he walked between two blazing fires, holding it aloft. He managed to complete the walk, but twelve days later he died of his burns.

This is evidence that Peter Bartholomew had come to believe by this time in the holiness of the Holy Lance, but it proves nothing more. We are never entitled to demand a miracle from God, even if we happen to be in the right. The advocates of Peter Bartholomew said with truth that he had walked through the fire; his opponents answered with equal truth that the fire had killed him. But henceforth Count Raymond gained no prestige from his guardianship of the Holy Lance.

At last on 13 May the army marched south, leaving Arqa untaken. It seemed absurd to waste the summer before this petty fortress, but there was something to be said for Raymond's view. Hitherto the Crusaders had succeeded in everything they undertook; even Antioch had been captured and held, against odds so great that success seemed a miracle. Now they had publicly admitted failure; the infidels might hope that Jerusalem would prove another Arqa.

Luckily the Emir of Tripoli was still frightened of these terrible Christians. He offered to provide food, pay a ransom, and release three hundred Christian captives if the army would march past his town without harming it. There was no fighting as the army proceeded down the coast road towards Beirut, where the Egyptians had a garrison. Genoese and English ships kept pace with the march as far as Beirut, but no farther. Off the coast of Palestine lay a strong Egyptian fleet, which they dared not encounter.

The march went well, though after they had left the fleet rations sometimes ran short. Beirut and Acre offered the same terms as Tripoli, ransom and supplies if the army did not harm them. At Caesarea under Mount Carmel the Crusaders kept Pentecost with fervour; at last they had reached the Holy Land.

At Arsouf they turned inland. The Moslems of Ramleh first destroyed the famous church of St George in nearby Lydda and then fled towards Sinai. The Crusaders erected Lydda into a Bishopric and appointed as Bishop a Norman, Robert of Rouen. This did not infringe the rights of any Greek prelate, for Lydda was a new diocese.

On the morning of 7 June 1099 the army climbed the hill of Montjoie and saw in the distance the Holy Sepulchre. That same evening they encamped before Jerusalem.

The Egyptian garrison was prepared. They had expelled all Christians, poisoned the wells outside the city, and laid in stocks of food.

After two years in the field the Crusading army had dwindled. The numbers who had crossed the Straits had impressed even the Greeks, accustomed to great crowds. Since then battle, disease, starvation and forced marches had taken their toll; and in addition garrisons had been left to hold Antioch and Edessa. The Christians encamped outside Jerusalem were no more than twelve hundred knights and eleven thousand foot, too few to encircle the place. They encamped before the northern and western walls, roughly from Herod's Gate to Mount Sion; a picket held the Pool of Siloam, the only source of clean water— an inconvenient source since it lay within range of the Egyptian machines.

At this hottest season of the year no food could be gathered from the sun-baked countryside. Even worse, there was no green forage, and the few remaining destriers were starving.

The Crusaders knew that a great army of relief was on the march from Egypt. There could be no question of blockade or scientific battery; they must speedily fight their way into the Holy City by brutal and bloody assault.

A hermit on the Mount of Olives advised them to attack at once, in expectation of a miracle. Five days after their arrival they tried to escalade the north wall. But for lack of timber there were not enough scaling ladders. After hours of heavy fighting the attack was beaten off.

No one knew what to try next, and the army was near despair. Then on 17 June a few Genoese and English ships anchored in the harbour of Jaffa, which they found deserted by the infidel. At once the Egyptian fleet blockaded the little squadron; so the sailors marched to Jerusalem, bringing food, tools, and materials for making siege-engines. On the road they were attacked by Egyptians from Ascalon, but they fought their way through. Then Tancred explored as far as the forests near Nablus, where he found timber and camels to carry it. At last there were scaling ladders in plenty, and Raymond and Godfrey each built a movable siege-tower.

On 8 July the whole army walked barefoot round the city, and Peter the Hermit preached a rousing sermon; to such effect that all swore to fight and die for the liberation of the Holy Sepulchre. Even Raymond and Tancred, those notorious enemies, went through a public ceremony of reconciliation.

It was decided to begin the assault at nightfall on 13 July, to avoid the terrible heat of midday. Until then everyone, knights, foot, clergy, women and children, worked at making siege towers and stone throwers, under the direction of ships' carpenters. All the machines must be covered with raw hide from newly slaughtered oxen or camels, lest they be burned by the Greek Fire of the infidel.

Greek Fire was a secret weapon which the Crusaders met for the first time in the orient. We do not know its exact composition, but evidently it had a petroleum basis (so it could not be made in the west, where there are no oil-fields). It had been invented by the Greeks just in time to save Constantinople from the first Moslem attack. For centuries its composition was a closely guarded state secret, but by this time it was known to the Arabs; though Alexius would not share it with the Crusaders. It might be used in several ways. Bellows might force out a long tongue of flame from a tube, or a package of the stuff might be thrown from an engine. Water would not quench it, for the burning oil floated on top. It might be smothered with sand, but the best protection was to cover exposed timber with wet hide.

At nightfall on the 13th three simultaneous assaults were launched. Godfrey's tower was pulled against Herod's Gate in the north wall, Raymond's against Mount Sion in the south, while Tancred led an escalade at the northwestern angle, near the Holy Sepulchre.

Before the towers could approach the wall the ditch must be filled in. This preliminary task took 24 hours of heavy and dangerous toil, within range of the arrows and stones of the defenders. By nightfall on the 14th Raymond's tower was in contact with the wall. But the best men in the garrison had been stationed at Mount Sion, and in stern hand-to-hand fighting they kept the Provençals at bay. On the morning of the 15th Godfrey got his tower into position, but not until midday could he fix his flying bridge to the battlements. Some knights from Lorraine fought their way across; once a stretch of the ramparts was in their hands others followed by scaling ladder.

The Lorrainers widened their hold until they could open the Gate of St Stephen. Then all Godfrey's men and Tancred's poured into the city. They expected hard fighting, for the garrison was at least as numerous as the attackers. But the best of the infidel warriors were holding Mount Sion against Raymond, and in the north resistance collapsed. The defenders of the northern wall fled towards the Temple in the southeast of the city, where they hoped to hold out in their principal mosque. Tancred followed them so closely that he got in before the doors could be barred and they surrendered to him. After planting his banner on the roof, to show that the mosque was under his protection, he returned to the fighting.

The infidels on Mount Sion were well-trained cool-headed soldiers. When they learned of the disaster behind them they disengaged smartly and withdrew to the Tower of David beside the Jaffa Gate, which contained their pay-chest. This they offered to Raymond in payment for their lives. The offer was accepted. The banner of Provence was hoisted on the tower, while the infidel soldiers rode out of the city in safety towards Ascalon.

Elsewhere bloody fighting continued, without quarter. The assailants had no supreme commander to whom the defenders could surrender; if they sought the protection of one leader his rivals might kill them to spite him. This was what happened to the fugitives in the Temple mosque. Naturally they had been disarmed; in the course of the day they were murdered by Crusaders who wanted to demonstrate that they did not take orders from Tancred.

The synagogue was burned, with the Jewish community inside it. The Egyptians had permitted them to remain in Jerusalem when the Christians were exiled; that was considered proof that they were allies of the infidel. All the Moslems were killed, men, women, and children. When the Crusaders gave thanks in the Holy Sepulchre where no priest remained to serve the shrine, they took over an empty city.

In fact there was a remarkable lack, in July 1099, of established authority in Jerusalem. The exiled Patriarch had recently died in Cyprus. No papal legate had been sent out, though Adhemar of Le Puy had been dead for nearly a year. The throne of St Peter was about to fall vacant; Pope Urban II died in the same July, before he knew of the liberation of the Holy City. The council of leaders who met to decide the future of the Holy Land began with a remarkably clean slate.

CHAPTER VII

The Establishment of Outremer

We do not know exactly who voted in the council of leaders, but in Jerusalem at that time there were only four noblemen grand enough to be considered for the supreme command: Raymond of Toulouse, Robert of Normandy, Robert of Flanders, and Godfrey of Bouillon. The obvious choice would be Count Raymond, one of the originators of the Crusading movement, a friend of the late Pope and the lord of the late legate, bound by oath to remain in the east. But his three rivals were united in dislike of him; partly because he had so obviously striven for the supreme command ever since they left Constantinople, partly because he was the partisan of the Emperor Alexius who had withdrawn from the Holy War. Nevertheless, in the interests of unity a halfhearted and reluctant council began by offering him the crown of Jerusalem.

Raymond was wise enough to know that he could never enforce his authority over these reluctant comrades. But he was the kind of cunning diplomatist who is sometimes too clever by half; he refused the honour, saying that the Holy City, the common property of Christendom, ought to be ruled by its Patriarch, with military defence entrusted to a commander nominated by the Pope. He did not know that the Pope who might well have nominated him, Urban II, was already dead; and he thought that his high-minded refusal would prevent the election of any other leader.

He was mistaken. Even though the council of war might continue to lead the army the Crusaders needed a commander to allot castles and fiefs; and they would not wait for an appointment from distant Rome. The Duke of Normandy and the Count of Flanders planned to go home as soon as possible, so that the only candidate remaining was Godfrey. He also refused the kingdom, saying that he would not wear a crown of gold where Our Saviour had worn a Crown of Thorns; but he accepted all the military and administrative powers of a king, with the title of Advocate of the Holy Sepulchre. Advocate was the title given in France to the lay protector of the lands of a monastery.

The Holy Sepulchre still lacked a Patriarch to govern it and clergy to serve it. The Patriarch Simon was dead in Cyprus and the rest of the Greek clergy had been expelled by the infidel. The Latin clergy then in Jerusalem proceeded to elect a Patriarch. Canonically their right to elect was doubtful; on the other hand they were the only clergy then present in Jerusalem, and in early days Bishops were often elected by the clergy of the diocese.

It would have been a sound move if they had elected a sound Patriarch. Unfortunately they could not find one. All the outstanding Bishops with the army had died of hardship or disease during the long halt at Antioch. Perhaps as part of a deal to reward the Duke of Normandy, who had behaved very gallantly throughout the war and got nothing from the victory, they chose one of his Norman chaplains, Arnulf. He was an eloquent preacher but inexperienced in administration, and his private life was not all that it should have been. He appointed twenty Latin Canons to assist him, and of course the exiled Greek clergy were permitted to return; for the schism of Constantinople did not extend to the Patriarchate of Jerusalem. But he expelled the downright heretics, Jacobites, Copts, Armenians, whom the infidel rulers had allowed within the shrine; which gave offence to the numerous heretics among the Christians of Syria.

All this had to be done very quickly, for a great Egyptian army was on the march. Early in August the Egyptians reached Ascalon, their fortified advance-post in Palestine. They were confident of victory, for they outnumbered the Christians many times over. They halted in their great camp outside Ascalon, while they decided whether to march first against Jerusalem or Jaffa.

They never dreamt that the outnumbered Christians would take the offensive; but for the last time the invincible army of the First Crusade went into action. At dawn on 12 August the Crusaders charged right through the camp of the infidels, who were completely taken by surprise. Robert of Normandy captured the tent of the Egyptian commander, containing his standard and his sword. A few infidels found refuge within the walls of Ascalon, but the great majority were killed in the rout.

The dismayed garrison of Ascalon offered to surrender; but they would yield only to Count Raymond in person, because he had saved the lives of his captives at the taking of Jerusalem. Duke Godfrey would not permit this slight on his authority, and the deal fell through. That was a pity, since the infidel fortress of Ascalon continued to endanger the pilgrim route from Jaffa to Jerusalem for another fifty years.

Now that the Egyptians had been beaten Jerusalem was safe; for the collapse of Turkish power had left the other infidels hopelessly disunited. Each city of infidel Syria had its own ruler on bad terms with all his neighbours. The Crusaders had fulfilled their vow, and those who wished might go home.

The Duke of Normandy left at once, to misgovern his Duchy until his brother, King Henry I of England, shut him up in a dungeon for the last thirty years of his life. During the Holy War, fighting for a cause in which he believed, he had behaved like a responsible leader and a true knight; but he could not keep it up. The Count of Flanders went home with him.

Count Raymond, who had sworn to remain in the east, journeyed slowly northward. In Latakia he was made welcome by the Greek commandant. He left his followers there, under the command of his wife, to help defend the city against Bohemond of Antioch; he himself went on to Constantinople to confer with his friend the Emperor.

Tancred easily overran the central plateau of Palestine, where few infidels remained. He took the title of Prince of Galilee, which might imply that he was independent of Jerusalem and subject only to the Pope; but in fact he recognised Godfrey as his overlord. Godfrey himself began a slow conquest of the seaports, whose infidel garrisons escaped to Egypt by sea; for the Egyptian fleet was still supreme in coastal waters.

At Christmas 1099 Bohemond of Antioch and Baldwin of Edessa came south to fulfil their Crusading vow by hearing Mass in the Holy Sepulchre. With them they brought Daimbert, Archbishop of Pisa, who had been sent out by the late Pope Urban to succeed Adhemar as legate. When Daimbert reached Jerusalem he expelled from the Patriarchate the Norman Arnulf, as uncanonically elected; and immediately elected himself. He then tried to make the Patriarch temporal lord of Jerusalem and Jaffa. Godfrey, busy with his sieges on the coast, did not bother to oppose him; but the lay Crusaders would not submit to the rule of a clerk. However, the whole Pisan fleet had escorted their Archbishop oversea; so that Venice, the bitter rival of Pisa, sent her fleet to watch their doings. The Egyptian navy no longer commanded the sea.

Outremer, the land over sea, as the French called the string of little Frankish states from Cilicia to Sinai, had now taken shape. In the north lay the independent Principality of Antioch, perpetually menaced and coveted by the Greek Emperor; on its western border the Armenian chieftains of Cilicia paid tribute either to Antioch or Constantinople, whichever course seemed more prudent at the time. Eastward of Antioch lay the precarious County of Edessa, with infidels to the north, south and east. Its army was more Armenian than Frankish though its Count was Baldwin of Boulogne. He described himself as a vassal of Jerusalem, though he lived too far away to help or hinder the ruler of the Holy City.

South of Antioch Count Raymond had conquered the County of Tripoli for himself, after Bohemond had driven him from Latakia. It was the only district of Outremer in which southern French, the Langue d'Oc, was spoken; everywhere else north French was the official tongue, to the vexation of German pilgrims who pointed out that Godfrey had been a German Duke, born of a German mother.

At Beirut began the Kingdom of Jerusalem proper, extending at one time as far south as Sinai and the Gulf of Akaba. But to the eastward none of these states had a fixed frontier; there was a perpetual seesaw with the infidel. In 1100 the Egyptians still held Ascalon and a great part of the coast. The greatest fief in the Kingdom was Tancred's Principality of Galilee; but it was always reckoned a part of the Kingdom, not an independent state on its own.

There were not nearly enough western knights to hold this long frontier. When the Duke of Normandy and the Count of Flanders went home, as they had every right to do, they were begged to appeal for permanent settlers. Outremer needed immigrants from Europe, not just pilgrims who would worship in the Holy Sepulchre and then go home. But the infidels saw Frankish knights as invincible; had they not destroyed a great army of Turks at Dorylaeum and a great army of Arabs at Ascalon? Also the infidels assumed that if ever the Christians were really in a bad way the mighty Emperor of Constantinople would march to their rescue. In the course of the year 1100 Bohemond, whose military success may have brought on swollen head, proceeded to throw away both of these intangible advantages.

He knew that his Greek subjects were disloyal, regarding themselves as servants of the Emperor who had never abandoned his claim to Antioch. He therefore expelled his Patriarch, the traditional leader of the local Greeks. That was severe, but there were precedents for such political intervention in ecclesiastical affairs. But Bohemond then appointed a new

Patriarch, the Latin Bishop of Artah, as though the secular power could of itself declare a Patriarchate vacant. The expelled Greek Patriarch resigned his See and entered a monastery in Constantinople; but Alexius appointed a successor. There were now two rival Patriarchs of Antioch, Greek and Latin. The schism of Constantinople had spread to Outremer.

Then Bohemond set out with a small force to answer an appeal for help from the Armenians of Melitene, beyond his northern frontier, who were menaced by the Turks of Sivas. On the way he fell into a Turkish ambush; after most of his men had been killed he was captured. He was taken off to be held for ransom in a distant fortress towards the Black Sea. The belief that Frankish knights were invincible had vanished for ever.

With great initiative Baldwin of Edessa at once took over the defence of the Principality of Antioch; he even managed to drive the Turks from Melitene. When he came back from this expedition, in August 1100, he learned that his brother Godfrey had died, probably of dysentery, after holding the office of Advocate of the Holy Sepulchre for just a year.

There followed a general post among the Frankish leaders. Baldwin of Edessa set out from Antioch to take over Jerusalem; on the way he defeated the Emir of Damascus in a savage two-day battle up and down the narrow pass where the Dog River reaches the sea north of Beirut. He gave the County of Edessa to his cousin Baldwin of Le Bourg. Tancred left Galilee to take up the regency of Antioch on behalf of his imprisoned uncle. King Baldwin, crowned in Jerusalem on 11 November 1100, gave the vacant fief of Galilee to Hugh of St Omer.

King Baldwin I was a stern and resolute soldier, the real founder and preserver of the tottering Kingdom of Jerusalem. It is odd to recall that during the First Crusade he had set the bad example of making war on Tancred, a fellow Crusader. Since then his sense of duty had increased. He fought the Holy War with devotion and ferocity; but he fought only for the common cause, never for his own hand.

His task was made more difficult by the collapse of Frankish military prestige. After the Turks of Sivas had captured the mighty Bohemond they no longer feared the charge of mailed knights. During the year 1101 their cousins the Turks of Iconium, the horde who had been driven from Nicaea and routed at Dorylaeum, scored a series of easy victories over western armies which restored their morale also.

When Europe learned that Jerusalem had been liberated, but that reinforcements were needed to man the new frontier of Christendom, thousands took the Cross. But the brief summaries which they had heard of the exploits of the First Crusade made their task seem far too easy. While they marched through the Empire the Greeks would feed them; then after a few brushes with skirmishing Turks while they crossed Asia Minor they would be in touch with the invincible Normans of Antioch; then they might journey safely through Christian territory as far as Jerusalem. They forgot that the battle of Dorylaeum had very nearly been a disaster, and that during the terrible leaguer of Antioch brave knights had fled in despair. The overland journey to Outremer was still a very dangerous undertaking.

In the autumn of 1100 a great company of Lombards set off for the east, led by the Archbishop of Milan with the Count of Biandrate as military commander. From Belgrade to Constantinople they had the usual disputes with their Patzinak escort. At Constantinople they resented the efforts of Alexius to hurry them over the Straits before other Crusaders had arrived. Presently, growing really angry, they tried to sack the Imperial Palace. In default of more trustworthy guards Alexius turned loose on them the lions of his imperial menagerie; until Count Raymond of Toulouse, who happened to be staying with the Emperor while his men held Latakia against the Normans of Antioch, persuaded them to go back to camp. Eventually they crossed the Straits, to wait near Nicomedia for reinforcements.

In the summer of 1101 they were joined by the army of Stephen Count of Blois; he had come back, on the orders of his forceful wife, to redeem his cowardly flight from the siege of

Antioch. With him came a smaller band of Germans led by Conrad, Constable of the Holy Roman Empire. Lombards, French and Germans united in a single army, and appointed to supreme command the veteran Count Raymond. They then set out to follow the route of the First Crusade, by way of Dorylaeum and Iconium.

But when the ordinary Crusaders heard that their hero Bohemond was held captive by the Turks of Sivas they insisted on marching northeastwards to rescue him. The fact that Count Raymond advised against the detour made them all the more set on it, for the enmity between Raymond and Bohemond was notorious. At first all went well. They captured the important fortress of Ankara, and loyally handed it over to the Greeks in fulfilment of the treaty they had made with Alexius before they left Europe.

East of Ankara they were within the Turkish grazing lands, where there were no crops for their foragers to gather; and soon they could not forage, for the Turks beset them closely. Count Raymond proposed that they turn north to seek refuge among the Greek fortresses on the coast of the Black Sea; if on the way they could capture Castamuni, the famous Castra Comnenon which had been the cradle of the Comnenan dynasty, Alexius would perhaps reward them by sending them to Outremer in his ships. But before they reached Castamuni heat, thirst and starvation had driven them to despair. Raymond still advised a breakthrough northward to the fertile coast; but the pilgrims shouted that he was a traitor, in league with Alexius for the destruction of all Crusaders. They turned east again, across the river Halys; perhaps still hoping to rescue Bohemond, perhaps merely trying to get away from the pastures of these terrible Turks into cultivated ground. At Mersivan, beyond the Halys, the Turks shot them down from a distance without ever coming within reach of the heavy western swords.

Deserting their comrades in the field, Count Raymond and his bodyguard fled to a Greek port on the Black Sea. During the day all the foot, the clergy, the women and the children were killed or enslaved; but a number of knights fought their way out to Sinope on the coast. It was not that these knights fled too soon; only Count Raymond was reproached with cowardice. When a Crusading army met disaster the knights often escaped; Turks were not eager to close with a well-mounted warrior in stout mail while there were helpless noncombatants to be captured for the slave-market. After all was lost a resolute knight might gallop away unpursued.

Following the Lombards, and trying to overtake them, came a band of French Crusaders led by the Count of Nevers. At Ankara they lost the trail, turned eastward, and were wiped out at Heraclea. The Count of Nevers fled on towards the east, with two or three knights. In the Taurus mountains they found a castle garrisoned by Greeks, whose governor gave them an escort of Patzinaks to see them safe to Antioch. In the wilderness the Patzinaks robbed them of their arms, horses and money, but did not kill them. They reached Antioch naked, starving, and on foot, complaining to everyone they met that Greeks were traitors to the Holy War.

Behind the Count of Nevers came another army, southern French under the Duke of Aquitaine and Germans under the Duke of Bavaria. With them rode the Count of Vermandois, the brother of the King of France who had deserted the First Crusade at Antioch. This army also was destroyed by the Turks at Heraclea, and again the leaders fought their way free. But they did not seek help from the Greeks and arrived at Tarsus in fairly good shape. There the Count of Vermandois died of his wounds, without ever fulfilling his vow to hear Mass in the Holy Sepulchre.

Among those captured in these defeats were the Archbishop of Salzburg and the dowager Marchioness of Austria. For some reason, instead of seeking a ransom from the Archbishop the Turks ordered him to deny his faith on pain of death; and he was duly martyred. It was said afterwards that the Marchioness, a famous beauty, was sold into a Turkish harem where she became the mother of the famous infidel warrior Zengi. Crusaders often comforted themselves with the fancy that infidels who defeated them were really of European descent; but because a tale is told too often that does not prove that it is never true. No one knows what became of the Marchioness, or of countless thousands of other Christian captives in the hands of infidel slave-dealers.

These disasters did great harm to the Christian cause. The victorious Turks now closed the precarious overland route from Constantinople to Antioch. In 1099 and 1100 a little energetic campaigning by the Emperor Alexius would have opened it permanently for Christendom. The Greek navy, by attacking on suspicion of piracy every western ship they encountered, did their best to close the sea route also. Every Crusader in Outremer now regarded the Greeks as treacherous enemies, who had guided honest pilgrims into Turkish ambushes. That accusation was false; but it seems true that Alexius preferred Turks to Latins as neighbours, and was not sorry to see these expeditions destroyed. Of course Count Raymond incurred most of the blame. When he landed at Tarsus on his way to join his wife in Latakia the Normans of Antioch arrested him as a traitor to Christendom.

The pity of it is that these defeats were quite unnecessary. United, the three armies would have been strong enough to cross Asia Minor unmolested. But the Lombards were impatient to rescue their hero Bohemond, the Count of Nevers hurried to catch up with them, and the Duke of Aquitaine hurried to catch up with the Count of Nevers. No one had the patience to halt and wait for late-comers.

Meanwhile King Baldwin was engaged in desperate war with the Egyptians. The infidels still hoped that the Crusade might prove to be a mere raid, and that the Franks might be driven right out of the east. The ministers of the wealthy Caliph of Cairo sent army after army of Arab and Sudanese mercenaries north to Ascalon. Naturally, after each defeat the next army was made up of worse material.

The Egyptians were now employing a new type of soldier, the mamelukes. These were slaves, mostly from the Caucasus, bought young and carefully trained to arms. As slaves, they must obey orders; so they were more thoroughly trained and better disciplined than most free warriors. A successful mameluke might be entrusted with an important command; but he remained in theory a slave, to be killed or imprisoned at the whim of his owner. The theory broke down only when troops were willing to follow their mameluke leader against his lawful owner. Such a great career lay open to a mameluke that free men would sometimes offer themselves to the service; in later days the great Saladin once described himself as a mameluke of the Caliph of Baghdad, though he was never a slave in law. Man for man, a mameluke might be as mighty a warrior as a Frankish knight; but the other troops in an Egyptian army were still Arab light horse, or dismounted black archers.

Between 1101 and 1105 King Baldwin disposed of three Egyptian armies at the three battles of Ramleh, won against enormous odds. But at the second battle, in 1102, he was for a time in grave danger. He had attacked with only five hundred knights, including the surviving leaders of the expeditions across Asia Minor who were staying with him in Jerusalem. After fighting all day he took refuge in a tower, from which he escaped in romantic circumstances. A bedouin sheikh helped him to get away, because King Baldwin had spared his bride during a raid on an Arab encampment. Next day Christian reinforcements arrived and won the battle; but meanwhile the knights who had stayed in the tower, nearly all great lords, had died fighting. They included the German Constable Conrad and the Count of Blois, whose gallant death atoned for his flight from Antioch in 1098.

When King Baldwin was not repelling Egyptian invasions he raided the bedouin beyond Jordan, or continued the slow reduction of the coastal cities. In 1118 he even carried an impudent counter-invasion of Egypt as far as the Nile, with a force of only 216 knights and 400 foot; such was the terror of his name that the Egyptians would not meet him in the open field. He built castles to hold down the land he conquered. They were designed with all the ingenious refinements of western military architecture, which was more advanced than eastern fortification; but instead of timber palisades all was of

stone, either because the native workmen had been trained to
build in masonry after the eastern fashion or because in that
arid country there were no big trees.

King Baldwin was master in his own Kingdom, despite
efforts by the Patriarch Daimbert to restrict the lay government
to military matters only. After endless intrigues a church council in Jerusalem deprived Daimbert of his office. To satisfy
public opinion two aged Patriarchs were elected, one after the
other; and when the second of these had duly died of old age
Arnulf the Norman was restored to the position he had first
held in 1099. Arnulf knew himself to be unworthy of the high
honour, and was content to take second place after the secular
power.

Meanwhile Bohemond lay in a Turkish prison, where he
amused himself by flirting with the wives of his captor. Tancred, who enjoyed being regent of Antioch, did not offer a
ransom for his uncle; though in 1102 he ended the scandal of
open war between fellow-Crusaders by releasing Count Raymond in exchange for the city of Latakia. Raymond agreed to
found a fief to the south of the Principality; and settled down
to besiege Tripoli from the great castle of Mount Pilgrim
which he built before its walls. In 1105 he died from burns
received in siege-warfare, and was honoured by his followers as
a Crusader fallen on the field of duty. A son came out from
Toulouse to succeed him. Tripoli held out until 1109, and then
became the capital of a County feudatory to Jerusalem.

In 1102 it became known that Alexius had offered to buy
Bohemond from the Turks of Sivas. If the famous hero of the
First Crusade fell into Greek hands he would lose his eyes, if
not his life. King Baldwin and the Patriarch of Antioch raised
contributions towards his ransom from all the veterans of the
First Crusade and from the Normans of Italy. Tancred did not
contribute. But in 1103 Bohemond was released, and took over
the government of Antioch.

Once more Bohemond made himself supreme in Cilicia,
where Greek garrisons had been encroaching. But in 1104
the joint armies of Antioch and Edessa were defeated by the

infidel in a scrambling fight near Harran. Each side had planned to ambush the other, and the infidel trap was sprung first. The Patriarch of Antioch, one of the first to flee, thought it prudent to cut off the tail of his horse lest a Turk should seize him by it. The army of Edessa was almost wiped out; Count Baldwin was among the captured, and remained in Turkish hands until ransomed in 1107.

With help from King Baldwin Edessa was saved. But the Principality of Antioch was now in a bad way. In Cilicia the Greeks were openly making war on their fellow-Christians; and though their army was not formidable their navy commanded the sea. The Turks of Sivas pressed on the Armenians to the north, the Turks of Mosul menaced the eastern frontier, to the south the Count of Tripoli could not be expected to behave as a friend. Bohemond was a subtle and ambitious politician, no more interested in the cause of Christendom as a whole than was the Emperor Alexius. He decided on a complete change of plan. The most dangerous foe to his own personal dominions was the Greek Empire; and the Empire was more vulnerable in Europe than on its war-torn eastern frontier. He would go back to Italy, recruit another great army of Crusaders, and overthrow Alexius. Then he might reign over the whole Christian east, securely in communication with his cousins in Sicily.

But to reach Europe he must pass through waters dominated by the Greek fleet. The story goes (it is only a story) that in 1104 he was smuggled on to a ship in a coffin, accompanied by a very dead cock to give off a convincing stink. It was said that he was being sent home for burial in the tomb of his ancestors. He got safely to Apulia, leaving Tancred as regent of Antioch; he then toured France and Italy in great glory as the most famous hero of the First Crusade. He was quite openly gathering recruits for an attack on Constantinople. But Alexius found an answer. In his turn he gathered an army of Turks, men who had fought against the Cross at Dorylaeum; and with them in 1107 he met Bohemond outside Durazzo. After a year of manoeuvre and countermarches Bohemond was surrounded.

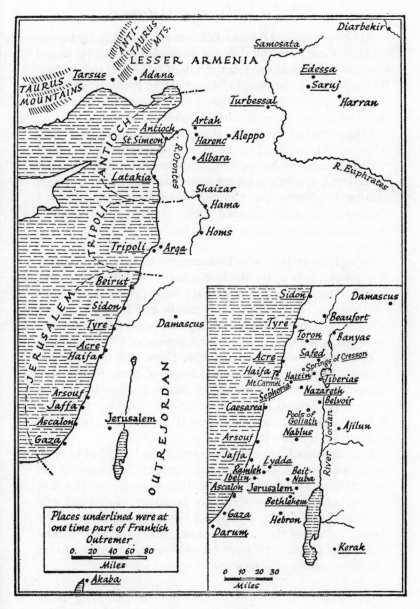

OUTREMER

Places underlined were at one time part of Frankish Outremer

0 20 40 60 80 Miles

0 10 20 30 Miles

LESSER ARMENIA

TAURUS MOUNTAINS

ANTI-TAURUS MTS.

Diarbekir

Samosata

Edessa
Saruj

Tarsus   Adana

Turbessal   Harran

Antioch
St. Simeon

Artah
Harenc   Aleppo
Albara

R. Orontes

Latakia

Shaizar
Hama

R. Euphrates

Homs

Tripoli   Arqa

Beirut

Sidon

Tyre

Damascus

Acre
Haifa

OUTREJORDAN

Arsouf
Jaffa
Ascalon
Gaza

Jerusalem

Akaba

Sidon   Damascus

Beaufort

Tyre   Toron   Banyas

Acre   Safed   Springs of Cresson
Haifa   Hattin   Tiberias
Mt. Carmel   Sephoria   Nazareth
Caesarea   Belvoir
Pools of   Ajilun
Goliath   Nablus   River Jordan
Arsouf

Jaffa   Lydda
Ramleh   Beit-
Ibelin   Nuba
Ascalon   Jerusalem
Bethlehem
Gaza   Hebron
Darum

Kerak

At Devol, outside Durazzo, Bohemond surrendered in person to Alexius and swore all that was demanded of him. He would evacuate Cilicia, and hold Antioch itself as a fief of the Empire; he would install the Greek claimant to the Patriarchate. If the Normans now in Antioch refused to be bound by these terms then Bohemond in person would make war on them.

After swearing these oaths Bohemond went back to Apulia, where until he died in 1111 he lived happily with the highborn French princess he had married after his return from the east. He claimed, of course, that the oaths sworn at Devol had been extorted by duresse, and therefore did not bind him. Tancred the regent naturally ignored them. Alexius did not really understand the customs of western feudalism so thoroughly as he supposed.

In his lifetime Bohemond was revered as a hero and a brilliant soldier; and rightly. But he was never a dedicated Crusader, and his intervention did more harm than good to the cause of the Holy War. It is perhaps a pity that he ever fought under the banner of the Cross, though if things had gone a little differently he might have made a competent Emperor of Constantinople.

Tancred died a year later, aged 36. There were the inevitable rumours of poison, but in the climate of Syria Franks died suddenly. His nephew Roger of Salerno succeeded to the regency of Antioch, though he held it only in trust until Bohemond's infant son, Bohemond II, should come from Italy to claim his inheritance.

King Baldwin I and the Emperor Alexius both died in 1118. In Constantinople John Comnenus peacefully succeeded his father; the cousin of Baldwin I, Baldwin of Le Bourg, Count of Edessa, became the second King of Jerusalem. His official style was 'King of the Latins in the Holy City of Jerusalem', to show that he was rather the leader of a foreign army than the natural lord of the country. He gave his old County of Edessa to his kinsman Joscelin of Courtenay.

CHAPTER VIII

Troubles in the North

King Baldwin II was crowned in Jerusalem on Easter Sunday, 14 April 1118; and almost immediately had to face the customary invasion from Egypt. The Egyptians attacked whenever there was a crisis in Jerusalem. Egyptian money could raise an army at short notice, but an Egyptian army was not a good army.

King Baldwin II, who had been a prominent leader during the First Crusade, had thought out tactics for meeting infidel armies which afterwards became the standard practice of Outremer. Jerusalem was now full of middleclass Frankish merchants and craftsmen; so he had plenty of trustworthy infantry, better men than mere peasants. These foot marched in a hollow square with the knights inside it. Thus the irreplaceable destriers were protected from arrows; the crossbows carried by the Christian foot could outrange the short horseman's bows of the Turks. If the infidels were massed and willing to fight the knights would suddenly charge out through an opening in the square. But often the skirmishing infidels would not stand, and then there was a danger that the destriers would be shot down before the knights got back to the shelter of their infantry. The way to deal with this was to allow the infidels to encamp beside the only water within miles, and then advance across the desert to attack them. This might seem hazardous;

if the attack failed the Christians would be thirsty during their retreat. But the infidels must stand to defend their water; and if the Christian square got to close quarters it could be certain of cutting its way through. Then the infidels would suffer from a thirsty retreat on top of a lost battle.

That was the best plan if the Crusaders were anxious to fight. But they might be so greatly outnumbered that fighting was too risky. In that case they took advantage of their knowledge that in all infidel armies the bulk of the troops were irregular volunteers who had come out for a brief raid not too far from their own homes, in search of good plunder. If a considerable Christian force hovered near them they dared not scatter to pillage. After some weeks of boredom in the safety of their camp the volunteers would go home.

That was what happened to the Egyptian invasion of 1118. For three months the two armies faced one another without fighting; then the infidels dispersed to their homes.

The other Crusading states, Tripoli, Antioch, Edessa, recognised King Baldwin II as suzerain; but he did not rule all the inhabitants of his own Kingdom. The Venetians maintained a great fleet in the Levant, which destroyed the Egyptian navy and in 1124 captured Tyre after a long siege; but in return for naval help all the Italian merchant cities received separate quarters of their own in every city of Outremer. In these colonies Italian traders might live under their own laws, administered by a consul sent out from the mother-city. They paid no taxes to the crown, they used their own weights and measures instead of those of the Kingdom, and though they turned out to fight the infidel they fought rather as allies than as subjects of the King of Jerusalem.

In 1118 was founded the Order of the Temple, in imitation of the slightly older Order of St John. When the Crusaders liberated Jerusalem in 1099 they found already existing in the city a hospital run by Benedictines from Amalfi in Italy, where Latin pilgrims might rest and recover from the hardships of the pilgrimage. Some Crusading knights joined the community as lay-brothers, with the special task of guarding pilgrims on

the road from the coast to the Holy Places; for this road was
exposed to attack from the Egyptian garrison in Ascalon. Soon
the knights became more important than the nursing brothers,
until the Pope recognised the Knights of the Hospital of St
John as a separate Order, independent of the Benedictines. In
Europe pious landowners gave them rich endowments. The
Templars, whose headquarters lay in the 'Temple of Solomon'
beside the royal palace in Jerusalem, had a similar history.

These knights remained laymen, though they took the triple
monastic vow of poverty, chastity and obedience. They were a
valuable reinforcement; for they were all trained, fit warriors of
military age; veterans past fighting were sent home to manage
the estates of the Order in Europe. An ordinary lay fief of the
Kingdom of Jerusalem might at any given time be in the hands
of a widow or a child. But on the battlefield the knights of the
Orders obeyed only their elected Grand Masters, and their sole
feudal superior was not the King of Jerusalem but the Pope.

At this period the army of Jerusalem consisted of about five
hundred knights who were the feudal vassals of the King, about
the same number of knights from the Orders who were the
King's allies but not his subjects, and several thousand excellent
foot who were mostly Italians serving under their own consuls.
During the reign of Baldwin II that did no harm; he was
admitted to be the supreme leader of all the Franks in Outremer. But if the King should happen to be a weakling, or if
the succession should be disputed, the Kingdom might fall
apart.

In 1119 Ilghazi, the Turkish lord of Aleppo, very nearly
destroyed the Principality of Antioch. He invaded with a great
army from the east. Prince Roger, regent for the child Bohemond II who was still with his mother in Italy, asked for help
from Jerusalem and Tripoli; but in the meantime he marched
against the Turks with only the army of Antioch, in accordance
with the accepted principle of warfare that a small army
concentrated nearby would limit the ravages of invaders.
But he encamped too close, and his scouting was slack. On
28 June 1119, at a place ever after known to the Franks as Ager

Sanguinis, the Field of Blood, his men woke up to find themselves surrounded by overwhelming numbers. A few great lords charged out through the ring, but most of the Norman knights of Antioch fell fighting round their sacred standard. Those of the foot and camp-followers who were not lucky enough to die in battle were taken captive. It seemed that Antioch and Edessa must fall.

But Ilghazi preferred to march back in triumph to Aleppo, where for some weeks he entertained the populace by torturing to death one batch of prisoners after another. King Baldwin hurried up from the south with the armies of Jerusalem and Tripoli, and fought a drawn battle against the Turks at Hab. The Christian prisoners taken at Hab were also tortured to death in Aleppo, but that was the end of the invasion. In place of the late Prince Roger, King Baldwin accepted the regency of Antioch, still on behalf of young Bohemond II.

In 1122 Count Joscelin of Edessa, travelling with a small escort, ran across a party of infidel raiders. At once the Christians charged; but at the same moment the weather broke, the desert turned to deep mud, and the destriers were bogged down. The Count and sixty of his knights were carried into captivity. King Baldwin took over the regency of Edessa also while he negotiated for the Count's ransom.

In the next year the King himself was surprised and captured, while hawking on the banks of the Euphrates within the County of Edessa. His companions were promptly martyred, but the King was taken to join Count Joscelin in the strong fortress of Kharpur. The Patriarch of Jerusalem summoned a council of barons who elected the lord of Sidon as regent; and so efficient was the government which Baldwin had set up that law and order continued undisturbed throughout the Kingdom.

Both Baldwin and Joscelin, married to Armenian ladies, had favoured the native Armenian nobility of the north. Now the Armenians undertook their rescue. Fifty Armenian heroes came to Kharpur disguised as pedlars, but with swords hidden under their clothing. Once inside the castle they surprised the garrison and seized the defences. Count Joscelin was sent off to fetch help. In disguise and on foot he slipped through the besieging Turkish army, crossed the Euphrates on an inflated goatskin though he could not swim, and reached his wife in the Edessan castle of Turbessel. The Patriarch of Antioch dared not march to the rescue with only the small remnant of the army of the Principality, so Joscelin rode on in haste to Jerusalem. From Jerusalem the united army of all Outremer, under the standard of the True Cross, set out by forced marches for Kharpur.

Meanwhile the Turks had offered the King his freedom if he would surrender the castle. But that would have meant death by torture for his Armenian rescuers, and the King refused. The Turks mined their way into Kharpur. They martyred every Christian in the place, male or female, save for the King and two of his barons who were worth good ransoms. These three survivors were removed to the immensely strong castle of Harran.

Next year, about the time the Venetians took Tyre in the name of the captive King, the Turkish leader died. His successor decided that he preferred a rich ransom to the honour and glory of holding captive the King of Jerusalem. Negotiations were opened, and Baldwin was sent to be held in custody at Shaizar, whose ruler acted as intermediary in the bargaining.

The rule of Shaizar at this time was an Arab of ancient lineage, and thus a man of honour. No Christian trusted a Turk sufficiently to pay over a ransom before the prisoner was free, and no Turk would free a prisoner until he had received the ransom; but both sides could trust an Arab nobleman.

The ransom of the King was agreed at 80,000 dinars, and after 20,000 had been paid he was released; though hostages were given for the payment of the remainder. His two companions were martyred, because the King would not buy their freedom by the surrender of Christian fortresses in addition to money. Among the hostages was the King's daughter Yvette. Although she was only four years old this stay among the infidels damaged her reputation. In after years no one would marry her; so that she ended her life, in great comfort, as Abbess of a convent specially founded at Bethany to receive her.

In 1125 King Baldwin defeated the infidels at the bloody battle of Azaz, and took such great booty that he paid off the balance of his ransom and freed the hostages.

The Moslem sect of Assassins appeared in Syria about this time. It had been founded about 1090 in Persia, by fanatics who held that the Caliph of Baghdad was a usurper. Their chief, the Old Man of the Mountain, lived in the fortress of Alamut in Persia. On this mountain-top he had laid out a splendid garden, peopled with beautiful women and furnished with exquisite food and drink. His followers, after being drugged with hashish (whence the name Hashishin = Assassin), woke up to find themselves in this lovely garden. Later they were drugged again, and taken home. Afterwards they were told that they had visited Paradise, and that if they died in the service of the Old Man they would return there for all eternity. Then they would be sent out to assassinate some enemy of the Old Man, and would do it fearlessly. To begin with the Assassins murdered only adherents of the Caliph of Baghdad, and did not bother Christians. In later times the successors of the original Old Man turned to common blackmail and arranged the murder of any lord, Christian or infidel, who refused to pay tribute. Throughout Syria and Outremer the Assassins were greatly feared, for it is impossible to guard against a murderer who does not mind being killed so long as he gets his man.

In 1126 Prince Bohemond II, aged 18, came east to take up his inheritance. King Baldwin handed over Antioch without making any difficulty, and in return the young Prince married the King's daughter Alice. In 1127, for the first time since the siege of Nicaea in 1097, there was no serious fighting between Christians and infidels.

In 1128 King Baldwin, who had no son, chose a successor. He married his eldest daughter Melisande to a middle-aged widower, Fulke, Count of Anjou; whose son and heir, Geoffrey, had just married the Empress Matilda, only child and heiress of King Henry I of England. Count Fulke handed over all his French fiefs to his son, and then came out to live and die in Outremer. But no Crusader could ignore that in the ordinary course of nature a grandson of their future King would rule England, Normandy and Anjou. Surely such a mighty Prince would send help to his cousin in Outremer.

In 1130 young Prince Bohemond II fell in battle against the infidel. At once the most frightful demoralisation showed itself in Antioch, whose stout Norman conquerors had perished on the Ager Sanguinis. The next ruler must be Bohemond's only child, the baby Princess Constance; and by feudal law it was the duty of her suzerain and grandfather, King Baldwin II, to nominate a regent.

But the widowed Princess Alice, Baldwin's daughter, proclaimed herself regent on her own authority. It was widely believed that she would never willingly resign her power; she had only to force or persuade her baby daughter to enter a convent and Antioch would be hers for life. Alice, child of an Armenian mother, had a following among the native Christians; but the Franks of Antioch disliked female rule and invited her father to come north and look into affairs.

When King Baldwin set off at the head of the army of Jerusalem Alice looked round desperately for allies to preserve her independence. She offered to do homage to the Turkish ruler of Aleppo, Zengi, if he would guard Antioch from the King of Jerusalem. King Baldwin intercepted the message, and after hanging the messenger marched on in wrath. His daughter was prepared to stand a siege. She closed the gates of Antioch against him; but her Norman subjects opened them in spite of her. So she took refuge in a tower and bargained for her life. It was agreed that she should retire to her dower, the city of Latakia. King Baldwin himself took over the regency of Antioch on behalf of his infant granddaughter, and named Joscelin of Edessa as his resident deputy.

All this took place in the early summer of 1130. By August King Baldwin II was back in Jerusalem, where he died. He was succeeded by his daughter and son-in-law, Queen Melisande and King Fulke.

About the same time died the famous warrior Joscelin of Edessa. The doctors had warned him that he was dying of an injury received in siege-warfare when he learned that the Turks of Sivas were attacking one of his castles. He ordered his son, Joscelin II, to relieve it; but the young man explained that he dared not march with only the small army of Edessa. Thereupon the dying veteran himself led the army, from a litter. Such was his fame that the Turks retired when they heard of his approach. When a messenger brought the good news the old man halted his army, climbed out of his litter to pray, and died in the midst of his prayers; perhaps the last survivor of the famous knights who had ridden in the glorious First Crusade.

With Baldwin II died the supremacy of the King of Jerusalem over all the Franks of the east. His sudden death had left a legal tangle. The barons of Antioch would not admit that his regency descended as of right to his son-in-law King Fulke; still less that the deputy-regency descended from old Count Joscelin to his son. Princess Alice was invited back to rule her daughter's city; Joscelin II of Edessa and Pons of Tripoli joined her in denying that King Fulke was their suzerain.

King Fulke sailed up the coast with the army of Jerusalem, since he dared not force his way through hostile Tripoli. After a little friendly fighting it became apparent that he was stronger than his enemies, but not strong enough to destroy them. All concerned kept their fiefs and did homage to the King; a homage extorted by force which none of them considered binding.

The Christians were losing their unity just as Zengi was trying to unite the infidel by adding Damascus to his original holding of Mosul and Aleppo.

Princess Alice, still powerful in Antioch as leader of the native Christian faction, still sought allies. Her own followers, who were Christians as well as Syrians, would not accept Zengi as protector. So in 1135 she sent a message to Constantinople, offering the hand of her daughter Constance to Manuel, the youngest son of the Emperor.

For nearly forty years the Greek Emperors had maintained on paper their claim to the allegiance of Antioch; but the Frankish knights and the Latin clergy were horrified at the prospect of a Greek ruler. They sent urgently to King Fulke, acknowledging him to be their suzerain and begging him to find a husband for Princess Constance; which was the right and duty of every suzerain when a fief descended to an unmarried girl. King Fulke chose Count Raymond of Poitiers, younger brother of the Duke of Aquitaine; who agreed to the match and landed in Antioch in the spring of 1136.

He was warned that Princess Alice might arrest him; so he gave out that he had come to propose marriage to the dowager, aged 28, and not to her 9-year-old daughter. While Alice waited in the hall of her palace to receive the handsome stranger he went instead to the cathedral. There he found little Princess Constance, still asking why she had been so suddenly brought to church. The Patriarch married them; and after that, by the feudal code which governed all western Christendom, Count Raymond was in right of his wife unchallenged Prince of Antioch. The wicked Princess Alice slunk off to Latakia, where she died.

Prince Raymond was a famous knight and a gallant soldier; but his chief aim was to secure the independence of his Principality, not to defend Outremer from the infidel. He began by fighting the Armenians of Cilicia, so that Antioch should have a strong barrier against the Greek Empire; when he ought to have made war on Zengi, who was slowly absorbing the other infidel states.

In the same year the Count of Tripoli was defeated and killed by the infidel, which was almost a natural death for the ruler of a Crusading County. But the circumstances were ominous. After his defeat Pons fled alone into the mountains of Lebanon, where the local Christians betrayed him to the Turks. His son and successor Count Raymond took vengeance on the traitors, but here was a dangerous warning that some Lebanese would rather be ruled by fellow-orientals who happened to be Moslem than by fellow-Christians who happened to be Franks. Without the support of the native Christians Outremer would hardly endure.

In 1137 King Fulke led the army of Jerusalem northwards to

help the new Count of Tripoli; but the result was another lost battle in which the Count of Tripoli was killed. The King with a handful of survivors took refuge in the castle of Montferrand. With great energy the Patriarch of Jerusalem raised an army of relief, so that every town and castle was stripped of its defenders and infidel raiders sacked Nablus and ravaged the suburbs of Lydda. But before help could arrive King Fulke had begged for terms. Zengi asked only the surrender of Montferrand. The King gladly accepted such lenient terms. He must endure the humiliation of appearing as a suppliant before Zengi's tent, but it might have been very much worse.

The reason King Fulke got off so lightly was that Zengi, like every other leader in northern Syria, wished to keep his hands free to deal with a new threat which had suddenly appeared among the mountains of Taurus. The Emperor John Comnenus, son of Alexius, was in Cilicia at the head of a large army.

Throughout the East the Emperor of Constantinople enjoyed enormous prestige. He lived in almost superhuman state, he received a very large revenue, he was always surrounded by thousands of attendants. He was believed to be immensely powerful.

As a matter of fact this splendour was largely a sham. The Emperor seemed to be rich because his subjects paid their taxes in money, not in service or in kind as men did elsewhere; but his expenses were so great that he was frequently insolvent, even when his treasury was heaped with gold and silver. The Greek military heroes of the past had come from Asia Minor, now overrun by the Turks; so his enormous army was made up of foreign mercenaries, who could not always be trusted to fight the enemies of the Empire. When the Emperor was away on campaign he must always be looking over his shoulder, for Constantinople was so much the centre of his realm that a palace revolution might unseat even the leader of a victorious army. During this expedition the Emperor John behaved with caution and prudence.

His object in marching east was not to push back the infidel, but to add to his dominions Christian Cilicia and Christian

Antioch. He could advance strong legal claims to these provinces. Undoubtedly the leaders of the First Crusade, while in Constantinople, had promised them to his father Alexius. But most Franks held that Alexius had forfeited his right when he withdrew from the Holy War after the surrender of Nicaea.

Cilicia, disputed by rival Armenian chieftains, soon submitted to the great Imperial army. By the end of August 1137 the Emperor reached Antioch. Immediately his powerful siege-engines began to batter it. Prince Raymond was absent on duty, attempting to rescue King Fulke from Montferrand; but he quickly slipped back through the lines of the besiegers and opened negotiations.

The Christians of northern Outremer were already hard pressed by the infidel; this stab in the back was more than they could endure. Raymond must yield, but he was determined to remain a Prince. Soon it was agreed that he should continue to rule Antioch for the time being, as a vassal of Constantinople; after the Emperor had conquered Aleppo from the infidels Raymond should be installed there, while Antioch became an ordinary tax-paying city of the Empire. Raymond probably guessed that he was safe in Antioch for life; the Greeks were not in the habit of conquering cities from the infidel. But he had to kneel and do homage to the Emperor before a large crowd, and that was always an unpleasant ceremony for a proud Frankish knight.

By the time all this had been fixed up autumn was drawing near; and the Greek soldiers, like most mercenaries, were unwilling to campaign in bad weather. Instead of marching on Aleppo the Emperor returned to pass the winter in Cilicia.

In April 1138 he did march against Aleppo, in company with the sulky Franks of Antioch. But Aleppo was a strong fortress, strongly held by warlike Turks. Presently John turned aside to besiege the isolated Arab city of Shaizar. The Greeks excelled at siege-warfare. Their engines soon smashed the houses of the town and damaged the walls. But to capture the citadel called for a full-scale bloody assault, and the Franks could not be trusted to fight for their new master; the mercenaries, as usual, were reluctant to face heavy casualties. Presently Zengi appeared at the head of a small army, and the Emperor retired to Antioch. To save face all round the Emir of Shaizar paid an interesting ransom, certain Greek crown jewels which had been heirlooms in his family since they were taken on the field of Manzikert in 1071.

The Emperor rode in state through his vassal-city of Antioch to hear High Mass in the cathedral, Prince Raymond and the Count of Edessa walking humbly on either side of his horse. Afterwards, at a meeting in the palace, John demanded that the citadel be handed over to his troops. But at that moment the Frankish burgesses began to riot in the streets, and the Emperor prudently withdrew to his camp beyond the Orontes. Soon afterwards he marched back westwards.

In 1142 he was back in Cilicia. He summoned Prince Raymond and demanded that he yield the city of Antioch, promising to compensate him with some great city of the infidels. Raymond played for time, saying that first he must consult his vassals in accordance with the code of western feudalism. After arguing all summer the Emperor lost patience. His army marched on Antioch and pillaged the suburbs. But winter was approaching, during which his mercenaries expected to be comfortably housed; he returned to Cilicia without seriously attacking the town.

During these negotiations the Emperor wrote to King Fulke, to say that next year he would visit Jerusalem with all his power, and after praying at the Holy Sepulchre wage war on the infidel. The King of Jerusalem answered that of course the Emperor would be welcome, but please would he come without his army? The Kingdom was barren, and could not find provisions for such a great host.

Now the Emperor had never claimed Jerusalem, and King Fulke had no reason to fear him. Furthermore, Jerusalem was always clamouring for Christian reinforcements. If King Fulke did not want the Greek army it can only be because he knew that when it came to the point the Greek army would not fight.

During his first incursion the Emperor had planned to expel

the Latin Patriarch of Antioch in favour of his Greek rival.
The Pope put a stop to that, by proclaiming that any Catholic
who helped to install a Greek Bishop in a Latin see would incur
excommunication. The mercenaries John used in the east were
mostly Latins; his Turkish soldiers were employed more often
against the Hungarians.

In March 1143 the Emperor was accidentally wounded while
hunting in Cilicia. The wound appeared slight, but blood
poisoning proved fatal. His army hastened back to Constantinople, to take part in the fascinating exercise of crowning his
younger son Manuel instead of his elder son Isaac. A disturbing
influence was removed from the political affairs of Outremer.
The Emperor had done the infidels no harm whatever, but
he had gravely weakened the Armenians of Cilicia.

In the winter of 1143 King Fulke died suddenly from a fall
in the hunting field. His 13-year-old son Baldwin succeeded,
with Queen Melisande as regent. The Kingdom obeyed them
willingly, but the Franks of the north would not recognise a
female regent as their suzerain.

Therefore when in November 1144 Zengi laid siege to the
city of Edessa the Franks did not unite for its relief. When the
Turks appeared Joscelin II was absent on a raid. The Latin
Archbishop took command of the defences, assisted by the
Armenian and Jacobite Bishops. Count Joscelin was not strong
enough to challenge Zengi with only his own followers.
Queen Melisande had mustered the army of Jerusalem but it
would be some time before it could arrive. Prince Raymond,
who was busy trying to reconquer Cilicia, refused to help
Count Joscelin.

Nobody hurried. It was assumed that the immensely strong
city of Edessa could hold out at least until the spring. But its
garrison contained few competent soldiers. On Christmas Eve
Zengi's engines battered a breach, and at once his Turks moved
in to the assault. Archbishop Hugh, inexperienced though
personally brave, made a serious tactical error. He was anxious
that the burgesses should not seek refuge in the citadel when
they ought to be holding the outer wall. He ordered that the

gates of the citadel be locked, while he himself remained out-side. But while the burgesses were gathered in the main square to discuss the crisis the Turks broke in. In the fighting that followed the Archbishop, and the bravest of the burgesses, were killed. Two days later the last frightened refugees in the citadel surrendered.

If a fortress resists until it falls by assault its defenders have no right to mercy. Zengi applied the full rigour of the laws of war. The Frankish defenders of Edessa were massacred on the spot, and their women and children sold into slavery. But if Zengi had killed all the Christians in Edessa he would have been left with an empty city, for no infidels lived there. So the native Armenians, Jacobites and Greeks were spared.

At the news that Edessa had fallen there was panic through-out Outremer. Count Joscelin kept his small army together in his castle of Turbessel, west of the Euphrates; but very little of his County remained to him. The Prince of Antioch went in person to Constantinople to beg help. But the new Emperor Manuel, who remembered him as the enemy of his father, would give him no troops and very little money, and for that niggardly help the Prince must perform various humiliating ceremonies.

Still Prince Raymond would do nothing to help Count Joscelin. It seemed that for lack of a field army the whole north would fall to the infidel, castle by castle.

But Zengi learned of trouble in his city of Mosul, and marched eastward to restore order. Then he moved south to attack Damascus. In 1146, while campaigning in Damascene territory, he was murdered in his bed by one of his eunuchs, a slave of Frankish origin. Outremer had a breathing space, but Europe must send help.

CHAPTER IX

The Second Crusade

Rumours of the fall of Edessa brought consternation to all Europe; but the formal appeal for help, sent by Queen Melisande of Jerusalem, did not reach Pope Eugenius III until the autumn of 1145.

The Pope saw at once that he must arrange a General Passage. That was the new name for an international Crusade; in contrast to the little pilgrimages, led by some Count or Baron, which set out during every year that a Christian foothold remained in Outremer to pray at the Holy Places and kill a few infidels.

It was a bitter disappointment. Everyone had taken it for granted that the First Crusade had done its work for all time, and that nothing more was needed than a regular flow of reinforcements. But at least in the planning of a second expedition the mistakes of the first might be avoided. The Pope, a clear-headed organiser, sat down to plan it.

This time the Normans of Italy must be left out. Roger of Hauteville, their leader, had just proclaimed himself King of Sicily; in derogation of the rights of his suzerain, the See of St Peter, and to the annoyance of all the other crowned heads of Christendom. Besides, he claimed Antioch in opposition to Prince Raymond, since he was the nearest surviving kinsman of Bohemond the conqueror. He was also the foe of both

Emperors, the German and the Greek. Luckily at that time the Normans of Italy were occupied in fighting for a foothold on the African coast near Tunis, and were not particularly anxious to go on Crusade.

The Spaniards also were busy fighting the infidel in their own country. The English were engaged in the great civil war between King Stephen and the Empress Matilda. That left only the French and the Germans. But the German Emperor was needed in Italy, to protect the Pope from his local enemies who had driven him from Rome to Viterbo. (Conrad of Hohenstaufen was never crowned, so his title should be King of the Romans. But many contemporaries called him Emperor, and to avoid confusion I shall do so.)

Only the French could be spared, and perhaps that was a good thing. They were the best knights in the world, and most of the settlers in Outremer were their kinsmen. Besides, it would avoid any quarrel about the leadership. This Second Crusade would consist of Frenchmen only, commanded by the King of France.

A Crusade by a national army of Frenchmen would have many advantages. Discipline would be good; any Frenchman would willingly take orders from his young and gallant King, who had already shown himself to be a good knight.

King Louis VII was a Godfearing Christian of unblemished private life, willing to be guided by the Pope in all religious matters; he would have no disreputable clerical friends to be provided with Bishoprics overseas. Best of all, the Greek Emperor would not fear him. Such a great ruler would not be seeking more territory in the east; after a little diplomatic preparation the Greeks would be glad to see him and eager to help him on his way. This Crusade would not repeat the disasters of 1101; instead it would improve on the glorious record of the first great expedition.

There was only one snag. At Christmas 1145, when King Louis proudly announced the glorious enterprise, the French lords would not volunteer and indeed begged him to stay at home. Never before, they said, had a King abandoned his

Kingdom to go on Crusade. The Church had laid down all sorts of paper safeguards for the lands of an absent Crusader, but those safeguards had not protected Duke Robert of Normandy from his greedy brothers in England. It would mean a regency in France, and the government of a regent nearly always led to disorder and civil war.

Neither King Louis nor the Pope would take No for an answer. For Easter 1146 the King summoned his lords to meet him at the holy shrine of Vezelay, the tomb of St Mary Magdalen. There Abbot Bernard of Clairvaux preached in the open air, for the crowd was too great to get into the basilica. St Bernard was the most eloquent preacher in Christendom, and accustomed to telling the laity what they must do. When he had finished speaking there was not cloth enough to provide the crosses which volunteers wore on their mantles, so that St Bernard cut up his own cowl to make more.

It was agreed that the French should set out in the following spring, and march overland to Constantinople by way of Hungary and the Balkans. Ships plied frequently between Italy and the ports of Outremer; the sea passage was known to be the best way to move destriers to Syria without heavy loss on the journey; many small companies of pilgrims went by sea. But the Italians charged heavily for the passage, and even the King of France could not pay for the sea-transport of such a great army.

Everything seemed set fair. Then the enthusiasm got out of hand and the Pope's plans were wrecked. While St Bernard was preaching the Crusade in Flanders a message reached him that another monk was inciting the faithful of the Rhineland to massacre the local Jews before setting out for the Holy Sepulchre. St Bernard hastened to Cologne and suppressed the fanatic. Then he was invited to tour southern Germany; and the movement grew until at Christmas 1146 he was preaching the Crusade to the Emperor and his court at Spires. Conrad and all his men took the Cross.

Now there were two Crusades, King Louis's and the Emperor's. The Emperor, at the very summit of the feudal pyramid, could not take orders from anyone; no Frenchman would permit the King of France to take orders from the Emperor. They could only be rivals. The Germans were first off the mark, entering Hungary in May 1147.

Meanwhile a third force had gathered, common men without famous leaders. Sailors and fishermen from both shores of the Channel assembled in the Kentish ports to sail through the Straits of Gibraltar to Outremer. England provided the largest contingent, but there were also many Flemings and Frisians.

Early in the spring of 1147 the fleet sailed. But the ships of those times could not carry enough drinking water for long passages at sea, and they met bad weather in the Bay of Biscay. They put in to refit at the mouth of the Douro, the last port in Christian hands before the narrow and dangerous passage between infidel Andalusia and infidel Morocco. There they found the Count of Oporto at the head of an army, about to attack the great infidel fortress of Lisbon on the Tagus.

Alfonso Henry, Count of Oporto, was a famous hero, who had already won many victories over the infidel; if he could push them back a bit farther he would be justified in elevating his County into an independent Kingdom. Experienced sailors would see the advantage of driving the infidels from Lisbon, a base from which corsairs set out to prey on the Christian shipping of Biscay and the Western Channel. The Crusading fleet agreed to help him.

After a siege of four months, marked by heavy fighting, the garrison of Lisbon surrendered on terms. The terms were not kept; most of the prisoners were murdered after their surrender. This may have been one more example of the difficulty of concluding a binding agreement with an international army which obeyed no single commander.

The result was a permanent and valuable gain for Christendom. Lisbon, whose first Bishop was an Englishman from Sandwich, became the capital of a new Kingdom from which in after centuries the Portuguese carried the Faith to Mozambique and Macao. We are inclined to see the infidel occupation of Spain and Portugal as a passing phase, doomed to inevitable defeat. But to the men of the 12th century it was a pressing danger, interrupting the passage between the Mediterranean and the North Sea to the great damage of Christendom.

The excellent commercial port of Lisbon needed more inhabitants, and nearby was unoccupied and fertile land. Most of the Crusaders settled down in Portugal, and though some pilgrims went on to Jerusalem the great war-fleet from the Channel never reached Outremer.

Meanwhile in 1146 the Emperor Manuel of Constantinople was making war on the Turks of Iconium. Manuel was a gallant young warrior, in his personal habits more like a western knight than a typical Greek. As a result of the First Crusade Manuel's father and grandfather had won back the western districts of Asia Minor and the entire coast from Trebizond right round to Cilicia. Manuel had a considerable army. Now, with help coming from Europe, there was a chance that he might drive the Turks right back to the Caucasus.

But as soon as the Emperor heard that a great Crusade had started he made a truce with Iconium. He feared Franks more than he feared Turks. He wanted all his troops ready in hand when this great host of pilgrims arrived in Constantinople.

Probably what frightened him most was that Conrad had taken the Cross. If King Louis had come with a purely French army, as the Pope had originally planned, he might have been made welcome. But relations between the eastern and western Emperors were always uneasy, since each claimed to be the only true Emperor in Christendom. Conrad outside Constantinople at the head a great host of Germans might be tempted to unite the two Empires.

All the same, the Greeks behaved correctly. They sent envoys to meet Conrad in Hungary and got from him an oath of friendship; though the German Emperor very sensibly refused to promise Manuel any towns he might liberate, because no one knew the boundaries of the ancient Greek Empire. After crossing the Danube without incident the Germans found guides and rations waiting for them. Until they reached Sofia all went well.

But Germans, though they revered their Emperor, did not obey him very diligently. Also, Germans thought it manly to get drunk, and excused the pranks of a drunken man because he did not know what he was doing. But the Greeks, like most Mediterranean peoples, saw drunkenness as a subhuman failing and an aggravation of any breach of the peace. From Philippopolis to Adrianople there were constant skirmishes between the Germans and their escort; drunken German stragglers were murdered by peasants, and in revenge the Germans sacked monasteries in violation of their Crusading vows. The trouble grew so serious that Manuel begged the Germans to cross into Asia by the Dardanelles without approaching Constantinople. Conrad refused, and in December 1147 he arrived at the capital.

In the suburbs there was looting and skirmishing; the Germans even sacked the hunting palace in which their own Emperor was lodged. Manuel wanted urgently to get them into Asia before they were joined by the French army which was coming up behind them. At first Conrad would not move, but then he had trouble with his contingent from Lorraine. These men were subjects of the Empire, but they spoke French and looked to Paris as the centre of civilisation. After a great deal of ill-feeling on both sides the Lorrainers waited behind to join King Louis while Conrad led the rest of his army over to Chalcedon.

The Germans must now plan their route. They could, at a pinch, travel all the way to Antioch through Christian territory, by going first southwest and then east along the coast. But besides being very roundabout that route was very toilsome, for they would be crossing an endless see-saw of river-valleys and mountain ranges; and the Turks, who did not often respect lines drawn on the map, would probably attack them just the same. On the other hand, the old main road over the central plateau led through wasted country, now little known to the Greeks; and the Turks would certainly attempt to bar their passage.

The Emperor Conrad compromised. By the long and mountainous coast road he sent all the noncombatants, the women and children and peasants and priests who encumbered every Crusading army; they were given a strong escort commanded by his trusted half-brother, Bishop Otto of Freisingen. He himself with his knights and foot-soldiers decided to make straight for Dorylaeum and fight his way through.

Bishop Otto thought it unnecessary to turn his back on Outremer and follow the west coast. Instead he headed more or less due south for the Greek fortress of Attalia. That meant that he was moving along the Turkish border, and his convoy of unarmed pilgrims suffered heavily from Turkish raiders. But in the end the bulk of his men reached Attalia.

Conrad's army advanced boldly into the unknown. But their discipline was sketchy and their scouting very slack. Ten days after leaving Nicaea, in October 1147, they finished an exhausting and waterless march which brought them to a stream near Dorylaeum. The knights dismounted to water their horses, the foot broke rank to crowd down to the stream, and no one would go out on picket until he had drunk. When the Turks charged down on them they never had time to form line of battle.

As usual in these disasters, many of the knights fought their way out of the trap. When the Emperor Conrad reached safety at Nicaea he still had a substantial force of cavalry. But he had lost the whole of his baggage, and all his foot were dead or enslaved. He could do nothing but halt on the Greek frontier until he received reinforcements.

King Louis was not far behind. The French army was smaller than the German, but it had an unusually high standard of discipline. Every man in it was following his natural lord, and they all loved and admired the gallant young King. Queen Eleanor, in her own right Duchess of Aquitaine, had accompanied her husband, with many other noble ladies; their presence may have helped to keep the army well behaved. With them came also the Grand Master of the Temple, bringing a draft of recruits to Outremer. Templars, who had sworn the monk's oath of obedience, were well known for their strict discipline;

and the veterans among them were experienced in Turkish tactics.

The French had marched through the Balkans a month behind the Germans; which meant, of course, that they found little food. But their discipline stood the strain, and in Constantinople they were received as friends. Then the old trouble came up, the question of restoring liberated towns to the Emperor. King Louis would not swear the oath demanded of him, so Manuel retaliated by letting him cross to Chalcedon and then cutting off supplies. King Louis gave way, and the flow of rations started again. Naturally, by this time hungry Frenchmen were asking whether the Emperor Manuel was really on the side of the Christians. At Nicaea they found the survivors of the German army, without food or baggage, practically besieged by Greek troops to keep them from plundering nearby villages. But still there was no open breach between Greeks and Franks.

Safety first seemed to be the wisest policy; for the Crusaders had set out to bring reinforcements to Outremer, not to liberate Asia Minor. King Louis decided to travel by the coastal route; he would be a long time on the journey, but he would bring his men intact to the front where they were needed. He marched southwestward by Smyrna to Ephesus and then up the valley of the Maeander. The German survivors followed behind, though at Ephesus the Emperor Conrad fell sick and was taken back by sea to Constantinople. There he passed the winter, and in March 1148 went on by sea to Outremer.

King Louis kept Christmas in the Maeander valley, and on New Year's Day 1148 encountered the Turks near Antioch-in-Pisidia. The infidels massed to defend the bridge, so the knights had a target for their charge. But when the Turks fled in disorder the Greek commander of Antioch opened his gates and gave them shelter.

When complaint was made to the Emperor Manuel he disavowed the act of his subordinate. He may have been telling the truth, but it was a significant action none the less. A Greek officer watched a fight outside the walls of his fortress between

Franks and Turks. Not only did he stand neutral during the fight; when it was over he helped the Turks to get away. Nothing could show more clearly that ordinary Greek soldiers preferred fellow-Asiatics to fellow-Christians who happened to be Franks.

Now the French turned south for Attalia and the sea. The road ran over high mountains, where January cold and Turkish raiders caused great hardship. One day the vanguard, after they had climbed a pass, saw below them a warm and sheltered plain; though they had orders to hold the crest until the baggage had reached the summit they felt too cold to stay there. It was said afterwards that Queen Eleanor, shivering in her litter, persuaded them to disregard their orders.

From the mountain above hovering Turks charged down into the gap. They reached the baggage in the middle of the army and began to kill the unarmed muleteers. King Louis and his household knights were with the rearguard, which in warfare against Turks was considered the post of danger. The King and his knights charged into the narrow, crowded pass, where the press soon brought them to a halt. Confused hand-to-hand fighting continued until dusk, when the disobedient vanguard again ascended the pass and the Turks withdrew.

In this chance medley the French very nearly lost their King. Louis had charged farther into the throng of Turks than any of his household knights, until his horse was killed under him. As he struggled to his feet the enemy pressed round him. He would certainly have been slain if he had not fought his way up the hill in full armour until he could set his back against a boulder. There he defended himself with his sword until nightfall.

Next day the angry King set up a court of inquiry, threatening to hang the man who had persuaded the vanguard to disobey orders. But the blame could not be fixed upon anyone (save perhaps the Queen), and nothing came of it; except that King Louis, with humility rare in a mediaeval monarch not yet 30 years old, handed over command of the column of march to the experienced Grand Master of the Temple.

In February the army reached the Greek fortress of Attalia and the Crusaders hoped that their troubles were over. But the stores of that remote outpost had been eaten by Bishop Otto's company, the commander would not allow them inside his fortress, and the peasants were so hostile that they guided the Turks on their raids into the Christian camp.

If the French remained where they were they would starve; but local guides assured them that the road eastward was even more rugged than that which they had just surmounted with such pain. In despair King Louis decided to hang the expense and finish the journey by sea.

The Greek commander agreed to find ships for hire. But this unsettled frontier was a dangerous part of the world, avoided by prudent seafarers. Only a very few ships appeared, though more were said to be on the way. King Louis and most of his knights embarked in these first ships, and in March landed at St Simeon outside Antioch. The Count of Flanders was left behind in Attalia in command of the main army. He had been instructed to bring on the foot and the unarmed pilgrims as more shipping arrived.

Without the King and his knights the Crusaders seemed less dangerous; the Greek commander allowed them to move within the walls of Attalia, where they might lodge in safety and reasonable comfort. When a few more ships arrived the Count of Flanders thought he might disregard the letter of his orders and move on to the scene of war. He took with him all the remaining knights, leaving only foot in the town.

By this time the foot were convinced that all Greeks were allies of the Turks. The rumour got about among them that the garrison planned to sell them in the infidel slave-markets of Syria. They set off to march overland to Antioch without leaders, without money, without supplies, without cavalry. Nearly all of them perished.

Thus the armies which had set out from France and Germany had been destroyed in Asia Minor; but the group of knights and barons who reached Antioch with King Louis was still in the eyes of the local Franks a valuable reinforcement. Prince

Raymond of Antioch, who was Queen Eleanor's uncle, was delighted to see them. During the feasts and tournaments organised to entertain them he discussed with King Louis the next move in the Holy War.

The Second Crusade had been mobilised to avenge the fall of Edessa, so it might seem that the first thing to do would be to march east and restore that town to Christendom. But Edessa, never mentioned in the Gospels, is not much of a Holy Place; and Prince Raymond was still on bad terms with Count Joscelin, lurking in his castle of Turbessel on the edge of his lost County. That objective was not seriously considered.

The Count of Tripoli wanted the French to help him recover certain castles on his eastern border, recently lost to the infidel. But that did not sound very exciting, and anyway the Count was bashful about pushing himself forward. For among the companions of King Louis was the Count of Toulouse, son of old Count Raymond of the First Crusade; he had a better claim to the County his father had conquered from the infidel than had the grandson of his bastard half-brother.

The Prince of Antioch proposed a reasonable objective. If all the infidels of Syria and Mesopotamia should ever be united under one ruler Outremer could not survive; therefore let the Christians attack the most powerful of the infidels before he had time to overcome his rivals. These rivals might join in the attack; at the very least they would refrain from helping him. At this moment the most powerful of the infidels was a son of Zengi, Nureddin of Mosul and Aleppo. Let the King of France help the army of Antioch to capture Aleppo, where they would find rich plunder, and Outremer would be greatly strengthened.

Queen Eleanor was hotly in favour of this plan. She was also fascinated by the heroic uncle, not much older than herself, whom she had not seen since she left the nursery. Usually King Louis took her advice. But she was so much in the company of her uncle that scandalmongers began to whisper of incest; and in April the Patriarch of Jerusalem arrived to invite the French to the Holy City and to tell them that the Emperor Conrad was there already.

The King of France could not for shame go off on a plundering raid while his rival the Emperor was fighting for the Cross. King Louis decided to march at once to Jerusalem. Queen Eleanor, accustomed to having her own way, announced that she for one would stay in Antioch. The King took her south by force; which so annoyed Prince Raymond that the army of Antioch took no part in the coming campaign.

The Count of Tripoli also stayed at home, anxious not to meet the Count of Toulouse. But just at this time the Count of Toulouse died suddenly; which seemed so convenient for the Count of Tripoli that everyone suspected poison, in particular Count Bertrand the bastard son of the dead man.

Nevertheless, even without the knights of Antioch and Tripoli, the army which gathered at Acre in June 1148 was the greatest Frankish host that had ever been seen in Outremer. After some discussion the leaders decided to march against Damascus.

The decision pleased the Crusaders from Europe because Damascus, often mentioned in the Bible, may rank as a Holy Place. It pleased 'the barons of the land', as the native-born Franks were called, because Damascus was a wealthy city, promising rich booty, and the centre of a fertile country which would make good fiefs for Christian barons. Strategic experts pointed out that Damascus in Christian hands would cut the great road between the two infidel capitals of Cairo and Baghdad.

But politically the decision was a mistake. The emir Unur of Damascus was the only infidel ruler who dared to stand up to the dangerous Nureddin, and in the past he had not been unfriendly to Christian Jerusalem. Fighting on the defensive against his Turkish rivals he had sometimes accepted surreptitious help from the Franks to preserve his independence. Since the rival Caliphs of Cairo and Baghdad were bitter personal enemies the two empires would never co-operate until one had conquered the other. Meanwhile an attack on Damascus might drive Unur into the arms of Nureddin, and set up the united infidel Syria which must prove fatal to Outremer.

The great Crusading host marched against Damascus, and by hard fighting drove back the defenders from the suburban date-groves to the walls of the city. Then it became known that Nureddin was leading a great army of relief; and other information leaked out which caused quarrels among the Christians.

The barons of the land had agreed that Damascus, when captured, should be ruled by the lord of Beirut, one of themselves. But the Emperor and the King of France had agreed to grant it to the Count of Flanders, to be another semi-independent Crusading fief on the lines of the County of Tripoli. The barons of the land did not see why they should fight for a Fleming, and anyway the siege must be broken off before Nureddin arrived. On the fifth day after they had arrived the Christians began their retreat, and suffered heavily from Turkish raiders until they got back to Galilee. By August the great army had dispersed, with nothing accomplished. The French and Germans blamed the cowardice of the barons of the land, whom they called by the opprobrious nickname of 'Poulains' or 'Colts'; the latter blamed the foolish impetuosity of the newcomers from Europe.

Almost at once Conrad left Outremer; but instead of going home he wintered in Constantinople where his brother married a Greek princess. By the time he reached Germany in 1149 he was a close friend of the Emperor Manuel, with whom he had concerted a plan for a joint attack on King Roger of Sicily.

King Louis remained in Outremer until the summer of 1149, though he undertook no more active campaigning. The Sicilian squadron which took him home happened to get mixed up in a battle between the main Sicilian and Greek fleets. The Greek admiral captured the ship which carried Queen Eleanor, and though she was soon released with apologies King Louis regarded this as another Greek outrage. He, and the other surviving French Crusaders, proclaimed to all who would hear them that the next Crusade should be directed against those perfidious Greeks rather than against the infidel.

The Second Crusade

The disastrous Second Crusade brought about yet another minor disaster. Young Bertrand, the bastard son of the late Count of Toulouse, seized a castle from which to make war on the Count of Tripoli, whom he accused of the murder of his father. The Count sought help from Nureddin and Unur. After the Turks had captured the castle Bertrand and his knights were sold as slaves in Aleppo.

Two great armies had left Europe, commanded by the two most powerful monarchs of the day. After suffering appalling loss of life they had accomplished nothing, except perhaps to increase the hatred between Frank and Greek.

CHAPTER X

The Warrior Kings

W hen the last Crusaders had gone home, in 1149, 18-year-old King Baldwin was faced by grave problems. Perhaps the most tiresome, because unexpected, was the ambition of his mother. Queen Melisande, heiress of the Kingdom, was reluctant to resign power even though her son was of age. She suggested seriously that she should remain ruler of the Kingdom, while Baldwin commanded the army in her name. After this plan had been turned down she tried to hold Jerusalem against her son; but the burgesses would not support her. Various compromises were discussed, including a joint coronation of mother and son. At last Baldwin III got himself crowned in due form, alone; but it had to be done surreptitiously, without his mother's knowledge. For the rest of her life Queen Melisande controlled church patronage, the branch of government which interested her most; but the King ruled all the laity, military and civilian, and did remarkably well at it.

The defence of the north was a constant drain on his resources. The Emperor Manuel had made peace with the Turks of Iconium, leaving them free to attack Antioch from the west while Nureddin attacked from the east. In 1149 Nureddin surrounded and destroyed the whole army of Antioch. Prince Raymond himself fell by the sword of Shirkuh, a Kurdish general in Nureddin's army. His skull, mounted in silver, was sent as a trophy to the Caliph of Baghdad; oriental civilisation in the 12th century was not so superior to that of Christendom as some historians maintain.

In 1150 Count Joscelin of Edessa was captured by an infidel band, who sold him to Nureddin. He was blinded and then chained in a dungeon until he died. It was obvious that the fortress of Edessa would never be restored to Christendom; in despair its Countess sold her remaining castles to the Emperor. Manuel paid a good price for them, in gold; but he did not strengthen their garrisons, and within a year the infidels had captured them all. Presumably the Emperor still nursed the hope that one day he would feel strong enough to attack Nureddin. If ever he should conquer Edessa the Franks must now recognise his title to it.

Young King Baldwin took over the defence of Antioch, not as its suzerain but as next of kin to the widowed Princess Constance. There would be a long regency, for the new Prince, Bohemond III, was only five years of age. But the King could not stay in the north and neglect Jerusalem. Princess Constance must marry again, so that her second husband could rule on behalf of his stepson.

It was the right of a suzerain to arrange the marriage of his vassal heiress, and now it was universally agreed that the Greek Emperor was suzerain of Antioch. Manuel nominated as bridegroom his charming but raffish cousin, Andronicus Comnenus. But on his journey to Antioch Andronicus was defeated by the Armenians, and fled back to Constantinople. Manuel then despatched his widowed brother-in-law, the Caesar John Roger. The Caesar was a Norman of Sicily, yet loyal to the Emperor, a most suitable choice. But he was also old and fat and ugly, and the Princess would not marry him.

All this had taken time. At last, in 1153 the Princess Constance married to please herself. The husband she chose was Reynald of Chatillon, a younger son of the Count of Gien in France; he had come out to Outremer in the following of King Louis, and stayed on because there was no fief for him at home. King Baldwin gave his consent, in his double capacity as

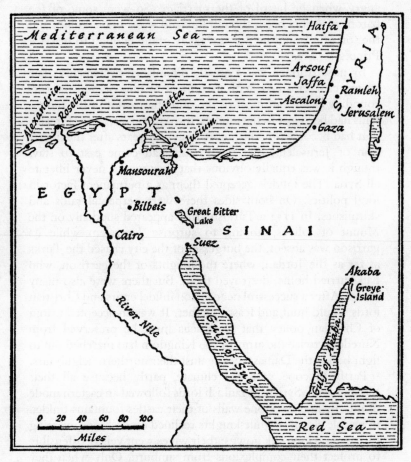

EGYPT AND JERUSALEM

Reynald's lord and head of Constance's family. But nobody remembered to seek the consent of the Emperor, who was very angry when he heard of the marriage. So were some of the barons of Antioch; for though Reynald was a brave knight and the son of a Count he was not really grand enough to marry a Princess.

By now Antioch was a greatly diminished principality. The strong city remained, with its port of St Simeon and the surrounding plain; but most of the outlying castles in the mountains had been lost to the infidels, the Armenians, or the Greeks.

It had become obvious, more than fifty years after the liberation of Jerusalem, that the Franks had come east to stay; though it was equally obvious that they would never liberate all Syria. The infidels accepted them as a permanent factor in local politics. On both sides there were perpetual raids and skirmishes. In 1152 a Turkish army appeared suddenly on the Mount of Olives, hoping to surprise Jerusalem while its garrison was absent; the burgesses of the city chased the Turks as far as the Jordan, where the knights of the garrison, who had hurried home, destroyed them. But there were also many truces. After a successful negotiation infidel emirs and Christian lords would hunt and feast together. It was an accepted axiom of Christian policy that Damascus must be preserved from Nureddin; twice the army of the Kingdom had marched out to fight beside the Damascenes against their northern neighbours.

Partly to cope with the climate, partly because all their servants were Syrians, Frankish lords followed an eastern mode of life. Behind the stone walls of their castles fountains tinkled in marble cloisters while knights reclined on cushions, wearing turbans and long silk gowns: their wives went veiled, ostensibly to protect their complexions from sunburn. Only when they put on armour did they look like proper Franks.

Noble pilgrims who came out for a few months, to hear Mass in the Holy Sepulchre and kill a few Turks, did not like this at all. They might have to go home without drawing their swords because a truce was in force; they objected to stumbling over an infidel guest as he crouched to pray facing Mecca in some corner of a Christian castle. To them all infidels were enemies, and they could not understand this local distinction between good Damascenes and Nureddin's wicked Turks. It began to be whispered in Europe that 'the barons of the land' were half-way to being infidels themselves, no better than those double-faced Greeks.

Meanwhile the power of the Templars and Hospitallers increased by leaps and bounds. They always had knights in plenty, supported by estates safe in Europe. If a castle lay in such an exposed position that raiders always took the harvest no lay lord could afford to live in it, but one of the Orders would be glad to hold it. By 1150 the two Orders combined supplied more than half the knights in the army of Jerusalem. They need not obey the King, for the Pope was their only superior; and they did not always consider themselves bound by truces concluded in the King's name.

In spite of these difficulties, and the uncertain temper of the Greek Emperor, young King Baldwin managed to extend his dominions. In the desert of Outrejordan a line of Christian castles extended as far as the Gulf of Akaba, cutting the overland communication between Baghdad and Cairo. Normally an infidel army could push its way through, but trading caravans must pay tribute to pass. In Outrejordan there were no peasants, but at certain seasons bedouin grazed their flocks there; they were as willing to pay rent to Christians as to Turks.

But the most promising field of expansion was Egypt, which seemed to be falling into anarchy. The Caliph of Cairo was too holy to do anything except appoint a vizier to govern in his name. This vizier held all power until the Caliph chose to dismiss him. In practice either a vizier who feared dismissal murdered the Caliph and chose another from the correct sacred family, or a nervous Caliph first murdered his vizier. The death-rate was such that the Caliph was usually a boy in his teens. Egypt was a very wealthy country, and under such a system of government incapable of self-defence.

In 1153 King Baldwin laid siege to Ascalon. After stiff fighting it was captured; but the course of the siege displayed

Tomb of a 12th century Knight Templar
from the Temple Church, London

the dangerous independence of the Orders. The first breach was made in the sector allotted to the Templars. In the hope of keeping Ascalon for themselves they mounted their own private assault, after posting guards to prevent the royal army from taking part. But the storming column was too weak; the garrison drove them out with the heavy loss of forty knights. Soon the Egyptian garrison surrendered to the King, on condition they might depart unharmed. A great booty was taken. King Baldwin gave the famous fortress, the gateway to Egypt, to his brother Amalric, Count of Jaffa.

But in 1154 Nureddin at last took Damascus; whose people had risen against their rulers, as traitors to the Holy War. Now all the infidels on the eastern frontier of Outremer obeyed one lord, from Aleppo down to Sinai. In the next great war the Christians would be greatly outnumbered.

Severe earthquakes, which destroyed the castles of infidel and Christian alike, suspended the war for a few years; until the new Prince Reynald of Antioch, in mere greed for money, brought back the Greeks to Outremer. Because he felt hard up he demanded a ransom from the Patriarch of Antioch, and tortured him until he got it. The ransom was not enough to satisfy the Prince, but with it he gathered a fleet which plundered the peaceful Greek island of Cyprus. He took valuable plunder, but of course the Emperor Manuel must intervene.

In the spring of 1158 King Baldwin with the army of Jerusalem bumped into Nureddin with his huge army somewhere in Outrejordan. At once the Franks charged, and luck was with them. Nureddin, who was sick, fled after a brief skirmish; and soon his whole army was pelting after him. It was not a serious battle, but King Baldwin won great renown as the man who had put to flight the mighty Nureddin.

In that same autumn the Emperor Manuel marched into Cilicia at the head of his imposing but noncombatant army. Prince Reynald was terrified. Standing humbly before the Emperor's tent, bareheaded and barefoot, he begged for peace at any price. Manuel let him keep Antioch on three conditions: a Greek garrison must hold the citadel, a contingent of Antiochene knights must serve with the imperial army, a Greek Patriarch must rule the Church of Antioch.

King Baldwin hurried north to give what help he could to the Franks. Nobody could maintain that he was Manuel's vassal; they met as fellow-sovereigns, and got on well together. As a result no Greek Patriarch was installed in Antioch, though the Emperor reserved the right to appoint one at pleasure. On Easter Sunday 1159 the Emperor made a state entry into his obedient city; Prince Reynald, walking humbly on foot, led his horse; behind him rode King Baldwin, without his crown.

The Emperor remained a week in Antioch. He was gracious to the Franks, and deigned to take part in a tournament. Then he marched out towards Aleppo at the head of his great army.

But he had come to frighten Nureddin, not to fight him. When infidel envoys asked for a truce it was immediately granted. Nureddin handed over six thousand Christian slaves, mostly Germans captured during the Second Crusade; and Manuel hurried back to Constantinople for fear that a rival Emperor might be proclaimed while he was so far from his capital.

The rich and famous Emperor at the head of his great army impressed the Turks; but this truce marked the end of his prestige among the Christians. At last they recognised him for a coward. But his wealth still made him a good match; now that his German wife was dead Maria of Antioch, sister of the young Prince, was glad to become his Empress. The troublesome Prince-regent Reynald had recently been captured by the infidel, and no one made a move to collect his ransom.

In February 1162 King Baldwin III died after a brief illness, in his 33rd year. There were the inevitable rumours of poison, but in the climate of Syria many young Franks died suddenly. He had been a gallant knight and a competent general, who had conquered Ascalon and seen the back of the mighty Nureddin. But the morale of his subjects was decaying, so that they had become very difficult to govern. The fear of sudden death in battle, or, what was even worse, mutilation followed by long years in an infidel dungeon, haunted every Frank night and day. In the open field they fought as well as ever, but in

council their strained nerves made them reckless and un-
scrupulous. They swore oaths they never meant to keep, they
robbed the Church they were vowed to protect, they intrigued
to snatch power from their own kin. They were unworthy
descendants of those steadfast warriors who had stormed
through Asia Minor to liberate the Holy Sepulchre.

King Baldwin, though married to a Greek princess, had died
childless. The heir was his brother Amalric, Count of Jaffa and
Ascalon, then 23 years of age. As soon as he was crowned he
got an annulment of his marriage with Agnes, daughter of the
Count of Edessa. She had borne him two children but her
reputation was shady, and none of the barons wished her to be
Queen. Some years later he married a Greek princess, Maria
Comnena, Manuel's great-niece.

King Amalric pursued a coherent foreign policy. To keep
Nureddin in check he advertised his alliance with the Emperor,
who was a more frightening figure on his throne in Constantinople than wandering timorously through Cilicia at the head of
his parade-army. So long as the Emperor made threatening
noises Nureddin must remain in the northern parts of his
great realm. But Amalric's main object was to win control of
masterless Egypt before it was snapped up by Nureddin. In its
conquest he hoped for help from the Greek fleet, which was
manned by Greek sailors and more willing to fight than the
mercenaries of the army. There was also a Venetian fleet
cruising in the Levant; but the Venetians had concluded a
profitable commercial treaty with the Caliph of Cairo and would
not help anyone to upset the present state of affairs.

In September 1163 King Amalric marched through Sinai
and laid siege to Pelusium in Egypt. But the invasion had been
badly timed, and the flooding of the Nile forced him to retire.
As soon as Nureddin learned that the King had gone south he
invaded Tripoli in force. The weak County was saved by the
lucky chance that two French Crusaders, Hugh of Lusignan
and Geoffrey of Angouleme, happened to be marching through
it at the head of their men. They held up the Turks until
Bohemond of Antioch and Coloman, the Hungarian who

commanded the Greek forces in Cilicia, could hurry to the rescue. Before the united Christian army Nureddin fled in some disorder.

In 1164 a deposed vizier of Egypt managed to get away alive; he fled to Nureddin and asked for an army to reinstate him. In return he offered to hand over certain fortresses, to recognise Nureddin as suzerain of Egypt, and to pay a large annual tribute. This was a remarkable reversal of policy. The only excuse for the existence of Egypt as an independent state was that Cairo had a Caliph of its own, who claimed to be the rightful Caliph of all Islam. If Egypt should submit to Nureddin, in religion a faithful servant of the rival Caliph of Baghdad, the Nile Valley would not need a separate government. But Shawar, the fugitive vizier, thought only of his immediate future.

Nureddin himself dared not leave his threatened northern frontier; after some hesitation, for Egypt was a long way from Aleppo, he despatched an expeditionary force under his favourite general, the Kurd Shirkuh. Shirkuh took with him his nephew, a young man of 27 named Saladin. It is said that Saladin was reluctant to join the expedition, which seemed to him hazardous in the extreme.

After a little skirmishing Shawar was restored to power, and immediately repudiated his sworn engagements. When Shirkuh refused to leave Egypt until he had been paid Shawar sought help from King Amalric. By forced marches the King hurried across Sinai to join Shawar. Together they besieged Shirkuh in the strong fortress of Bilbeis.

Shirkuh and Saladin were in grave danger, until Nureddin made a diversion to draw off the besiegers. Again he invaded Tripoli at the head of a great army. The Christian leaders of the north once more gathered to expel him: Bohemond of Antioch, Thoros the Armenian ruler of Cilicia, Coloman the Greek general, and Hugh of Lusignan who was still in Outremer. In a great battle at Artah Nureddin defeated them; all the Christian leaders were taken as prisoners to Aleppo.

King Amalric must hurry home. After he had made a truce

with Shirkuh the two armies marched side by side through Sinai to Syria. For the first time Saladin met Christian Franks, whose manners and point of view he understood so well in later life.

Nureddin might perhaps have captured Antioch; but that would have brought the Emperor Manuel into the field, and Nureddin was still afraid of the Greeks. Instead he set himself by careful diplomacy to drive a wedge between Constantinople and the Franks. The Greek general Coloman was released for a nominal ransom; Bohemond and Thoros, as vassals of the Greek Empire, were released also, though a full ransom was demanded for them. But no money could buy the freedom of the Count of Tripoli, or of other Crusaders not under the protection of the Emperor.

Prince Bohemond, ruined by his heavy ransom, visited Constantinople to beg money from his sister the Empress. It was given to him, but when he came home he brought with him a Greek Patriarch, who drove out his Latin rival and restored the liturgy of the Greek Church. The Principality of Antioch was on the way to becoming an ordinary province of the Greek Empire.

In 1167 Nureddin sent back Shirkuh and Saladin to Egypt, with express orders to overthrow the Caliph of Cairo and enforce the spiritual authority of the Caliph of Baghdad. At once Shawar and his Caliph appealed to King Amalric, and the army of Jerusalem occupied Cairo. Christian envoys had a personal interview with the sacred Caliph, and swore to uphold him against his enemies; a curious situation for Crusaders engaged in the Holy War.

King Amalric and his Egyptian allies attacked Shirkuh on the Nile above Cairo, and got the worst of it. But even after this defeat they still outnumbered the Syrians, and Shirkuh felt very nervous. All the fortified cities of Lower Egypt, and the guarded frontier of Sinai, cut him off from Nureddin. In a lightning march he hurried over the desert to the strong city of Alexandria; whose inhabitants, disliking Shawar as an ally of Christians, opened their gates to him.

King Amalric followed in pursuit. He could not breach the mighty walls of Alexandria, but he kept up a strict blockade and there was little food in the populous city. Shirkuh feared to be starved into surrender. In desperation, he slipped out by night with most of his men, leaving Saladin to hold the town with only a thousand mamelukes. Once safe in the desert he sent envoys to King Amalric.

It was clear that neither side could crush the other. The Franks were secure in Cairo, but they could not expel Shirkuh from Egypt. After lengthy negotiations terms were agreed.

Saladin, who was now in grave danger, was to evacuate Alexandria unmolested. After he had joined his uncle the whole Syrian army must leave the country. At the same time King Amalric would go home. The vizier Shawar had promised that the Alexandrians who had admitted Shirkuh should not be punished for their treason, that a small Frankish garrison should control one of the gates of Cairo, and that Egypt should pay to Jerusalem an annual tribute of 100,000 pieces of gold. By August 1167 both armies were out of the country.

During the long negotiations Saladin got to know Frankish knights; for the barons of the land, and many Templars, spoke Arabic fluently. The Franks liked him, and he developed an interest in the code of chivalry. In after years it was rumoured that about this time he was knighted by the Constable of Jerusalem, Humphrey of Toron. That is a tall story, incapable of proof; but not quite absurd on the face of it. Western chivalry, beginning about the time of the First Crusade, had increased in influence during the last sixty years; but it depended so heavily on devotion to Our Lady and reverence for the female sex in general that no polygamous infidel could follow its code. Yet trust and honour between warriors can exist without any higher sanction. Saladin, though an unrelenting foe, was a man of honour who never broke his word. He was on the way to becoming a knight; and had he been a Christian he would have been a good knight. Perhaps the Constable gave him some kind of non-religious accolade.

That there was considerable social mobility between Greeks, Franks, and infidels was shown at this very time by the adventures of Andronicus Comnenus. This gallant cousin of the Emperor had recently been appointed governor of Cilicia, principally to get him away from the dissipations of Constantinople. But he preferred to live in gay Antioch, where he soon began to pay court to the beautiful Philippa, sister to Prince Bohemond and to the Greek Empress. When Bohemond complained Manuel ordered Andronicus to come home. Instead he seized all the cash in the provincial treasury and with it fled south to Jerusalem. King Amalric, like everyone else who met Andronicus, was charmed by his courage and wit; the exile was soon installed as lord of Beirut, a fief of the Kingdom.

In Acre, not far from Beirut, lived the dowager Queen Theodora, widow of King Baldwin III. She was a Comnena, cousin to Andronicus. Soon the two Greek exiles in Frankish Outremer were in love with one another. When the angry Emperor demanded the arrest of Andronicus the guilty pair fled to Damascus.

Andronicus could charm infidels as easily as he charmed Franks. Nureddin received him as an honoured guest; no one asked him to change his religion. For some time he wandered happily from one infidel court to another; until the Turks of Iconium gave him a castle on their frontier with the Greeks, where he lived happily and prosperously by preying on his fellow-countrymen. No more is heard of Queen Theodora. Andronicus may have given her the slip when he grew tired of her, or she may have been lucky enough to die young.

In 1168 King Amalric concluded a formal alliance with the Emperor Manuel; the Greek navy would help the army of Jerusalem to conquer Egypt, and the proceeds would be shared between the allies. Unfortunately Greek expeditions were never very quick off the mark. To mobilise the fleet took a whole year. But the barons of Jerusalem would not wait so long. At any moment a more able and popular vizier might replace the hated Shawar, and it happened that the Count of Nevers had brought from France a strong force of Crusaders.

These Frenchmen were eager to fight, but they could not remain indefinity in Outremer. The chance must be seized.

During a stormy council the barons of the land and the Count of Nevers persuaded the King to march at once. The Hospitallers concurred, so that automatically their rivals the Templars favoured delay. Only the Pope could command the Grand Master of the Temple, and there was no time to seek instructions from Rome; so that when the rest of the army set out, in October 1168, the Templars, about one-third of the knighthood of the Kingdom, stayed firmly behind.

Nevertheless, after stiff fighting the invaders stormed the border-fortress of Bilbeis. Unfortunately the Frenchmen, leaderless after the death from fever of the Count of Nevers, massacred all the inhabitants, including many local Christians. Fear caused all the Egyptians to rally behind Shawar, whose government did not collapse as had been expected. Instead the cunning vizier played for time. He threatened to burn Cairo rather than see it fall into Christian hands, and meanwhile sent envoys to offer tribute; but they haggled over the amount. Suddenly Shirkuh and Saladin arrived in Egypt at the head of the army of Damascus, proclaiming that they had come at the invitation of the Caliph of Cairo.

The young Caliph must have been a fervent Moslem, since he would rather see his own dynasty extinguished than Egypt under Christian rule. His public-spirited action was completely successful. King Amalric could not cope with Shawar and Shirkuh in alliance. In January he led his army home through Sinai. Shawar, who was still very rich, tried to buy off his supplanters; but Saladin murdered him with his own hands during a friendly conference.

Shirkuh took over the government of Egypt. Soon, in the unaccustomed luxury of Cairo, then the most civilised city in the Moslem world, he ate himself to death. He had been a very great soldier and, what was much more remarkable among infidel soldiers, completely faithful throughout his career to Nureddin his master.

Saladin inherited his uncle's personal estate, which included his army; for mamelukes were literally personal property. He ruled Egypt by a curious double title. He was the general of Nureddin, who was the faithful adherent of the Caliph of Baghdad; he was also the chosen vizier of the Caliph of Cairo, Baghdad's deadly rival.

Luckily for the peace of Egypt the young Caliph of Cairo was so sacred that he might never leave his palace. He remained in happy ignorance that in all the mosques of Cairo prayers were being offered in the name of the opposition Caliph. He was dying of some obscure disease, and Saladin allowed him to die on his throne. But after his death no successor was appointed from among his numerous cousins. Saladin now governed Egypt in the name of Nureddin.

King Amalric was dismayed at this concentration of infidel power, as well he might be. He sent envoys throughout Europe, begging for an immediate General Passage. But King Henry of England was so fiercely at war with King Louis of France that neither dared to leave his dominions, and the German Emperor was at odds with the Pope. Nothing came of the mission.

In the summer of 1169 the great fleet from Constantinople arrived punctually at Acre, as promised. This time it was King Amalric who was not ready. After the unsuccessful campaign of the previous autumn his army needed reorganisation, and the Templars still stood aloof from the war. The combined expedition did not start until October, by which time the Greeks had eaten most of their supplies. They planned to capture Damietta, the port at the mouth of the eastern branch of the Nile; and then move up by the river to Cairo.

The defenders of Damietta had received ample warning. They stretched heavy chains across the river to bar the passage of the Greek ships. The Greeks suggested that the army should storm the walls, but the Franks would not assault until Greek engineers had battered a breach. Food ran short, and winter rains flooded the camp of the besiegers. In December the Christian allies burned their siege engines and retired. King Amalric kept Christmas in Ascalon, but a storm wrecked many

Greek ships before they could reach Constantinople. This, the only combined operation between Greeks and Franks against the infidel, had accomplished nothing.

In 1170 Antioch was smitten by a terrible earthquake. The choir of the cathedral collapsed, killing the Greek Patriarch and most of his chapter. After this clear demonstration of the Will of God the delighted Franks fetched back the deposed Latin Patriarch. The Emperor had other troubles at that time, and no further Greek Patriarch was sent out from Constantinople.

In 1171 King Amalric paid a state visit to the Emperor, who received him with all due honour; for Manuel, who himself aspired to be a gallant knight, always got on well with gallant knights. Perhaps plans were explored for another attack on Egypt, certainly the Emperor gave the King great sums of money, and sent more to Jerusalem for the repair of the Holy Places. But nothing of importance was decided, though a good time was had by all.

Meanwhile the King was concerned about the succession to his Kingdom. By his first marriage with Anne of Edessa, which had been annulled before his coronation, he had a son and a daughter, Baldwin and Sibylla; by his second marriage with the Princess Maria Comnena he had one daughter, Isabella. Now it had been discovered that the 9-year-old Baldwin was a leper. He could not live long, and would never father children.

By feudal custom the husband-to-be of the unmarried Princess Sibylla would be King after little Baldwin. Or would he? Not if Sibylla, born of a dissolved marriage with a commoner, were ranked below Isabella, daughter of an imperial Princess who had also been crowned Queen. All that the wisest lawyer could say was that both Princesses would be well worth marrying.

On the other hand, the barons of the land might claim the right to elect a King unrelated to Amalric. Godfrey of Bouillon had been elected. No formal Assize of the High Court, which declared the customary law of the Kingdom of Jerusalem, had ever decreed that the crown was hereditary in Godfrey's kindred. The future was uncertain.

But then the future of the infidels was also uncertain. Nureddin had united all Syria, and for the present Saladin in Egypt acknowledged his authority. But Nureddin was old and infirm. Like every other Moslem magnate he maintained a well-stocked harem, and he would leave plenty of warlike sons to fight among themselves for the succession. Saladin seemed to be on the brink of declaring himself independent; at the moment his soldiers were loyal to old Nureddin, but that loyalty would not descend to the heir. The delicacy of the position had been demonstrated in 1171 when Saladin laid siege to the Christian castle of Montreal, in Outrejordan south of the Dead Sea. The Christians were about to surrender when Nureddin marched south to link up with his lieutenant; whereupon Saladin abandoned the siege and went home, ostensibly to quell a disturbance in Upper Egypt. It was whispered that he feared to meet his suzerain, lest Nureddin should entice away his mamelukes.

The Kingdom of Jerusalem could not long survive attack from a united infidel realm of Syria and Egypt. But infidel unity hung on the lives of two remarkable men, Nureddin and Saladin; and in the east great men died suddenly. Perhaps in a few years' time every infidel city would obey its own separate dynasty, as in the good old days of the First Crusade.

In May 1174 Nureddin died after a brief illness. At once his realm fell to pieces. In Mosul, Aleppo and Damascus local generals declared themselves regents on behalf of his young sons. Saladin, after his offer to take over the regency of the whole realm had been refused, declared himself independent ruler of Egypt. King Amalric immediately marched against Damascus, the weakest of his enemies; and was bought off by a large ransom and the release of all Christian captives.

In July 1174, just two months after the death of Nureddin had brought fresh hopes to the Franks, King Amalric died of dysentery in his 39th year.

CHAPTER XI

The Struggle with Saladin

King Baldwin IV, the 13-year-old leper, succeeded his father without opposition; for all the Franks of Jerusalem knew that they must close their ranks against the threat from Egypt. In one sense this threat was nothing novel; since the foundation of the Kingdom Egypt had been a wealthy land, all its resources concentrated in the hands of its ruler. But the army of the old viziers had been a miserable force. Saladin was a competent general, and his army of Turks and mamelukes had been recruited in warlike Syria. Besides, he might soon conquer the rest of the huge realm of Nureddin, which had extended from Upper Egypt to Mosul.

The unfortunate King Baldwin was a selfless hero, perhaps the noblest hero who ever wore the crown of Jerusalem. He knew that soon he must die an agonising death; but without thought of his health or his comfort he devoted all his energies to the Holy War. In the beginning he tried to rule without a regent, relying on the advice of his father's seneschal, Miles of Plancy. But Miles of Plancy was a French Crusader, lacking roots in Outremer, and unpopular with the barons of the land.

For by this time the division between the parties had hardened. On one side were the Crusaders from Europe, the Templars, and a few landless native-born younger sons. Their programme was war against the infidel, against all infidels everywhere; with the help of God they would defend the Holy Places against all comers, and conquer more land until the Kingdom was strong enough to stand alone. In the other party were the barons of the land, many of them the third generation born in Outremer, speaking Arabic, living after the eastern fashion.

They saw the Christian states of Outremer as merely one factor in oriental politics, and understood the feuds which divided their infidel neighbours. Their policy was to play off one infidel ruler against another, to make truces so that their peasants might till the soil in peace, to retire into their strong castles when invasion came and by cunning diplomacy make trouble for the invaders at home until they turned back. To their minds Outremer was big enough already, since they held good fiefs. They were supported by the Italian merchants in the seaports, who wanted peace so that they might trade with the farther East; and by the normally warlike knights of the Hospital, who without thinking opposed any policy favoured by their rivals of the Temple.

After a few months this native peace party compelled young King Baldwin to choose as regent Count Raymond of Tripoli, their most eminent leader. If there had to be a regent Raymond was indeed the best candidate. In the female line he was first cousin to the late King Amalric, and thus the nearest male kinsman of little King Baldwin. He was also the very exemplar of a baron of the land. Recently ransomed after a long captivity, he was personally known to many infidel leaders and his favourite amusement was the study of Arabic literature. He saw the problems of Jerusalem as exactly on a par with the problems of Damascus. The immediate task was defence against Saladin. All the foes of Saladin, no matter what their faith, must pull together.

Unluckily Miles of Plancy was murdered soon after he had resigned his office. The murderer was never identified, but all the members of the opposition took it for granted that he had been put away at the instigation of the new regent.

One advantage brought by the alliance with Saladin's infidel enemies was the release of all Christian captives held in Aleppo. Among those set free was Reynald of Chatillon, the former regent of Antioch. Princess Constance was now dead, and it was thought that such a famous warrior should be kept in Outremer by marriage with another heiress. He was given the lady Stephanie, widow of Miles of Plancy and in her own right heiress of Outrejordan. Since she blamed Count Raymond for the murder of her first husband she encouraged her second husband to defy him. In any case, no ruler in Jerusalem or Acre could control what went on in the distant frontier castles stretching out to the Gulf of Akaba.

The young Queen dowager, Maria Comnena, made a happy second marriage with Balian of Ibelin. The Ibelins were the most prominent of the barons of the land, perhaps because their great castle of Ibelin lay near the coast, remote from infidel raids. They were not an ancient house; for lack of a surname their founder, in the days of the First Crusade, took his name from his new castle. But by this time they had become the most noble and the most powerful of the native families of Outremer.

In 1175 the King's sister, the Princess Sibylla, was given in marriage to William of Montferrat. It was a political alliance, not a love-match. William was the eldest son of the Marquis of Montferrat, a powerful magnate of northern Italy, cousin to the German Emperor and the King of France. When the poor young leper-King died Sibylla's husband would be regent, and William could bring the knights of Montferrat to reinforce the army of the Kingdom. But luck was running against the Christian cause. After a few months of marriage Count William died of fever. He left a baby son, next heir to the crown; but there was now no obvious candidate for the regency when King Baldwin died, as he must within a few years.

Meanwhile Saladin had conquered Damascus, in spite of all the Franks could do to hinder him. But Aleppo and Mosul were still held by rival generals purporting to act for the infant sons of Nureddin, so that Saladin was too busy campaigning in Mesopotamia to have time to threaten Christian Outremer.

The Struggle with Saladin

In 1176 luck dealt the Christian cause another blow. After a long and glorious reign, in which he had conducted great armies from the Danube to the Orontes, the Emperor Manuel was rash enough to fight a battle. With all his mercenaries, his famous siege-train, and his numerous supply-wagons, he had marched against the Turks of Iconium; and the Turks of Iconium, instead of buying peace as they had always done in the past, met him in arms at the far end of the defile of Myriocephalum in Phrygia.

When Manuel saw the enemy ready to fight he hesitated; but his officers persuaded him to attack. His vanguard went forward to pierce the Turkish centre while the main body of his army was still struggling through the pass. The vanguard charged to victory, driving the Turkish centre before it; but the Turkish wings, according to custom, edged forward until they could sweep down the hills on either side of the road.

To clear one flank Manuel sent out his best troops, the Frankish contingent from Antioch. They rode into the mass of Turkish horsebowmen and perished, borne down by overwhelming numbers. As soon as the Emperor saw this disaster he was the first Christian to flee. Though he had reigned for twenty-three years of incessant armed bullying this was the first time the foe had come near his sacred person. Few of his troops were able to follow him; jammed among the siege-engines in the narrow defile, they were massacred by the Turks. Until dark the victorious Christian vanguard remained in their captured position. Next day, riding back to look for their Emperor, they found the pass carpeted with the bodies of their comrades.

The Turkish Sultan might have pursued as far as the Bosphorus, but he was more eager to expand his dominions towards the east. Within a few days Manuel was able to buy peace from him, by the surrender of his most important frontier fortresses. The Emperor got back safe to Constantinople; but he was now too poor, and too disheartened, to set about hiring another mercenary army.

Myriocephalum marked the end of the Greek empire as a

141

Saladin

military power. For the Franks of Outremer that cut both ways. Asia Minor was now securely in Turkish hands, which blocked the overland route to Europe; but Antioch was safe from a Christian stab in the back, such as Manuel had twice administered. Constantinople had withdrawn from Syrian politics.

The Emperor Manuel died in 1180, to be succeeded by his 11-year-old son Alexius II. In accordance with Greek custom the Empress-mother, Maria of Antioch, became regent. She favoured the Italian merchants who had settled in Constantinople during her husband's reign, which made her unpopular with the Greeks. In 1182 Andronicus Comnenus, the exiled brigand, returned to the capital and overthrew her. The revolution was marked by a terrible massacre of Italians. The Empress Maria was executed, and soon after the boy-Emperor was murdered.

Andronicus as Emperor proved a bloodthirsty tyrant, so fearful of rebellion that he killed any man of distinction among his subjects. In 1185 he was overthrown and tortured to death amid great public rejoicings. The mob chose as his successor a pious and ineffectual nobleman, Isaac Angelus, who had barely escaped the tyrant's executioners. During these troubles the Slavs of the Balkans rebelled against their Greek masters, and the kingdoms of Serbia and Bulgaria achieved independence. Henceforth the Emperor in Constantinople ruled only Hellas and Thrace in Europe, and in Asia Bithynia as far as Nicaea and a few scattered ports on the Black Sea. He maintained no army save a few mercenary palace guards; and his navy, though manned by excellent Greek sailors, decayed for lack of money.

The Italians never forgot the treacherous massacre of 1182, all the more treacherous because the merchants had settled in Constantinople at the express invitation of Manuel Comnenus.

In 1177 King Baldwin, aged sixteen, was old enough to reign by himself. His envoys had toured Europe to urge another General Passage, and it was learned with joy that the Kings of France and England had taken the Cross. But nothing came of their vows. King Henry II of England rarely kept a sworn promise, and such was his ferocity that while he reigned no King of France could neglect the defence of his realm to go on pilgrimage.

But in the autumn of that year the Franks of Jerusalem won a glorious victory. Saladin marched from Egypt through Sinai at the head of a great army. Though the Templars tried to block him at Gaza he slipped by and continued to Ascalon. He came so suddenly that there had been no time to assemble the full army of the Kingdom; young Baldwin, with the five hundred knights of his household, just got into Ascalon before it was invested. So large was the infidel host that Saladin could leave enough troops to blockade Ascalon and still march on Jerusalem with his main body. No Christian army was in the field to meet him. It seemed that the Holy City must perish, and with it the Kingdom. But King Baldwin the leper showed himself to be a great general, or, what was the same thing in the 12th century, a great captain of horse.

He managed to send a message summoning the Templars from Gaza. While they attacked the besiegers in the rear he broke out from Ascalon. At the head of his combined force he picked up the barons of the land who had mustered at Ibelin; then he rode hard after Saladin. By the castle of Montgisard, outside Ramleh, he charged the Egyptians from the rear just as they were disordered by the crossing of a steep ravine.

St George himself was observed leading the Christian array, as he had led their ancestors at Antioch eighty years before. The mamelukes fled in panic. Saladin himself would have been captured or killed if his bodyguard had not sacrificed themselves to delay his pursuers. Enormous booty was taken, and many Christian captives set free.

As the Egyptians struggled home through Sinai they suffered further heavy loss, for the bedouin of those parts will fall upon a defeated army of any faith. When the rumour reached Egypt that Saladin had been beaten Cairo very nearly rose in rebellion; the native Egyptians hated their conquerors and the spiritual authority of the Caliphs of Baghdad which they had imposed. But Saladin sent messages by carrier pigeon to say that he still led a great force of mamelukes, and all was quiet. This pigeon post, an Arab discovery, was one of the wonders of the east which impressed every visiting Frank.

If King Baldwin planned the timing of the charge at Montgisard he was a cavalry tactician of the stature of Cromwell or Murat. But perhaps it was just a piece of good luck; after so much undeserved bad luck the Christians deserved a change.

All this time there had been peace in the north, where Antioch and Aleppo and the Armenians of Cilicia were united against Saladin. In 1180 a general truce was concluded for all Syria, to last two years; because there was such a severe drought that the whole country, Christian and infidel, was in danger of starvation.

In the same year the widowed Princess Sibylla married Guy, a younger son of the Count of Lusignan. No great prince had come forward to marry the mother of the heir to Jerusalem, a match which must carry with it the regency between the death of Baldwin IV and the coming of age of Baldwin V. So great was the menace of Saladin that no ruler with a good fief of his own would leave it to undertake the defence of the tottering Kingdom. In the end Sibylla married for love; and in the opinion of the barons of the land she married beneath her. The Counts of Lusignan came very low in the feudal pyramid of France. They were vassals, very unruly vassals, of the Count of Poitou, who held of the Duke of Aquitaine, who held of the King of France; and Guy was not even the heir. Furthermore, he was weak and foolish, unable to make up his mind; he had a trick of following the advice of the last man who had shouted at him in council. But by feudal custom he must be regent for his stepson when the unlucky leper-King should die; there was nothing to be done about it.

A few months later the Canons of the Holy Sepulchre met to elect a Patriarch. Under the influence of the Lady Agnes, the King's scandalous mother, they chose the Archbishop of Caesarea. Heraclius was a Frenchman of little education and openly immoral life; but because he was very handsome and well-mannered he was popular with the ladies. His current mistress, the wife of an Italian shopkeeper, was soon known throughout Outremer as Madame la Patriarchesse.

In the north the Prince of Antioch had quarrelled with the Armenians of Cilicia; and in the confusion attending the downfall of the Emperor Alexius II a Greek provincial governor, Isaac Comnenus, had set up as an independent Emperor in Cyprus. The united front called into existence to withstand Saladin had vanished.

In 1181 Reynald of Chatillon, in right of his wife lord of Outrejordan, plundered a rich infidel caravan travelling from Damascus to Mecca. It was a naked breach of the truce. Reynald was a brave and daring warrior, but not an honourable knight.

Saladin complained to King Baldwin. The young King agreed that his vassal was at fault, but then had to admit that he could not control Reynald. After a formal declaration of war Saladin marched from Egypt through Sinai.

It was shown that the Franks could still defend the Holy Places when overwhelming danger made them forget their internal quarrels. After calling at Damascus to gather reinforcements Saladin invaded the Kingdom by way of the south shore of the Lake of Galilee. Near the castle of Belvoir he met the army of Jerusalem; a stubborn battle ended in the retreat of the infidels, though their ranks were unbroken. Then Saladin made a hasty dash at Beirut, hoping to find it ungarrisoned. But King Baldwin hurried up to the relief of the city and once more the infidels retired, baffled.

In 1182, while Saladin made war on his infidel rivals in Aleppo and Mosul, King Baldwin raided right up to the walls of Damascus and brought home rich plunder. But in the spring of 1183 he fell ill, too ill to lead his army. Meanwhile Bohemond III of Antioch, desperately afraid, concluded a truce for four years; and in July Saladin at last conquered Aleppo and was ready to turn all his forces against Jerusalem.

King Baldwin, bedridden and almost blind, must appoint a regent. He therefore appointed the man who would be regent when he died, Guy of Lusignan. The barons of the land did not like his choice, but they could not object.

About this time Reynald of Chatillon carried into execution a daring project which had been long in his mind. His favourite trick was to raid districts whose inhabitants thought themselves secure, as once he had raided peaceful Cyprus. His new expedition was as simple, and as effective, as Drake's raid up the west coast of America, where the Spaniards had never seen a hostile ship. He marched south through his fief of Outrejordan, bringing on camel-back shaped timbers from the forests of Moab; at Akaba he fitted the timbers together, and sent out the ships thus made to prey on the pilgrim-traffic of the Red Sea. He himself stayed behind in the Gulf of Akaba with two galleys, to blockade the little Egyptian island of Greye.

No Christian warship had cruised in the Red Sea since the Moslems conquered Egypt. Unopposed, the pirates sacked many harbours on the African shore, then crossed over to plunder Yambo, the port of Medina. It was about the time of the annual pilgrimage to Mecca, and there were many unarmed pilgrim-ships.

Hastily Saladin manned local vessels with sailors brought overland from his Mediterranean fleet. These professional sailors soon found and captured the Christian ships, whose crews must have been landlubbers from inland Outrejordan. Many Christians were taken alive. Some were sent to Mecca, to be executed as the climax of the pilgrimage. (This was Saladin's personal contribution to Moslem ritual, which does not in general countenance human sacrifice.) The remainder were killed in the main square of Cairo, for the entertainment of the populace. There were no survivors, except that Reynald himself and the crews of his two galleys got away safely to inland Outrejordan. Saladin vowed solemnly that for this sacrilegious attack on the Holy Places of Islam he would one day kill Reynald with his own sword.

In September 1182 Saladin mounted another full scale invasion of Galilee. He killed some of the monks on Mount Tabor, and pillaged the open country. The army of the Kingdom gathered to oppose him, encamped by the Pools of Goliath.

The forward party, led as usual by Reynald of Chatillon, proposed to attack the infidel camp; but the barons of the land said that against such odds the army should remain on the defensive. Guy of Lusignan, in command, could not make up his mind whose advice to follow; as a result the army did nothing, which proved to be the right policy. Paid mamelukes formed only a small proportion of Saladin's army; many of his followers were volunteers, who came out to kill Christians and win plunder. If there was no battle in prospect, and no chance to scatter for pillage, these volunteers went home. Soon Saladin, weakened by desertions, withdrew to the territory of Damascus.

But though the campaign had gone well it had shown that Guy of Lusignan was too irresolute to be entrusted with the defence of the Holy City. On the advice of his council King Baldwin dismissed Guy from the regency. He declared that he would govern his Kingdom in person, though he was now completely bedridden.

In an effort to heal the breach between the factions Reynald of Chatillon decided to marry his stepson, the heir to Outrejordan, to the Princess Isabella, daughter of Queen Maria. At 17 Humphrey of Toron should have been ruling his own fief; but he was a young man of artistic tastes who liked a quiet life. Queen Maria was now married to Balian of Ibelin, the leading baron of the land; as Reynald himself was the leader of the foreign-born Crusaders. During November 1183 all the nobles and ladies of the Kingdom assembled at Kerak in Outrejordan for a great marriage-feast.

Saladin had not been invited, but he came at the head of his army. While infidel engines battered the castle the wedding festivities continued. The mother of the bridegroom, the Countess Stephanie, sent out a share of the feast to Saladin as though he were another guest. In return for this friendly gesture he inquired in which tower the happy couple were passing their honeymoon, and commanded that no stones should be thrown at it.

Presently the army of the Kingdom marched to the relief of

Kerak. Raymond of Tripoli commanded it; but King Baldwin came also, carried in a litter. Saladin retired, reluctant to fight a pitched battle with a hostile castle in his rear.

In 1183 Saladin made another unsuccessful pounce on Kerak. But his main objective was still the conquest of Mosul, and in the winter of 1185 he fell dangerously ill; so the unfortunate leper-King passed his last years in peace. At a great council he expounded to his barons his plans for the future. The next King must be his young nephew, the son of Sibylla. But the regency would not go, as custom decreed, to Guy of Lusignan, the boy's stepfather. Instead the regent should be Raymond of Tripoli. Since little Baldwin was notoriously weak and delicate it was probable that he would die in childhood. Then the direct line would be extinct; and the best way of choosing another King would be by international arbitration. It was agreed that the Pope, the German Emperor, and the Kings of France and England should decide between the claims of Sibylla and Isabella.

Arbitration would be needed, for this was a knotty problem. Feudal law laid down that where there was no son, daughters should share an inheritance equally, without regard for seniority. By strict law there should be two joint-Queens— which was absurd, since these two half-sisters could never agree on anything. But if one sister must be chosen, which should it be? Sibylla was the elder; but her mother's marriage had been annulled, and to choose her would be to choose the unpopular Guy of Lusignan. Isabella, though the younger, was the daughter of a Princess; and if she reigned the regent would probably be her stepfather, Balian of Ibelin, the most respected baron in Outremer.

The appointment of Raymond as regent for the next King was a triumph for the native party; achieved all the more easily because the leaders of the opposition, the Patriarch and the Grand Master of the Temple, were touring Europe to beg help for the Holy Places.

In fact there was urgent need of a General Passage; but the restless ambition of Henry of England made it impossible for the King of France, or any other great French lord, to neglect home defence. Henry himself took the Cross, and then arranged that his councillors should beg him not to go. The scandalous life and unconcealed cowardice of the Patriarch Heraclius weakened the force of his appeal. Jerusalem must of course be saved from the infidel, but was this the kind of prelate the knighthood of Europe had a duty to protect?

In March 1185 died Baldwin IV, the most noble and most unfortunate of the Kings of Jerusalem. Seven-year-old King Baldwin V was crowned in his stead, with Count Raymond of Tripoli as regent. There was truce between Saladin and all the states of Outremer. Trade flourished; the Italian merchants did good business.

But during 1186 Saladin at last absorbed Mosul into his empire, though he permitted its ruler to remain as his vassal. In August of the same year died little King Baldwin V, leaving no obvious successor.

In the course of some confused double-crossing the Patriarch Heraclius, supported by the Templars, crowned Sibylla in Jerusalem; while at Nablus the assembled barons of the land proclaimed young Humphrey of Toron as their King. But Humphrey feared to undertake the dangerous honour. Instead he rode off to Jerusalem and did homage to Sibylla. There was nothing for it but to accept Sibylla as Queen, with Guy of Lusignan as her regent.

Rather than do homage to Guy, Balian's younger brother, Baldwin of Ibelin, handed over his fiefs to his son and emigrated to Antioch; other good knights followed him. Raymond of Tripoli retired to his wife's fief of Galilee without doing homage as he should. The Franks of Outremer were bitterly divided.

The truce with Saladin remained in force, until at the end of the year Reynald of Chatillon broke it. To Reynald there was something absurd and undignified in Crusaders living at peace with their infidel neighbours; and he could not believe that he owed obedience to that ridiculous Guy of Lusignan. Plain greed, and a reckless disregard of consequences, impelled him to pillage a great caravan of infidels as it crossed Outrejordan from Egypt to Damascus.

Saladin observed with care the procedure for such a case laid down in the truce. First he asked Reynald, politely, to return the booty. After Reynald refused he took up the matter with King Guy; who very properly commanded Reynald to return the stolen goods, but took no steps to enforce his command. With international law on his side, Saladin prepared to invade the Kingdom.

All Outremer trembled in terror. Bohemond of Antioch renewed his truce, announcing that he would stand neutral in the coming war. Raymond did the same for his County of Tripoli, which some lawyers might reckon to be an independent state. But Raymond went further; he suggested that his wife's fief of Galilee might also stand neutral, though it was undoubtedly a part of the Kingdom of Jerusalem.

King Guy decided that this was a suitable moment for an attack on Tiberias, the capital of Galilee, as punishment for the treason of Count Raymond. While the enemy massed on the frontier the Franks were about to fight a civil war, until Balian of Ibelin raged at the King and insisted on peace. As always when someone shouted at him, King Guy changed his mind.

Balian and the Grand Masters of the two Orders went to Count Raymond to arrange terms of peace. Balian was delayed overnight at one of his castles. Next day, hurrying to catch up with the Grand Masters, he reached the Templar castle of La Feve and found it deserted save for two sick knights. He was still puzzling over this strange state of affairs when news reached him of a terrible disaster.

Saladin had jumped at the chance to conclude a private truce with Count Raymond. He was determined to keep it to the letter, and thus embitter the quarrel among the Christians. At the same time he wished to reconnoitre the castles of the Kingdom. So he politely asked permission for a party of horse to cross neutral Galilee, and promised that they would commit no hostile act during their passage.

The Struggle with Saladin

Count Raymond's treasonable dealings with the enemy had put him in an awkward fix. He disliked the proposal; but if he broke with Saladin before he had made terms with King Guy he would be crushed between two mighty armies. Reluctantly he gave the required permission, on certain conditions.

The mamelukes must enter Galilee after sunrise, and return to their own land before sunset on the same day. He must have time to warn his vassals, so that they could shut up their flocks and themselves stay behind walls and in general present no temptation to plunderers.

Raymond's warning reached the Templars of La Feve while the two Grand Masters were within it. Since the Templars were not parties to the truce they resolved to attack what they thought would be a small body of scouts. The Grand Master of the Hospital advised caution, but after he had been accused of cowardice he naturally had to come too. At the Springs of Cresson one hundred knights of the Temple, with forty lay knights who had rallied to their standard, charged against seven thousand mamelukes. Three of them got away badly wounded, including the Grand Master of the Temple; the remainder perished on the field.

Count Raymond, shocked at the consequence of his treason, made haste to denounce his truce and join the King's army. But by muddle and misunderstanding the Kingdom had lost more than a hundred good knights before the opening of the decisive campaign.

CHAPTER XII

The Fall of Jerusalem

In the later battles of the Holy War much turned on the actions of individual lords, and this may be a convenient place to explain why every knight on the field could be recognised at a glance by both friends and enemies.

Basically armour was still the same as it had been at the time of the First Crusade, a covering of linked mail; but the appearance of the armed knight had greatly altered. Armourers, grown more skilful, handled steel almost as a tailor handles cloth. Closefitting mail covered the knight's legs from toe to hip; where it was fastened to the inner side of the mail shirt, so that a spearman could not slaughter a fallen rider by stabbing upward inside the shirt to the belly. Since the thigh was protected by mail leggings the shirt need be no longer than a modern jacket. Neck and ears were still covered by a mail hood. The shield had become much shorter and lighter; the knight could move it to parry a blow, instead of crouching immovable behind it. Above the mail, but confined by the swordbelt, came a linen surcoat, intended to shade the metal from the heat of the sun which might otherwise have made it glow too fiercely to be touched. It seems that the surcoat originated in Outremer, and may have been copied from a similar garment worn by Greek cavalry.

Thus in outline the knight of 1190 seemed to be wearing a tight suit of clothes, whereas the knight of 1090 had seemed to be muffled in a loose overcoat; though both were protected by the same kind of mail.

Technically, the most important change was in the shape of the helm. The conical steel cap with nasal had gone out in favour of something safer but much less comfortable. The new 'great helm' was a round flat-topped box of steel which covered the whole head. A slit before the eyes permitted limited vision straight ahead, and holes before the mouth admitted some fresh air. But the great helm was desperately hot, stuffy and heavy. A knight wearing it could not blow his nose or wipe sweat off his face. On the march it was slung from the shoulder, and put on only at the last minute before a charge. For anything less than a stubborn pitched battle many knights preferred to wear a round steel cap.

The development of heraldry had changed the outward appearance of the knight. The leaders of the First Crusade could be distinguished only by the banners borne behind them. Since the early 1100s, perhaps as a direct result of the confusions of the First Crusade, personal hereditary arms had spread through Christendom with the speed of an epidemic. Every warrior of gentle birth displayed his personal arms as conspicuously as he could: painted on his leather shield, on the breast and back of his surcoat, on the trappings of his horse and the pennon of his lance. Above the flat top of his great helm rose his personal crest, modelled in leather and brilliantly coloured. Note that these armorial bearings were strictly personal; the arms of a dead knight might descend to his heir, but younger sons must bear a different device. Arms and crest did not tell the world: 'Here is one of the Jones boys.' They said: 'This is William Jones and none other.'

Since the great helm hid the face heraldry was necessary for recognition in battle. It was part of a gentleman's education to know at a glance the arms of his neighbours and comrades. The infidels, who went into battle with faces uncovered, did not use heraldry. But any infidel who thought it might be useful could

The True Cross at Hattin

easily learn the blazons of leading Frankish knights. Before the first encounter on a day of battle warriors on both sides might say with certainty: 'There rides the lord of Ibelin, there the lord of Tripoli, there the lord of Outrejordan.'

During the summer of 1187 both sides mustered their forces for the crucial battle. The barons of the land stripped their castles of the normal garrisons to increase the field army. The Orders, eager to avenge the disaster at the Springs of Cresson, sent every available knight. The large sum of money sent by King Henry II of England in penance for the martyrdom of St Thomas was used to hire visiting Crusaders from Europe. Raymond of Antioch, son of Prince Bohemond, brought a small contingent in breach of the truce concluded by his father. By the end of May King Guy had assembled at Acre twelve hundred knights, some thousands of the light horse known as Turcopoles because they were trained to skirmish after the Turkish fashion, and ten thousand foot. It was by far the largest army that had ever been mustered in Christian Outremer. The True Cross would serve as its standard, as was customary when the whole army of the Kingdom marched to battle. But on this occasion the Patriarch did not bear it. Heraclius, pleading ill health though most people suspected plain cowardice, had entrusted the precious relic to the Bishop of Acre.

On 1 July Saladin crossed the Jordan at the head of an innumerable army gathered in all the lands of the infidels, from Persia to Cyrene. He moved north up the western shore of the Lake of Galilee to besiege Tiberias. In Outremer it was not the custom to campaign during the greatest heat of summer; but the tension had risen so high that neither side could bear to wait for autumn.

Soon the infidels stormed the town of Tiberias, but in the castle the lady Eschiva maintained a stout defence. She managed to send a message to Count Raymond her husband, who was with the royal army at Acre. King Guy called a council of war to consider it.

Count Raymond advocated a defensive strategy, although his wife and his greatest castle were in grave danger. In this heat the infidels would find no fodder for their horses, and if the Christians camped nearby they would not dare to pillage in small parties. Presently lack of supplies and increasing hardship would force Saladin to retire, as in 1182 he had retired from the Pools of Goliath. A battle would be too risky, since the Franks had no reserves. The lady Eschiva, and the garrison of Tiberias, must be sacrificed to the needs of the Holy War, as in the past other gallant Crusaders had been sacrificed.

But Raymond could not live down the memory of his private truce with Saladin. His rivals, Reynald of Chatillon and the Grand Master of the Temple, could assert with some show of plausibility that recently he had put the welfare of his lands above the interests of the Kingdom. They urged an immediate attack.

Their arguments were attractive. This time, perhaps, Saladin could be blockaded into retreat; but he would come back again in the autumn, and Outremer could not live under perpetual threat of invasion. Here was the strongest army that had ever been gathered under the True Cross, gathered by a special effort which could not be repeated year after year. If the army of Jerusalem dared not encounter the infidel in battle it was useless to continue the Holy War; they might as well all go home to Europe. King Guy, convinced as usual by the last speaker, ordered an advance to Sephoria.

The Christians were still not committed to an attack. Sephoria was a strong position with ample water and, a rarity in a Syrian summer, abundant pasture for the horses. If Saladin should attack he would probably be beaten. At a council on 2 July it was agreed to halt at Sephoria; but that same night the Grand Master of the Temple came privately to King Guy in his tent and shamed him into making an effort to relieve Tiberias.

Therefore on the morning of the 3rd the Christians continued their advance. The day was very hot, even for Galilee in July. The road climbed uphill to the range which divides the coastal plain from the Jordan valley, and no water was to be found on it. Since they were within Raymond's fief of

Galilee feudal etiquette gave him the right to command the van. Balian of Ibelin and the Orders had the post of greatest danger in the rear. The King commanded the centre.

The army of the Kingdom was not attempting anything unusual. An attack on a water-point in parched country was a standard Crusading manoeuvre; it ensured that Saladin must stand to meet them in fair fight instead of skirmishing all over the countryside. It was taken for granted that the steady infantry of the cities, well-armed Italian spearmen and cross-bows, could cut their way through the infidel line to the Lake of Galilee; after a hasty drink the knights would charge and scatter the mameluke light horse. Saladin must then retreat through waterless country, while the Christians rested secure in Tiberias.

There was nothing novel about the plan. But, as in every military operation, success depended on the leader asking no more from his men than they could perform.

As soon as the Christians left camp Turkish horsebowmen harassed them at long range, concentrating as usual against the rear. The dry grass of the hillside was set on fire, so that they must march through choking clouds of smoke and a shower of fine black ash. Heat and smoke slowed up the horses. By mid-afternoon the army was still on the western slope of the range, below a ridge which was crowned by two little hills known as the Horns of Hattin; from this ridge the road descended for about three miles to the Lake of Galilee. The time-table had gone wrong. It would be dark by the time they were in in position to charge the infidel.

At this point the Templars in the rearguard sent word to the King that their horses could go no farther. In the centre the foot also were suffering severely from heat and thirst. A commander with any drive would have pressed on at all costs; three miles of downhill road and one vigorous charge would have brought the whole army to the Lake. But King Guy lacked drive; and he saw below the Horns the little hamlet of Hattin. Where there are houses there must be water. Convinced as usual by the man who was shouting at him, in this case the Templar from the rearguard, King Guy gave orders that the whole army should halt short of the ridge.

Count Raymond hurried back from the van, furious at the halt and crying that all was lost. But the King could not be persuaded to change his mind. The whole army would pass the night beside the well at Hattin, and resume its advance at sunrise.

In that unusually hot summer the well was dry.

At sunrise it was the infidels who attacked. During the cool of dawn Saladin brought up his fit and well-watered army to encircle the thirsty Christians. The first probing attack was beaten off. But then discipline collapsed, chiefly because none of the Franks respected the King's military judgement. In defiance of orders the foot surged forward in a mass to reach water. They pushed back the infidel a little way and then were brought to a standstill. On a little hilltop they formed square. After many had been shot down by infidel arrows the remainder surrendered, too thirsty and exhausted to continue the fight.

Knights without foot to protect their horses were an easy mark for arrows; but of course the mamelukes wanted the honour and glory of defeating them hand to hand. The knights took refuge on one of the Horns of Hattin, where they rallied round the True Cross and the King's scarlet tent. They beat off charge after charge, killing many mamelukes. But after the foot had surrendered the Christians had no hope of victory; all they sought was to save some part of the army from the wreck. At the King's suggestion Count Raymond gathered his followers and tried to open a way through the circle of infidels.

Of course Saladin could recognise Raymond by his arms. He knew of the rumours of treason current among the Christians, and cunningly reinforced them. When Raymond charged the enemy opened their ranks to let him pass; after he had escaped they closed the circle again.

Later in the day Balian of Ibelin and Reynald of Sidon fought their way out, by their own prowess without infidel collusion. On a hilltop surrounded by the infidel they left their King and, what was more important, the True Cross. But afterwards no one reproached them for desertion. By the time they escaped all hope had gone.

Presently the Bishop of Acre was killed, and the True Cross captured. Last of all the King's scarlet tent was overthrown. When the mamelukes advanced for another charge they found the surviving knights lying on the ground beside their dying horses; thirst, heat and exhaustion had left them too weak to stand. They did not beg for quarter, but as the infidels bound them they made no resistance. All were taken prisoner, including the King, his brother Amalric, Reynald of Chatillon, Humphrey of Toron, and the Grand Master of the Temple (the Grand Master of the Hospital had been killed at the Springs of Cresson).

Before nightfall Saladin interviewed his prisoners, in his great tent which had been erected on the battlefield. He hoped that this decisive defeat might be the end of Christian Outre-mer; but he feared the mustering of an avenging army in Europe, so he wished to wind up the Crusades without hard feelings. He drew a distinction between ordinary land-holding knights of the Kingdom, who might go home to the west and never come back, and warriors dedicated to the Holy War.

With his own hands he gave water to King Guy, and assured him that in captivity he would be well treated. Then he rounded on Reynald of Chatillon and abused him until the prisoner answered back. That gave him an excuse to draw the sword he never used in battle; for Moslem rulers, unlike Christian Kings, led their armies from the rear. On the carpet of his state pavilion, in the presence of his court and all the other prisoners, he struck off Reynald's head.

The remaining captives were divided into two groups. The barons of the land were held for ransom, as was the valuable Grand Master of the Temple. But the other knights of the Orders were hacked to pieces on the spot, for Saladin knew that if they were released for ransom they would continue the Holy War.

The foot and the numerous camp-followers were sold as

slaves. In Damascus the price of a strong man fell to three dinars, and one infidel soldier swapped a slave for a pair of old shoes.

On the following day the castle of Tiberias was surrendered on terms. The Countess and her garrison were permitted to retire to Tripoli. Saladin always fulfilled the terms agreed at a surrender. Now that there was no Christian army in the field this persuaded the garrisons of many strong places to surrender their undamaged walls.

Wisely, Saladin next marched to the coast. Jerusalem, and the castles of Outrejordan, were very strongly fortified; but they could not hold out if no seaports remained in Christian hands. The merchants of the coast, stunned by news of the disaster, made little effort to defend themselves if they were offered generous terms. By the end of July Acre and all the other towns and castles of Galilee had capitulated. Farther south Jaffa, besieged by Saladin's brother Saphadin, made a gallant resistance until taken by assault. All its inhabitants were sold into slavery.

Continuing northward, Saladin sat down before Tyre. But Tyre lay on a peninsula, so that only one short stretch of wall could be battered; its garrison included most of the survivors of Hattin, under the command of Balian of Ibelin. After one assault had been repelled the infidels moved on to Sidon and Beirut, which soon yielded. Tripoli and Antioch were protected by truces, which Saladin was scrupulous to observe. He knew that these partial truces encouraged dissension among the Christians. By the middle of August he had conquered the whole Kingdom of Jerusalem; save for Tyre, Ascalon, Gaza, the remote castles of Outrejordan and the Holy City itself.

Before turning inland Saladin delayed to mop up Gaza and Ascalon, whose lords were among his prisoners. The Grand Master of the Temple was offered his freedom in return for his city of Gaza. In breach of the Rule of his Order he told the garrison to surrender; though Templars were expressly forbidden to yield strong places to buy their own release. Unfortunately the knights of the garrison observed their Rule, which bade them do whatever their Grand Master commanded. It was generally agreed to be a poor exchange. Yet the Grand Master had witnessed the massacre of Templar knights after Hattin, and knew that his life hung by a thread. Before we blame his cowardice we must be quite sure that in similar circumstances we ourselves would choose martyrdom.

The lord of Ascalon was King Guy, who seldom got willing obedience from his vassals. The garrison first ignored his command to surrender and then beat off an assault with heavy loss. Yet their position was hopeless; their valour gained them no more than favourable terms of surrender. They were escorted, with all the property they could carry, to Alexandria in Egypt; whence after some delay Venetian ships took them safely to Europe. King Guy remained in his easy captivity until the spring, when Saladin released him without ransom because he knew the unpopular King would embarrass the Christian cause.

Saladin hoped that by remaining on the coast, where he blocked all avenues of relief, he would frighten the burgesses of Jerusalem into surroundering their city undamaged. But the envoys whom he summoned to Ascalon answered proudly that they, and all their fellows, would die sword in hand rather than surrender the Holy Sepulchre. In return Saladin swore that he would win Jerusalem by the sword; which by the laws of war would give him the right to massacre all its inhabitants. On 20 September his army appeared before the city.

The burgesses had been strengthening their walls since the beginning of July. But though the city was very strong it lacked a competent garrison. Its resident knights, and the best part of its burgess-militia, had fallen at Hattin. Women and children, including refugees from the open country, outnumbered the able-bodied men by fifty to one. In the absence of the King command normally devolved on the Patriarch; but nobody would trust the timid Heraclius. The noncombatant financial officials of the Orders were doing their best to organise the defence, but they were not trained for war. In the nick of time a worthy commander appeared.

Balian of Ibelin was a very gallant knight and a true Crusader. But he was also a baron of the land, speaking fluent Arabic and accustomed to negotiation with his infidel neighbours. At Hattin he had done more than his duty, and he had saved Tyre; but he thought it quite natural to ask a favour from his old acquaintance Saladin. His wife, the Queen-dowager Maria, was in Jerusalem with her children. He sought a safe-conduct to fetch her back to Tyre before she was shut in by the coming siege. Saladin granted his request, on condition Balian did not bear arms and remained only one night in Jerusalem.

While Saladin was still in Ascalon Balian reached the Holy City. The burgesses, desperate for a trained commander, would not let him go. So Balian wrote to Saladin explaining what had happened; and Saladin, pleased by his honesty, agreed that he might stay. A guard of well-disciplined mamelukes escorted Queen Maria and her children to Tyre; and Balian took over the direction of the defence, though he still held himself bound by his promise not to bear arms in person.

Among Balian's measures one may seem to our eyes strange. In Jerusalem he found only two knights, who must have been sick when their fellows rode to Hattin. To strengthen the garrison he knighted all youths of noble birth above the age of fifteen, and thirty chosen burgesses. Here is a reminder that in the 12th century any knight could make another knight; whereas at the present day this privilege is reserved to sovereign princes. It is even more curious to speculate what gain was expected from this promotion. To Balian, that true knight, knighthood must have seemed something like a lay sacrament, a mystical ceremony which would make even a brave man fight better after he had received it.

The future that awaited these new-made knights makes this incident one of the most tragic in all the long tragedy of the Holy War. Some of these burgesses and boys will have fallen in the breach after enjoying for a few days their unexpected glory; others perhaps were ransomed. But some, let us hope only a few, will have fallen into slavery with the bruise of the accolade still on their shoulders. For a free man to be enslaved is horrible enough; for a youth who had just been honoured by knighthood the degradation must have been almost unbearable.

After nine days of battery the Egyptian engineers opened a breach in the wall. For a whole day of fierce fighting the Christians held the breach against savage assaults. But they could hold it only by putting every man into line. There were no reliefs, no reserves.

The fall of the city was inevitable, and its inhabitants made their several preparations. The Franks wished to open a gate, sally out, and die fighting. The Patriarch vetoed this plan, pronouncing it to be suicide; perhaps it would have been sinful suicide, but that may not have been the reason why Heraclius forbade it. The Greeks also planned to open a gate if they could get control of one; after all the Latin clergy had been martyred there would be vacancies for Greek Canons in the Holy Sepulchre. Only Balian kept his head. On 30 September he visited Saladin to ask for terms.

While Balian was negotiating the second day's assault raged. Saladin began by repeating that he had sworn to win Jerusalem by the sword; in any case there was no more room for bargaining, for the city was already his. He pointed to his banner, just planted on the crest of the breach.

At that moment the Franks counter-attacked, and the banner fell.

Balian replied that unless the Franks were offered quarter they would destroy Jerusalem; in particular they would destroy the Moslem shrine which marks the spot from which Mahomet is alleged to have ascended into Heaven. In addition they would kill all their numerous infidel prisoners.

There was a good deal of money in the city, Balian continued: the treasures of the two Orders, and part of the large sum paid by the King of England as penance for the murder of St Thomas. Would it be possible to fix a flat rate for individual ransoms?

While the battle raged in the breach they haggled, until a figure was agreed. All Franks might buy their freedom at the rate of ten dinars a man, five for a woman, one for a child.

Balian remarked that the city held twenty thousand penniless refugees; could the city treasury ransom them all for a lump sum? Saladin demanded one hundred thousand dinars, which was more than Balian could pay. At length it was agreed that thirty thousand dinars would ransom seven thousand paupers.

Balian then commanded the defenders of Jerusalem to lay down their arms. On 2 October 1187 Saladin entered the Holy City. The Greeks sat at home unmolested, but every Frank was immediately expelled. Those who could pay their ransoms set off westward to the coast, those who could not were driven eastward to the slave-market at Damascus. Saladin's brother Saphadin, a merciful man, asked for a thousand slaves as a present and immediately set them free. Saladin, now in a generous mood, gave seven hundred to the Patriarch and five hundred to Balian. The Patriarch caused unfavourable comment by paying ten dinars for himself and taking the rest of the treasure of the Holy Sepulchre with him to the coast. He could argue that the money had been given for the service of God, not for the ransom of Christian captives; but it is hard to give Heraclius the benefit of any doubt. Every other Frank who had money ransomed as many fellow-Christians as he could. Nonetheless, many thousands went into slavery.

Saladin's counsellors advised him to demolish the Holy Sepulchre, so that the Christians would have no incentive to recapture Jerusalem. He answered very sensibly that Christians valued the site of the Crucifixion, the plot of ground; not the masonry of the shrine. They would fight on for as long as they thought their Faith worth fighting for. Soon the Greek Emperor, Isaac Angelus, sent a letter to congratulate Saladin on his great achievement; he begged also that the Holy Places might be restored once more to Greek control, and the request was granted. But the Emperor's friendly message was not soon forgotten in the west.

Raymond of Tripoli died before the end of the year, perhaps of grief and shame. Many Franks believed him to have been a traitor, though Balian stood by him. In Outrejordan the garrisons of the castles sold their lives dearly, for these followers of Reynald of Chatillon could expect no mercy. Kerak held out until December, and Montreal until the following spring. There were no survivors.

Farther north most of the castles inland from Antioch surrendered at the first summons, until Bohemond begged for another truce. Of all Christian Outremer there remained only a few seaports. In the autumn of 1188 Saladin dismissed his army, supposing his task concluded. But in Tyre there was still the nucleus of a Crusade; and a new leader had arrived, almost by miracle, to inspire them to fresh efforts.

CHAPTER XIII

Counter Attack

The rulers of Montferrat, though their fief lay in northern
Italy, had many ties with the east. The elderly Marquis
had settled in Outremer. Though past military age he
had joined King Guy's army, where every knight was needed;
and had been captured at Hattin. His eldest son William had
married Queen Sibylla, and died after fathering the boy-King
Baldwin V. William's brother Conrad had settled in Constantinople where he married the Princess Theodora Angelina. But
in the spring of 1187 he was implicated in a charge of murder.
Fearing arrest, he decided to go on pilgrimage to the Holy
Places. He secretly took passage on a ship carrying a company
of French Crusaders from the Golden Horn to Acre.

During the campaign of Hattin he was at sea, where he
could hear no news. But when the ship reached Acre the master
noticed something odd about the place; the bell which normally
announced the arrival of a Frankish ship was not rung. Perhaps
the master recalled that bell-ringing, though not specifically
forbidden by the Moslem faith, is offensive to infidel sentiment.
He furled his sails, but cautiously did not drop anchor.

A customs officer put out in a little skiff, according to the
usual routine. The Crusaders saw with horror that he was an
infidel. Conrad, who spoke Greek, posed as a Greek merchant
and called out to learn the news. The infidel answered that the

army of Jerusalem had been destroyed, and that four days ago Acre had yielded to Saladin.

When the ship left Constantinople Acre, the chief port of Galilee, had been far from the infidel border. It was astonishing and terrible news, but the Crusaders kept their heads. Quickly they unfurled their sails and got out of harbour before the infidel could board them. They decided to sail north along the coast, for surely Antioch and the Cilician ports must still be in Christian hands? At the next harbour, Tyre, they crept in cautiously; to see Christian banners flying from the walls.

It was the 14th of July, only ten days after Hattin; but Conrad was barely in time to save the strongest seaport in the Kingdom. Already Saladin's army was entrenched on the isthmus and the survivors of Hattin were negotiating for surrender. In the absence at Jerusalem of Balian of Ibelin they were led by Reynald of Tripoli. He had come so near agreement on a capitulation that Saladin had sent into the town two of his banners, to be displayed on the wall as a sign that his terms were accepted.

Conrad at once took charge, helped by a shipload of knights who had not been shaken by the disaster at Hattin. He threw the infidel banners into the town ditch and defied Saladin to do his worst.

Saladin retorted by parading before the walls the captive Marquis of Montferrat, threatening to kill him unless his son surrendered. But when Conrad remained resolute Saladin did not carry out his threat. Though he was ruthless in pursuit of victory he did not delight in slaughter when there was nothing to be gained by it. Presently he marched away to capture Ascalon. In November he returned and once more laid siege to Tyre; but at the end of December a great assault by land and sea was repelled with heavy loss, and in January he retired inland. Already the hot and marshy coastal plain had been infected with deadly disease, which made it a most unhealthy seat of war throughout the subsequent campaigns.

In Tyre the barons of the land, frightened by their terrible experience at Hattin, waited anxiously for help from Europe.

Surely every good knight of the Frankish lands, which then included England, the Netherlands and the Rhineland as well as France proper, would hasten to take the Cross when he heard that the infidels had captured the Holy Sepulchre? This would be a greater General Passage even than the First Crusade. So it was, when it got under way. But for two years a chapter of accidents delayed it.

In the west no one had expected that the whole Kingdom of Jerusalem would fall to the infidel as the result of a single defeat. For forty years, ever since the fiasco of the Second Crusade, armed pilgrims had journeyed to Outremer. They were impressed by the splendour and state of the barons of the land, the strength of their castles, the riches of the Italian merchants in the coastal cities; too often they were cheated of participation in the Holy War by the conclusion of a friendly truce with infidel neighbours. It was hard to conceive that a great Kingdom more than ninety years old could vanish within less than a month. Surely every knight had ample time to settle his personal affairs before beginning the long ride to the Holy Places?

In addition, the Pope was the obvious leader to arrange a General Passage; and the Papacy kept on changing hands. In October 1187 Urban III died of grief on hearing the terrible news of Hattin. His successor, Gregory VIII, died in the following December. The work of organisation devolved on Clement III, who was himself to die before the armies he raised had reached Outremer.

The German Emperor and the Kings of France and England took the Cross. But the Emperor Frederick Barbarossa was in schism, and it was some time before Clement III could reconcile him with the Church. Neither Philip Augustus of France nor Henry II of England were enthusiastic Crusaders; they would do their duty because their subjects expected it of them. Neither dared to go overseas while his rival was at large in France, and first they must agree on a truce to suspend the age-old war between Anjou and Paris. They met at Gisors, the traditional place where the Dukes of Normandy made peace with their overlords; but soon after the truce had been agreed fighting broke out again, and continued until King Henry died in July 1189.

The only Christian King who appreciated the need for haste was William II of Sicily; and he must wind up a bitter war before he could spare forces to fight in Outremer. In 1187 he was engaged in one of the traditional occupations of Sicilian Kings, an attempt to take the mainland of Hellas from the Emperor of Constantinople. Luckily it was never hard to get peace from the unwarlike Isaac Angelus. By the spring of 1188 the excellent Sicilian fleet was cruising in Levantine waters, carrying a landing force of two hundred knights. One result was that Saladin postponed his siege of Tripoli.

Saladin had won very nearly all he wanted, Jerusalem and the other Christian Holy Places. At this time he seems to have been willing to leave the Christians in their harbours on the coast, provided they gave up any attempt to win back the Holy Sepulchre. Italian ships were useful to his export trade, and he had no ambition to rule the seas. Through Tripoli he made overtures for peace. But the Christians answered that if he wanted peace he must first evacuate the whole Kingdom of Jerusalem, which in any case would be taken from him when the promised reinforcements arrived from Europe.

Rather curiously, Saladin continued to release the prisoners taken at Hattin. First they were ordered to surrender their castles; but if a garrison disobeyed its captive lord was freed all the same. The release of King Guy in July 1188 was probably intended to harass Conrad of Montferrat; but the old Marquis and young Humphrey of Toron were freed about the same time with no obvious advantage to the infidel. Perhaps Saladin, who could be humane with Christians whom he liked personally, saw that he gained nothing by keeping them and could not bring himself to murder them. King Guy joined his Queen in Tripoli, where most of his adherents gathered round him.

These captive knights, including King Guy, swore to leave Outremer as soon as they were free. As Saladin must have foreseen, they were absolved from these oaths in the first Christian town they reached; oaths sworn under duress, and especially oaths sworn to infidels, are invalid by Canon Law. But a true knight does not make a promise he does not intend to keep, whatever may be the legal position. King Guy was slightly ashamed of himself, and his adherents were slightly ashamed of their leader.

By late summer all was working out as Saladin had planned; the Christian remnant in Outremer was on the brink of civil war. King Guy led his followers south from Tripoli to Tyre; and when he demanded admittance to the chief remaining city of his Kingdom Conrad closed the gates in his face.

All Crusaders were keen amateur lawyers, delighted to apply feudal principles in a land which lacked a settled code. Conrad did not base his claim on force, like a pirate; he said that Guy had forfeited his throne by military incompetence at Hattin, and by the even graver fault of going into captivity without nominating a regent. The throne of Jerusalem was vacant. He, Conrad, would hold Tyre in trust until the German Emperor and the Kings of France and England should arrive in Outremer to appoint another ruler. Baffled, Guy withdrew once more to Tripoli.

In April 1189 he came back again, bringing Queen Sibylla in whose name he ruled the Kingdom. Still the gates of Tyre were shut against him. He encamped with his followers before the walls, though he did not attempt to break in by force. By now the worst of the danger was past. The Christians were beginning to forget that Conrad had saved them when all seemed lost; they remembered only that he had no legal right to Tyre. Guy's faction began to increase.

The Sicilian sailors recognised him as rightful King, though they refused to fight for him against fellow-Crusaders. Another fleet, from Pisa, joined his party. In the summer heat Conrad was too sick to take the field. Meanwhile a torpid state of war continued between Saladin and the Christians; many mamelukes had gone home with their plunder and the Crusaders would not move until help arrived from Europe. Suddenly, after the deadlock before Tyre had continued all summer, Guy ended it by leading his men to the siege of Acre.

It was a fantastically rash move, hardly to be expected from the weakwilled commander who had dithered into defeat at Hattin. Either Guy was following the advice of some bold counsellor whose name is lost to us, or his nerve had broken and he was anxious to end the stalemate at any cost. At once his bold initiative made him in the eyes of Europe the leader of the Crusade. But the garrison of Acre outnumbered its attackers, and Saladin could quickly gather his army in the hills to the eastward. Nevertheless, Guy sat down before Acre.

The town, built on a peninsula, was immensely strong. Its numerous garrison was well supplied. A squadron of infidel warships lay in the harbour. But by the beginning of September King Guy had fortified a camp on the hill of Turon, a mile to the eastward; this hill rose slightly above the malarial plain, and was well supplied with water.

Reinforcements from Europe were beginning to drop in, private parties of earnest Crusaders who would not wait for the dilatory Kings. First came a fleet of North Sea sailors, mostly Danes, who had fought their way through the dangerous Straits of Gibraltar. They were better seamen than any to be found in the Mediterranean. For the time being the Christians had command of the sea.

James of Avesnes, the most famous knight of Flanders, brought a group of French and Flemish volunteers. The Marquis of Thuringia, the Count of Guelders, the Bishops of Beauvais and Verona arrived with their followers. At the end of September Conrad of Montferrat left Tyre to join the army, though he would not serve under King Guy.

Saladin had encamped a mile or so to the east of the Crusaders. He was unable to raise the siege, though his troops fought their way to the north gate of Acre and passed in some reinforcements. On 4 October the Crusaders sallied out to storm his camp. In the course of a muddled engagement they broke in, so that the Count of Brienne captured Saladin's own tent. But as the Christians scattered to pillage the infidels counter-attacked and drove them back to their own camp with heavy loss, especially of famous knights who had charged too far. The Count of Brienne was slain; the Grand Master of the Temple was taken and immediately murdered; Conrad, surrounded and in danger of capture, was rescued in a gallant charge by his rival King Guy.

For the rest of the year the deadlock continued. The Crusaders blockaded Acre, and Saladin in turn blockaded their camp. As each side received reinforcements the balance of power, and especially the vital command of the sea, changed hands. Saladin sought help from as far afield as Moorish Spain, Crusaders came from Sweden and Hungary. In November a fleet arrived from London, after loitering on the voyage to fight for the King of Portugal. But in the same month the powerful Sicilian fleet was called home.

The sudden and unexpected death of William the Good, King of Sicily, was a severe blow to the Crusade. The Kings of France and England had planned to travel to Outremer by way of Sicily, counting on help from King William, the husband of King Richard's sister. But she was childless. The next heir was William's aunt Constance, married to Henry of Hohenstaufen, the Emperor's son. But the Normans of Sicily, unwilling to be ruled by a German, crowned William's bastard cousin, Tancred of Lecce. In fear of a German invasion he ordered his fleet back to Sicily.

Henceforth neither side commanded the sea. An infidel fleet could usually fight its way into Acre; a Crusading fleet could usually fight its way to the open beach which supplied the besieging army. But all three armies, the garrison of Acre, King Guy's, and Saladin's, were often hungry.

With the hot weather of 1190 disease raged in the foul, crowded camps. New arrivals from the west suffered from it in particular. But as the long stalemate persisted the bored armies began to fraternise. Children from the camps played together, mameluke emirs attended Christian feasts. The leaders on both sides got to know one another, personally or by reputation. Yet the war continued with bitter intensity.

Bedouin thieves crept into the Christian camp by night. For every man they murdered, for every child they stole, Saladin gave them a reward. But he was not utterly lacking in generous impulses; when he could see with his own eyes the suffering he had inflicted he might sometimes feel remorse. A brave Christian mother sought him out in the infidel camp, begging for the return of her baby girl stolen by these bedouin marauders. Saladin bought the child from her kidnappers and sent back mother and daughter to the Christian camp. Yet he continued to employ these bedouin who terrorised Christian noncombatants.

With great fortitude both armies sat it out for the whole of the year 1190. Saladin's doctors warned him that such a long stay in the feverish coastal plain might kill him. He answered with an Arab proverb: 'Kill me and Malek, kill Malek with me.' These were words first spoken by a hero of early Islam, as he struggled on the ground with the leader of a pagan army; after the same spear-thrust had killed both, the Moslems were victorious. Saladin knew well that the climate, though it might weaken him, would do much more harm to newcomers from northern Europe. For long periods he lay sick in his tent, but he continued to command his army.

Meanwhile Conrad had come to terms with King Guy. It was agreed that he should be lord of Tyre, and of Sidon and Beirut after they had been liberated from the infidel; but he should hold them as a vassal of the present King of Jerusalem.

Distinguished Crusaders continued to arrive; among them the Archbishop of Canterbury and Henry, Count of Champagne, a young man of distinguished family. His mother was a daughter of Eleanor of Aquitaine by her first marriage with King Louis of France; so that both King Philip and King Richard were his uncles.

The epidemic which raged in the autumn carried off Queen Sibylla and her children. King Guy had lost his title to the throne; the next heir was the Princess Isabella, Sibylla's sister. The barons of the land now proposed to marry Isabella to Conrad of Montferrat, and thus give the crown to the leader of their choice. It was a neat plan, but there were ecclesiastical obstacles.

It was widely known that Conrad had been married twice, in Italy and in Constantinople. He maintained that both his wives were dead, but not everyone believed him. However, what was a little bigamy when the recovery of the Holy City was at stake? No one could prove that either of these ladies was alive, and his partisans announced that Conrad was a widower.

The position of Princess Isabella took more explaining. Not only was she married; her husband, Humphrey of Toron, was present in the camp. Furthermore, she loved him and disliked Conrad.

Pressure was brought to bear by her mother, Queen Maria Comnena, now married to Balian of Ibelin. In due course Isabella testified that her marriage, contracted when she was eight years old, had lacked her free consent; and that the notoriously effeminate Humphrey had never consummated it. If she was telling the truth her marriage might be annulled.

The Patriarch Heraclius was unwilling to decide such a ticklish question. Pleading ill health, he appointed the Archbishop of Canterbury to judge it as his deputy. Without bothering to inquire into the facts Archbishop Baldwin decided that the marriage must stand; because every true Englishman ought to support King Guy, who had been a vassal of King Richard's Duchy of Aquitaine before he came to Outremer. Then, in November 1190, the Archbishop of Canterbury died of the fever; and five days later the Archbishop of Pisa, the papal legate, annulled the marriage and married Isabella to Conrad.

Because King Guy refused to drop his royal title Conrad withdrew to Tyre. Until he had been crowned Conrad might not call himself King, and his position was still so doubtful that no prelate was willing to crown him.

By the spring of 1191 King Guy was still blockading Acre with magnificent obstinacy. His army, much reduced in numbers by disease, was on the verge of starvation; for supplies could not be landed on the open beach during the storms of winter. Saladin, still encamped a few miles to the eastward, thought seriously of bringing on a pitched battle; he might win a victory even more crushing than Hattin. But he feared too great a victory. Hattin had brought out on Crusade the German Emperor and the Kings of France and England; another disaster might bring even more Crusaders. He decided to let time work for him. Presently these invaders would see that they could never regain the Holy Places; they would all sail back to Europe, and at last the Holy War would be over.

In March the weather moderated so that ships could unload on the open beach. These ships brought something better than food—they brought news that the Kings of France and England were nearing Outremer.

CHAPTER XIV

The Third Crusade

The first European ruler to set out for the east was the German Emperor. For many years he had been a mighty Emperor, so great that in German legend he still lives. Like our King Arthur, Barbarossa sleeps among his knights in a remote cavern, his red beard growing through the table before him. One day someone will be brave enough to blow the magic horn at the entrance, and Barbarossa will emerge to set the world to rights.

In his youth he had ridden to Outremer on the disastrous Second Crusade, and he was aware of the perils of the expedition. He gathered a large, well-disciplined army and a great treasure, and wrote in advance to all the rulers through whose lands he would pass. The King of Hungary and the Greek Emperor answered that he would be welcome, the Sultan of Iconium did not answer at all, and Saladin replied with a courteous defiance. When he set out, in May 1189, his army was the most formidable that had ever marched to Outremer.

But even the great Barbarossa had certain weaknesses. He was nearer seventy than sixty years of age, though he still intended to lead his men in battle; and he found it difficult to provide for the government of his Empire during his absence. His famous adversary, Henry the Lion, Duke of Saxony, had to be driven into exile. The Emperor's eldest son, another Henry, was appointed regent; but in theory the Empire was still an elective monarchy, so the young man could not be nominated as next Emperor. Barbarossa's second son, Frederick Duke of Suabia, accompanied the army as second in command.

All went well until the Germans reached Belgrade, where the officers of Isaac Angelus gave them food and guides. But in the west it was not yet understood that Constantinople had lost control of the Balkan Slavs. These rebels attacked stragglers from an army friendly to the Greek Emperor. When Barbarossa opened negotiations with the Serb and Bulgarian chieftains Isaac Angelus suspected he was encouraging the rebellion; as a reprisal he imprisoned the envoys Barbarossa had sent forward to Constantinople. At once Barbarossa wrote to the Pope, proposing that the Crusade should be preached against the Greek Empire as well as against Saladin; and ordered his ministers in Germany to raise a fleet among the Frisians which might protect his crossing into Asia if the Greeks should resist him by force. In terror Isaac Angelus released the envoys. In return for Greek guides and supplies Barbarossa agreed to avoid Constantinople and cross into Asia by way of the Hellespont.

By this time it was late in the year, and Barbarossa knew the winter climate of Asia Minor. He wintered in Adrianople, and cross the Hellespont in March 1190. In May he drove the Turks from Iconium, and thus reopened the overland route to Outremer. No obstacle remained, except the Taurus Mountains.

On 10 June the Germans descended into the Cilician plain, intending to cross the river Calycadnus. The elderly Emperor galloped ahead in full armour, eager to reach the cool water. Then either he jumped into the stream and was swept away by the current; or his horse slipped and put him in. When his troops reached the river bank they found him drowned.

Among Germans the Holy War had never been popular. They had come east to Cilicia because they would follow Barbarossa anywhere. Now that he was dead many of them went home by sea, and others sailed independently to Tyre. It was a much smaller army that Frederick of Suabia led to Antioch, where again many deserted. Eventually he also continued to Tyre. But he was not a reigning monarch, and when the Kings of France and England arrived he must take third place. Since Conrad of Montferrat was his cousin all the supporters of King Guy were his enemies. As a final touch of discouragement Barbarossa's corpse, though carefully pickled, had to be buried hastily in Antioch. The Germans had hoped that it would lead them to Jerusalem. The German Crusaders who finally joined the besiegers of Acre were a useful reinforcement; but they were hardly a shadow of the great army which had left Ratisbon in 1189.

King Philip of France and King Richard of England had hoped to start together in 1189. At the last moment the Queen of France died, so that mourning delayed them until autumn. Since it was unwise to travel in winter they finally set off from the holy shrine of Vezelay in July 1190.

The reluctant allies were personally incompatible. King Philip, aged 25, was an eccentric and unknightly figure; he never learned to ride properly, and clung to the only destrier he could manage until the beast died of old age. In his careful planning for the future of his Kingdom he was willing to run calculated risks; but when he could be persuaded to appear on the field he was usually the first Frenchman to flee. Ugly and meanly dressed, he never appealed to the emotions of his men. He was not interested in the Holy War, and had taken the Cross only because his vassals expected him to do so.

At 33 the tall handsome Richard Coeur de Lion was the most famous knight and the most flamboyant ruler in Christendom. Invincible in the charge, he was also a farseeing strategist and a remarkable military engineer; his skill in poetry was equally well known. He was so devoted to the Holy War that he neglected his Kingdom and robbed his subjects to lead a mighty army to Outremer. His followers adored him.

But he was not exactly the pattern of a Christian knight. In some respects he was barely a Christian at all. For years he would not receive Communion, because he refused to go through the form of forgiving his enemies in Confession. He was suspected of simony in his choice of bishops. Worst of all, his enemies could plausibly suggest that he was a homosexual. Certainly he preferred the society of handsome young men to that of beautiful ladies; his marriage, contracted for reasons of foreign policy, was childless. Though he was eager to liberate Jerusalem he got on very well with infidels.

In diplomacy he was his own worst enemy, invariably bested by the farseeing Philip. He thought of witty, unforgivable remarks about his allies, and he blurted out any witty remark that came into his head. When his pride was injured or his quick temper aroused he was utterly reckless of consequences. He was a magnificent commander-in-chief, but quite incapable of co-operation with equal colleagues.

To raise money for his army he would sell anything. He sold English sheriffdoms to the highest bidder, and encouraged the King of Scotland to buy back the vassalage he had sworn to England. Yet, however strong the force he led, while he marched in company with the King of France he must take second place; for in his capacity as Duke of Aquitaine and Normandy he had done homage to King Philip, who had done homage to no man.

The two kings planned to sail to Outremer by way of Sicily. It was the most expensive way to travel, but it would bring their forces fresh and undamaged to Acre. But they had looked for help from King William, who had invited them to come by this route. Now King William was dead, and his bastard cousin Tancred reigned in his stead.

King Philip and his fleet reached Messina in September. Richard, who suffered from seasickness, preferred to ride through Italy. He travelled without a guard, as usual, and his hot temper led him into undignified scrapes. Once when he saw a hawk in a peasant's cottage he tried to confiscate it; for the hawk of a landless man must be used only for poaching. The villagers very nearly lynched the famous King of England. By the time he crossed over to Messina he was very angry.

He was especially angry with King Tancred, who was oppressing the dowager Queen Joan, Richard's sister. Her dower was unpaid and she was under arrest, for fear she might adhere to Princess Constance and her German husband. To show his disapproval of King Tancred Richard sacked Messina.

King Tancred released Queen Joan and paid her dower. King Philip patched up a peace. Then a formal treaty was drawn up to regulate the conduct of the allies. Most of it was concerned with discipline among the troops, but one clause laid down that all gains made 'during the Crusade' should be shared equally between Philip and Richard. Richard chose this moment to repudiate his betrothal to Philip's sister Alice, giving as his reason that she had been seduced by his father, old King Henry. Philip swallowed the insult to his family in the interests of the Holy War; but henceforth he hated Richard as a man, not merely as a danger to France. Richard announced that he was about to marry Princess Berengaria of Navarre; which must be a political alliance directed against France.

During the winter of 1190 the three Kings lived in uneasy peace on the same island. They heard of the disaster which had befallen the Germans; but in Outremer Guy and Conrad seemed to be holding their own and there was no urgent hurry. At feasts and tournaments King Richard quarrelled with other eminent knights; but he was so obviously in earnest about the Holy War that other Crusaders made allowances for his hasty temper.

On 30 March King Philip sailed for Tyre. On 10 April Richard followed, bringing his sister the widowed Queen Joan and his betrothed the Princess Berengaria. While the fleets were at sea Clement III died and the new Pope Celestine III crowned as Emperor Henry VI of Hohenstaufen, Barbarossa's eldest son; who happened to be passing through Rome on his way to wrest Sicily from King Tancred. Thus ended the precarious European peace which had been arranged with such difficulty to allow for the General Passage.

The French Fleet met fair weather. By 20 April King Philip had joined the besiegers of Acre, and was soon on good terms with his cousin Conrad. The French built some powerful siege

Richard Coeur de Lion

engines, but it was agreed that the assault should be postponed until King Richard arrived.

The English ships encountered continual storms, until sea-sickness made Richard genuinely ill. To recover, he sheltered first in Crete and then in Rhodes, where he remained until 1 May. There he heard that some of his ships had been driven ashore in Cyprus, including that which carried his sister and Berengaria. The rebel 'Emperor' had plundered these ships and arrested all on board.

Through another frightful storm Richard sailed for Cyprus. Isaac Comnenus hurried to meet him at the port of Limassol, where he promised all Richard demanded of him. But after seeing the battered ships and the seasick Crusaders he changed his mind and defied the Franks to do their worst.

Richard received unexpected reinforcements. News of his doings had reached the camp before Acre, where King Philip had come out as a supporter of Conrad. King Guy and his friends, Bohemond of Antioch, the Armenian chieftains of Cilicia, Humphrey of Toron, sailed from Tyre to Limassol, all eager to put Richard under an obligation. Richard decided with their help to conquer the whole island of Cyprus.

The conquest was not difficult. The Greeks of Cyprus would have preferred to be ruled from Constantinople, but as between the rebel Comnenus and the Franks they were indifferent. Richard had promised not to put Comnenus 'in irons' if he yielded; so silver fetters were made for him. By June all the castles of the island were held by Crusaders, and two English barons had been appointed temporary justiciars until a permanent lord could be chosen. Best of all, Richard had taken an enormous treasure.

The conquest of Cyprus greatly strengthened Outremer, where the few remaining Christian ports could not even feed themselves so long as the infidels held all the open country. For supplies they depended on imports from other Latin lands, of which Sicily had been the nearest. Now that Cyprus could feed them the cities of Outremer were once more self-supporting.

Before Richard left Cyprus he married Berengaria. She was

crowned Queen of England by the Norman Bishop of Evreux in the Church of St George in Limassol; the Plantagenets had an international outlook. On 6 June Richard reached Tyre. But on Conrad's orders the garrison would not admit this strong force of strangers, so the fleet proceeded to the open beach near Acre; where at last they came ashore on 8 June 1191, eleven months after they had left Vezelay.

Since August 1189 Acre had been besieged, and it looked as though the siege would never end. The infidel garrison, though tired and often hungry, was not completely cut off; Egyptian warships could fight their way into harbour. The Christian camp was strongly entrenched; but after such long occupation disease raged over the filthy ground. Saladin with his great army was encamped only a few miles away. He could read signal-flags displayed on the walls of Acre; so that whenever the Crusaders assaulted the town he assaulted their camp and they must return to defend it.

Most newcomers fell sick as soon as they arrived in camp, and Richard was no exception. But he had a great curiosity to meet the infidel warrior who had conquered Jerusalem, and he may have genuinely believed that he could end the Holy War by a negotiated peace. After all, Jerusalem was not an especially holy place to the Moslems. Saladin might be persuaded to evacuate it, in return for a promise that the rest of his dominions would be left undisturbed.

As soon as possible Richard sent envoys to Saladin, suggesting a personal interview. Saladin answered that interviews between warring Kings were seldom fruitful, though he would be delighted to meet Richard in time of truce. Meanwhile the King of England should negotiate with his brother Saphadin. Saladin may have feared assassination, or he may have been very busy. But perhaps this was a barbed reminder that in the Crusading army Richard ranked second. Nearly all Crusaders were of French descent; in their eyes Philip was the natural ruler of all Franks, and Richard merely his greatest vassal.

Richard arranged to meet Saphadin, but was prevented by illness.

Meanwhile the arrival of the English fleet had given the Crusaders command of the sea. Acre was closed to infidel ships. The hungry garrison began to think of surrender.

Richard and Saladin conducted an odd long-range flirtation, though during the whole Crusade they never met. Richard had brought some falcons as a gift for Saladin; but the voyage had made them ill. For their recovery they needed fresh poultry, unobtainable in the blockaded camp. Saladin sent chickens to Richard, with snow and fresh fruit to help him in his own convalescence. Envoys continually passed between the armies bearing trifling presents. Some Crusaders murmured at this friendship, but perhaps Richard had a strategic object; the garrison of Acre had begun to treat with their besiegers, and he may have wanted to make sure that Saladin knew of it.

Probably the Crusaders might now have taken Acre by assault, if they had all attacked together. They did not, for they could not agree which lord should hold the town afterwards. While Philip's men attacked Richard's stayed in their tents, and vice versa. Great men continued to die of disease, including the Patriarch Heraclius and the Count of Flanders. The latter left no direct heir, so that by feudal law his County reverted to King Philip. About this time Philip reminded Richard of the treaty made in Sicily. Since all conquests made on Crusade were to be shared equally, when might he expect his half of the island of Cyprus?

Richard answered that when he had won Cyprus he had not been on Crusade; he had been avenging wrongs done to his betrothed and his sister. The treaty applied only to conquests won from the infidel. But if it ought to apply to all gains made while the Kings were on Crusade, then he would give Philip half Cyprus as soon as he had received his half of Flanders. That closed the discussion, but it left Philip with another grievance.

Saladin, hearing of the desperate condition of Acre, determined on fighting a pitched battle to raise the siege. But his army, discontented by the long static campaign in the unhealthy coastal plain, would not fight. That was a danger-signal.

Saladin had displaced Nureddin's rightful heirs. He had no legal or hereditary right to the allegiance of his men, who followed him only because he led them to victory. If he led them to defeat they would choose another leader. Acre must be sacrificed, to open up the campaign and permit him to fight in the hills or in the desert, where he had a better chance of victory.

On 12 July the infidels in Acre surrendered on terms. They were the flower of Saladin's army, led by his favourite emirs; they took it for granted that he would honour any promises they made. He must return the True Cross; he must pay a ransom of two hundred thousand pieces of gold; he must free fifteen hundred Christian slaves; lastly, he must hand over a hundred captives of noble birth, to be named by the Crusaders. Until all this had been done the infidels would remain in Richard's hands as prisoners of war.

The entry of the Christians into Acre was a quarrelsome business. The Duke of Austria, who commanded the Germans since the death of Frederick of Suabia, claimed that as representing his Emperor he ranked with the Kings. His banner was displayed beside those of France and England and Jerusalem until Richard had it thrown into a sewer. The Duke and his Germans promptly went home. Christian refugees from Acre wanted their own houses back, while Crusaders claimed them as booty won by the sword. Conrad was lord of Acre as a vassal of King Guy; so much had been agreed beforehand. But Richard took the Royal Palace as his headquarters, so that King Philip had to be content with the Templars' convent.

King Philip was genuinely sick, as well as very cross. At the beginning of August he sailed for France. Before leaving he swore not to attack Richard's French possessions, an oath easily evaded by claiming that they were not rightfully Richard's and never had been. The Duke of Burgundy took command of the numerous French Crusaders who remained in Outremer.

Conrad of Montferrat sulked in Tyre, because he would not serve in an army commanded by King Richard the friend of King Guy. The army in Acre was diminished in numbers; but

Richard was now its sole commander, and could lead it effectively.

It soon became apparent that Saladin would not fulfil the promises made by the garrison of Acre. When Richard's envoys visited him they were shown sacks of gold collected to pay the ransom. They were allowed to revere the True Cross, which otherwise Saladin kept under the threshold of his tent so that all who entered must trample on it. A number of Christian slaves had been assembled. But there was no sign of the eminent, named prisoners.

The most likely explanation is that the infidels in Acre, long besieged, did not know that these knights were already dead. It was not Saladin's custom to keep noble prisoners. Those whom he liked were released almost at once, often without ransom; those whom he disliked were killed. Public executions of Christian prisoners were a frequent entertainment at his court. Moslem writers praise him because, with parental forethought, he would not let his children join in the fun. He explained that if they fell into the habit of slaughter during their formative years they might grow up to slaughter Moslems as well as Christians.

On 20 August, therefore, in strict accordance with the laws of war, Richard killed all the prisoners taken at Acre, to the number of two thousand seven hundred. Saladin's outposts could see what was done, but their attempted rescue was beaten off. Many historians condemn Richard for this massacre; but his contemporaries agreed that, though stern, he was within his rights. The infidels had offered to buy their lives, and then failed to hand over the price. If Acre had fallen by assault, as must have happened if they had not yielded, no one would have been entitled to quarter.

Henceforth Saladin killed all his Christian prisoners, unless they were rich enough to pay a good ransom.

Saladin now barred the road to Jerusalem, expecting that the Crusaders would march inland. But Richard was a skilful strategist as well as a skilful tactician. He saw the weak spot in Saladin's empire; which was that his money came from Egypt while his soldiers came from Syria. He led his army south along the coast, hoping to sever communications between Cairo and Damascus.

The army marched along the shore, in the formation normally used by Christians against Turks, but with refinements of Richard's own devising. On the right the English fleet kept pace with them; next the sea came the baggage train, escorted by that half of the foot whose turn it was to rest; then rode the knights, divided into van, main battle, and rearguard; inland, nearest the enemy, trudged another column of foot.

The infantry wore arrow-proofed haquetons, jackets quilted with cotton or tow. (The word haqueton is derived from the Arabic al-coton, cotton.) The Moslems were disheartened to see these men walk on undisturbed, with arrows sticking in their haquetons until they looked like porcupines. Their crossbows kept the Turkish horsebowmen at a distance. In theory men wounded in the legs, or overcome by exhaustion, should be carried in the ships; in practice, at that hottest season of the year, many crossbowmen in their padded armour died where they fell. But the column of foot shielded the irreplaceable destriers of the knights.

The infidels marched beside them, a little way inland. Every step was delayed by perpetual skirmishing. On 5 September Richard, who was beginning to appreciate the difficulties of the campaign, had an interview with Saphadin. But since he demanded possession of all Palestine west of Jordan before he would take his army back to Europe the war continued.

On 7 September Saladin attacked in force, as the Crusaders passed the wood of Arsouf where the mamelukes could lurk unseen. For once the infidels placed their foot in the front line; their Sudanese spearmen drove back the Christian foot on the knights. Then the mamelukes rode in, concentrating on the Hospitallers who formed the rearguard. The Templars were in the van; Crusaders from France and England, under Richard's personal command, made up the main battle.

It was essential for the Christians to remain on the defensive until the mamelukes were too closely committed to retreat.

Richard's force of character kept his knights in line, though the Hospitallers sent more than once to say that they must charge, for they could endure no more. At last they charged without orders. But Richard, with his remarkable sense of timing, led all the knights of the main battle and the van to charge beside them. Since the charge was slightly premature the mamelukes fled so swiftly that few of them were slain.

The Crusaders' loss was also small, though the good knight James of Avesnes charged too far and was surrounded; he was killed, after he had killed fifteen infidels. But though Saladin's army rallied quickly, so that next day he was ready for another battle, he had suffered a grave moral defeat. He had lost Acre because his men would not charge; and when at last they charged they were scattered to the winds. Another such defeat and they might choose a different leader. He retired to Ramleh, ready to fight the Christians when they turned inland towards Jerusalem.

Richard did not turn inland. Perhaps an immediate advance would have given him Jerusalem; but only because its garrison was weak and its walls in bad repair. Once inside Jerusalem he would have been cut off from the coast. If Saladin did not besiege him most Crusaders would go home as soon as they had heard Mass in the Holy Sepulchre.

By this time Richard had seen that he could not free Jerusalem. A garrison for the Holy City must be found by the Orders and the barons of the land; and the barons of the land had deserted him to follow Conrad of Montferrat. That was why he sought peace, offering to go home if Saladin would evacuate the Holy Places. But so long as he remained in Outremer he would go on hammering at the weak spot in Saladin's dominions. He marched south to Jaffa and restored its fortifications.

Saladin feared to be cut off from Cairo, if Richard continued south. He lead his army from Ramleh to Ascalon, and entirely demolished that flourishing city. This was to pay a great compliment to Richard's prestige. Ascalon was strong, and might have been given a strong garrison. But Saladin knew that his men would not dare to hold it against Richard.

From Jaffa Richard sent Humphrey of Toron to negotiate with Saphadin. The terms he asked were still the old ones, the True Cross and the Kingdom of Jerusalem west of Jordan; in return he would make a firm peace with Saladin and lead his Crusaders back to Europe. When these proposals were once more refused Richard suggested a most ingenious compromise; whose only fault was that it ignored the religious aspect of the Holy War.

Let Saladin retire east of Jordan. But let him hand over the Holy City, with the title of King of Jerusalem, to his brother Saphadin. Saphadin would marry the widowed Queen Joan, Richard's sister; she would bring as dowry the Christian cities of the coast. The happy couple would reign in Jerusalem, which would be open to pilgrims of every faith, with separate wards for Moslems and Christians. The rural fiefs of the Kingdom would be divided; the Orders (who had fought gallantly at Arsouf) would get back their castles, but those of the barons of the land (who had stayed in Tyre with Conrad) would remain in Moslem hands.

When this remarkable proposal was laid before Saladin he gladly assented; at the same time he roared with laughter, for he knew that it would never be carried into effect. But discussion of it would inflame the quarrels of the Christians, which was all to the good.

Conrad of Montferrat secretly sent rival proposals. His plan was more modest. If Saladin would recognise him as 'King of Jerusalem' and guarantee him undisturbed possession of Tyre, Sidon and Beirut, Conrad would evacuate Acre and refuse to fight beside the Crusaders. But when Saladin inquired whether he would fight beside the infidels against Richard even Conrad scrupled at such treason to Christendom.

Saphadin, that able diplomatist, kept negotiations going until winter. About this time there was bad news from Richard's new and neglected conquest, Cyprus. One of his justiciars had died, and the Greeks had risen in revolt. The island was no use to Richard, though it was useful to Outremer as a whole. He was glad to sell it to the Templars for ready cash.

When Queen Joan heard of the husband her brother had chosen for her she was horrified. Never, she declared, would she marry an infidel. Richard, who was moving farther from reality as he pondered the beauty of his bright idea, asked Saphadin whether he would become a Christian. After Saphadin declined Richard continued to press his solution of the Holy War. Perhaps a dispensation from the Pope would persuade Joan to change her mind? (But would any Pope have given it?) If not, and Plantagenets did not easily change their minds, there was another Princess available, his niece Eleanor of Brittany. She was a child, and his ward. By feudal law he could make her marry anyone, willing or unwilling.

On 8 November Saphadin entertained Richard at a great banquet. All the company enjoyed themselves. But even Richard, who got on well with infidels if they were also gallant warriors, realised that his plan must be abandoned.

It was not in itself an absurd plan, if the aim of the Holy War was unhindered access to the Holy Sepulchre. But if that was the sole aim of the war there was no need to fight at all. Moslems, who revere the institution of pilgrimage, have normally been willing to admit Christians to any Holy Place on payment of a suitable fee. What every Crusader wanted, except King Richard, was something quite different: the expulsion of all infidels from the Holy Places of Christendom.

Saphadin's friendly negotiations had achieved their object. By November heavy winter rains had soaked the Judean hills, and Saladin considered that campaigning would be impossible until the ground had begun to dry. He dismissed half his army and with the rest retired from Ramleh to Jerusalem.

At this stage Richard had no long-term plan, no hope of ultimate victory. But a good general pursues the next tactical move, the best way to damage the foe and encourage his own side, even if ultimate victory is impossible. If the Crusaders hung about on the coast they would lose heart; they had left home to free Jerusalem, and they must try to free it. After all, something might turn up; Saladin might die, and then all his great realm might dissolve in civil war.

The Third Crusade

During November Richard advanced to Saladin's old position at Ramleh. By January 1192 he was at Beit-Nuba, only twelve miles from Jerusalem. The weather was frightful. The tents were blown down, rain rotted the biscuit and bacon. Saladin had summoned another army from Egypt; this force did not join him in Jerusalem but lurked outside ready to take any besiegers in the rear. The knights of the Orders, who knew the country, advised retreat. It was even more ominous that the Crusaders began to make plans for returning to Europe as soon as they had worshipped in the Holy Sepulchre. Before the end of January Richard led his army back to the coast, where he rebuilt the demolished walls of Ascalon.

On 20 March Saphadin brought an offer of peace, the first time Saladin had made the opening move. The offer was generous, for Saladin feared King Richard. He would recognise the present frontier of the Christians, and in addition cede to them the harbour of Beirut on condition they did not fortify it. The Holy Places would be open to Latin pilgrims, and Latin priests might serve in them. In return all he asked was that Richard should go home to Europe.

To Richard these seemed the best terms that could be had. He was anxious to go home, for he had heard of the trouble his brother John was making in England. He sealed no treaty with Saphadin, but he let it be known that his proposals were acceptable. One question must still be settled before the Crusaders could go home. Something must be done to quench the smouldering civil war between the partisans of Conrad and Guy.

In April Richard summoned a meeting of all the barons of the land. He announced that he would soon be leaving, and invited them to choose their next King. To his surprise, they voted unanimously for Conrad.

Richard himself thought Guy the better man, and was mortified to find himself in a minority of one. But he had asked for a vote, and he must abide by the result. He sent Henry of Champagne, his nephew, to tell Conrad the good news.

It was agreed that Conrad and his followers should march

from Tyre to join Richard in Ascalon; on the way Conrad would be crowned at Acre. A few days later, while he was still in Tyre, Conrad was stabbed to death as he walked in the street.

One of the two murderers was killed on the spot, but the other was taken alive. He admitted that he was an Assassin, as everyone had supposed. The murder had been planned with amazing patience. The two Assassins had come to Tyre nearly a year before, saying that they wished to turn Christian. After instruction they had been baptised. Their godfathers had been Conrad himself and Balian of Ibelin.

A wave of panic swept Outremer. If Assassins would pose as Christians, which no orthodox Moslem could bring himself to do, then there was no safety anywhere. A rumour went round that the Assassins had infiltrated the Syrian clergy; some Crusaders feared to kneel before the altar lest the priest stab them as he gave them Communion.

But why should the Old Man of the Mountains sacrifice two of his followers to kill Conrad of Montferrat? Ostensibly he stood neutral in the Holy War, but it was supposed that he hated the Caliph of Baghdad and his faithful servant Saladin more than he hated the Christians. On the other hand, he sometimes sold the services of his devoted murderers. Perhaps Saladin had bribed him?

But in the first place, though the Old Man was open to bribery, he was unlikely to accept a bribe from Saladin, his most bitter enemy. In the second place, why should Saladin desire the death of Conrad, when he profited so greatly from the divisions among the Christians?

One Christian leader had been Conrad's consistent foe since the siege of Acre. The partisans of King Philip were soon whispering that the man who had bribed the chief of the Assassins must be Richard.

It is impossible to disprove this accusation, but nowadays it is not generally believed. It is not the sort of thing Richard would do. He spent his life in war, and he could be relentless, as he was relentless with the garrison of Acre. But he was an honourable knight and of all the foes he killed not one, other

than Conrad, was murdered. A man whose last act as he lay
dying was to safeguard the archer who had killed him would
not arrange the secret murder of an opponent.

The most likely explanation of the gratuitous murder is that
the Old Man planned it to advertise his power. He lived by
blackmail, and from time to time he must show Christians as
well as infidels that it was prudent to pay what he demanded.

Though the Christians were even more divided than before,
the death of Conrad brought one advantage. Isabella was free
to marry again, and her next husband would be King of
Jerusalem; at least until her baby daughter by Conrad was
old enough to marry in her turn. After a week of widowhood
Isabella was married to Henry of Champagne. He was reluctant
to fight in Outremer for the rest of his life instead of returning
to his pleasant French County; but his uncle Richard persuaded
him to undertake the duty, and promised that one day he
himself would come back with an even greater army and help
him to recover Jerusalem.

Richard was still anxious to get back to Europe, but first he
must do something for his old friend Guy. Luckily the Templars
found Cyprus a liability instead of an asset; about this time they
offered to return it to the King of England. Instead it was
arranged that Guy should buy it. In May 1192 he landed in
Cyprus with the title of King. Some of the large sum of money
that changed hands found its way to Richard.

While ships were being gathered to take the Crusaders home
Richard filled in the time by an attack on Darum, the last
fortress on the coast before Sinai. After five days of savage
fighting he took it by assault, without a formal siege. The
victorious Crusaders now clamoured for one more attempt on
Jerusalem, and against his better judgement Richard consented.
There were rumours of rebellion in Mesopotamia, and it was
said that Saladin had been called east to suppress it.

On 11 June the Crusaders were back in Beit-Nuba, the
farthest point of their earlier advance. But Saladin was in
Jerusalem after all, and he had blocked up all the wells in the
neighbourhood. It was on this second occasion that Richard

refused to gaze on the distant Holy City which God would not permit him to deliver.

For nearly a month the Crusaders remained at Beit-Nuba. They captured a rich caravan from Egypt, and in various skirmishes western knights did mighty deeds. But Richard could see no way of capturing Jerusalem, and no way of holding it if it could be won. Unfortunately he knew nothing of what was passing in Saladin's camp. Military intelligence was never taken seriously by the Franks, though Saladin had spies everywhere. At that moment Saladin was considering whether to evacuate Jerusalem; not because it was untenable but because he could not trust his discontented mamelukes to fight for him.

On 4 July Richard led his army back to the coast.

Negotiations opened again. Saladin, aware that Ascalon in Christian hands might cut him off from Egypt, offered a great price for its return. He would be a friend to the new King Henry, he would maintain Latin priests in the Holy Sepulchre, he would evacuate Lydda. If the Christians would not withdraw from Ascalon perhaps they would dismantle the walls and hold it as an open city?

On this question of Ascalon negotiations broke down. But Richard was now most anxious to get back to Europe. He was in Acre, planning to seize Beirut as his port of embarkation, when Saladin made a sudden counter-attack.

His army marched from Jerusalem to Jaffa in one day, 27 July; within three days they breached the walls. When the mamelukes broke in they massacred the burgesses; but the garrison retreated, fighting desperately, to the castle. From its shelter they sought terms of surrender; but Saladin, unable to control his men, answered that they must wait until discipline had been restored after the sack.

Envoys from the garrison were in Saladin's tent when suddenly the mamelukes began to flee from the town. King Richard was driving them before him.

As soon as Richard heard that Jaffa was in peril he sailed from Acre with fifty galleys. His army was ordered to march along the beach beside him; but at Mount Carmel the ships met head winds and the army, unwilling to fight without its trusted leader, delayed until the ships were out of sight. Arrived off Jaffa Richard saw infidel banners on the wall. He hesitated to land, until a brave priest swam out from the castle to tell him that there were still Christians to be rescued. He waded ashore on foot, still wearing his sea-going slippers. At the head of eighty knights, two hundred foot, and two thousand sailors he drove Saladin's men from the town. What made it an especially famous feat of arms was that his landing party had only three horses.

Next morning Saladin sent an envoy to Richard. He found the King chatting with infidel emirs, captured yesterday and awaiting ransom. He was telling them that before he left Jaffa his garrison had promised to hold the town for at least three months; Saladin had captured it in three days and he himself had won it back in three hours. Everyone was friendly, but once more the talks broke down on the question of Ascalon.

Since Jaffa was littered with the decaying corpses of its burgesses, mingled with the decaying corpses of their pigs, Richard's little force camped outside the walls. By sunset his main army had not arrived. Saladin determined on a dawn attack.

As the sun rose a sailor heard the trampling of horses and gave the alarm. Richard had just time to array his men. But he must face Saladin's whole army with fifty-four knights, fifteen horses, and about two thousand foot, collected from the fleet and the rescued garrison; this was all that remained to him after the fighting of yesterday. For more than half the day his infantry withstood the onslaught of seven thousand mameluke horse. In mid-afternoon he actually led an attack. Saladin, watching from the security of his tent, was overcome with admiration for his gallant adversary. When he saw Richard fall as his horse was killed under him he sent a groom leading two fresh horses as a present from one King to another. By evening the infidels were in retreat. Saladin manned the defences of Jerusalem in fear that Richard and his little force might follow on his heels.

Instead the stalemate continued, and so did the negotiations. The stumbling-block was still Ascalon. Saladin would not make peace without it, and Richard would not yield it; until his nephew Henry of Champagne pointed out that when the Crusaders had gone home there would not be knights enough in Outremer to hold it.

On 2 September the final treaty was sealed. Saladin swore that for at least five years he would remain at peace with the Christians, who would hold all they now possessed except Ascalon. Unarmed pilgrims would be welcome at the Holy Places; unarmed infidels might trade in the Christian ports. As a parting present Saladin added that not more than four Latin priests might serve in the Holy Sepulchre.

Crusaders flocked to the Holy Sepulchre, though Richard's pride would not permit him to enter Jerusalem unarmed. Then the Crusaders went home. Many mamelukes visited the European shops of Acre. Then they returned to their colours. That was what had baffled Richard from the outset. His men were anxious to go home; the infidels were at home.

When Isaac Angelus heard that Latin priests were to be allowed in the Holy Places he protested to Saladin at this breach of the Greek monopoly; in the same letter he asked for mamelukes to help him reconquer Cyprus from the Franks. Both requests were refused. No one, whether Christian or infidel, now valued the friendship of the Emperor of Constantinople.

As we all remember, on his way home from the Crusade King Richard was kidnapped by the Duke of Austria. As an excuse for his detention he was charged with the murder of Conrad of Montferrat. But when a ransom was offered the charge was dropped.

For all his courage and skill in war Richard had given very little material help to the Christians of Outremer. But his victories, though barren, had restored Christian confidence and frightened the infidel. There was no more talk of ending the Holy War and going back to Europe, as there had been after Hattin. In addition Richard's almost inadvertent conquest of Cyprus gave Outremer a secure base which prolonged its life for another century.

CHAPTER XV

The Diminished Kingdom

A t some time unknown, probably soon after Richard's departure, Saladin gave the True Cross to the Greek canons of the Holy Sepulchre. The Latin canons still existed as a corporate body, with the duty of electing each Patriarch of Jerusalem; but both canons and Patriarch lived as exiles in Acre.

In March 1193 Saladin died, aged 54, worn out by the hardships of the Holy War. He was an adventurer who rose to power by treason and murder; but after he had won a great kingdom he governed it well. He was so charitable that at his death his treasury contained a single dinar. As he lay dying he sent his standard-bearer round Damascus, bearing a shroud on his pole instead of the standard; the man proclaimed that the great King of the East might take only this to his grave.

By his will Saladin divided his dominions between his two brothers and his seventeen sons, who at once began to fight among themselves. Not until 1201 did the wily Saphadin emerge supreme, with the title of Sultan of Egypt. For these eight years the Franks of Outremer were safe from infidel attack.

Suppose Saladin had died in 1191, when he was very ill, instead of two years later? Richard would have liberated Jerusalem, and the resultant loss of prestige might have destroyed Saladin's new Kurdish dynasty. The infidels of Syria might have remained disunited, and today the Holy Sepulchre might be under Christian rule. Chance, especially the chance of unexpected death, played a great part in the history of the doctorless Middle Ages.

Meanwhile the states of Outremer were constituted as follows: From Jaffa to Tyre stretched the 'Kingdom of Jerusalem', ninety miles long and never ten miles wide. Sidon and Beirut were held by the infidel. Northward the town of Tripoli and the small plain surrounding it were ruled by Bohemond, a son of Bohemond of Antioch. The infidels held Latakia. Antioch was a strong and thriving city, connected with the sea at St Simeon; but all its outlying towns and castles had been lost. These fortified bridge-heads, for they were little more, were strong in a military sense. Italian merchants, who lived by trading with the infidel, could man their walls. But for a field army they depended on the military Orders, supported by their estates in Europe, on the few barons of the land who still held castles near the coast, and on visiting Crusaders, anxious to complete the pilgrimage and go home.

Luckily two new Christian Kingdoms lay nearby and could provide reinforcements. Cilicia and the surrounding mountains were now known as Lesser Armenia. The Armenians had been heretics, with a liturgy of their own. But though they hated the Greek Emperor, who had persecuted them in the past, they were indifferent to the Pope; of whom they had never heard until the Franks arrived. The Armenian Catholicus was persuaded to submit to Rome; on the implied condition, which Rome was wise enough to observe, that the Pope would never send him any orders to submit to. In 1198 the new Kingdom of Armenia received international recognition. For the coronation of King Leo the Greek Emperor supplied a crown and the Pope a sceptre. The Chancellor of the German Empire, Greek and Jacobite prelates, envoys from the Prince of Antioch and the Caliph of Baghdad were all present at the ceremony.

Recognition from an Emperor or Pope was essential for the inauguration of a new Kingdom. Guy of Lusignan had been

King of Jerusalem, and while he ruled Cyprus he might continue to style himself King. But after his death in 1194 his brother and successor Amalric must look round for a sponsor to confirm his royal title.

He did not want the Pope for suzerain; even without that title the Pope interfered too frequently in the affairs of Outremer. He chose the German Emperor, Barbarossa's son. Henry VI is remembered in Italy as a bloodthirsty tyrant; but he was anxious to redeem the failure of his father's Crusade. He had sent his Chancellor, with a small party of German volunteers, to prepare the way for the great army he hoped to lead in person one day. When King Amalric was crowned in 1197 he did homage to the imperial Chancellor as proxy for the Emperor. Presumably the German Emperor was chosen as the potentate least interested in Cyprus and least likely to intervene in its affairs. Unfortunately King Amalric guessed wrong.

For some reason Henry of Champagne, ruler of 'Jerusalem', was never crowned; perhaps because his marriage with Queen Isabella, only a week after the death of her second husband, was held to be uncanonical.

In 1197 the infidels besieged Jaffa, and about the same time the vanguard of German Crusaders reached Outremer. Henry of Champagne prepared to march with them; but as he stood in an upper room of his palace he absentmindedly stepped back and fell through an open window. Queen Isabella was free to marry again.

During the confused interregnum Jaffa yielded to Saphadin after a perfunctory resistance. Then the barons of the land chose a new ruler (Queen Isabella was never given a voice in the choosing of her husbands). With great prudence they chose the newly-widowed King Amalric of Cyprus.

Unfortunately the union of the Kingdoms could only be temporary. The heir to Cyprus was Hugh, son of Amalric by his first wife; the heir to Jerusalem would be the husband of one of Isabella's daughters. She now had three, one by Conrad and two by Henry of Champagne. Later she bore two Lusignan daughters, but no son.

King Amalric did not try to recover Jaffa. Instead he captured Sidon and Beirut, until his northern border marched with Tripoli. The German Crusaders accomplished nothing. They boldly laid siege to the inland castle of Toron. But at the approach of Saphadin they fled without fighting, and in February 1198 sailed back to Europe. A few good knights among them stayed in Tyre to found the Order of Teutonic Knights, on the pattern of the Hospital and the Temple.

In general the permanent inhabitants of Outremer no longer hoped for victory. What they wanted was to hang on in their seaports, where they might grow rich by trading with the infidel. Most of them disliked Crusaders from Europe, who might start a war they would not stay to finish. The barons of the land, poor and bored, cooped up in walled cities, occupied their leisure in petty civil wars.

In Antioch, as usual, the moral decay was worse than elsewhere. The nobles were divided into Armenian and Norman factions, whose quarrels at last stirred the burgesses into setting up a Commune. A Commune was a self-governing corporation, with its own courts of law and especially its own armed forces; in legal theory it was a corporate vassal of the ruler. At that time it was a new political device, just beginning to spread from Italy into France. This suggests that the leading citizens of Antioch were Italians, though the idea of a self-governing city would appeal also to Greeks.

Prince Bohemond III of Antioch had married his son and heir Raymond to Princess Alice, heiress of Armenia; so that after his death Antioch would be united with Armenia. But Raymond died before his father, leaving an infant son, Raymond-Roupen. Of course his mother would bring up the boy as an Armenian; so the anti-Armenian faction declared for Prince Bohemond's younger son, Count Bohemond of Tripoli. There followed a nagging little war, marked rather by sudden coups and treacherous imprisonment of envoys than by open fighting. For more than twenty years the War of the Antiochene Succession occupied the languid energies of the decadent north.

Farther south communities of Italian merchants, each living

in its own quarter under the rule of a Consul sent out from the mother-city, were the only vigorous and self-supporting elements in the population. Unfortunately they imported into Outremer the disputes of their homeland; where Venice, Pisa and Genoa were engaged in a three-cornered struggle for commercial supremacy. Sometimes Acre and Tyre were disturbed by open war, as the merchants of one city tried to sack the warehouses of another; always King Amalric had to treat with them as equal allies, not issue commands as though to loyal subjects.

In 1205 King Amalric died suddenly, aged fifty. Cyprus passed to his son by his first marriage, Hugh, aged six. 'Jerusalem' reverted to Queen Isabella, who died before she could be married to a fifth husband. The heir was her eldest daughter, Maria of Montferrat, aged thirteen and not yet married. The regent who ruled on her behalf was her mother's half-brother, John of Ibelin, Balian's son.

But henceforth the internal history of the little remnant of Outremer is too complicated, and too unimportant, to be treated at length. Great events, bearing on the progress of the Holy War, could occur only when an army of Crusaders arrived from Europe. Unfortunately Crusaders from Europe, with a magnificent new field of expansion just opened to them, were reluctant to visit decaying Outremer.

CHAPTER XVI

The Fourth Crusade

In November 1199 young Theobald, Count of Champagne, held a great tournament. During the feast afterwards the knights discussed the troubles of Outremer; naturally enough, for Count Theobald was the younger brother of the late Count Henry, husband of Queen Isabella. By the end of the evening all present had taken the Cross, and a committee had been chosen to organise another General Passage.

Count Theobald's motives were religious and chivalrous. But many other French lords had political reasons for going abroad for a few years. In the spring King Richard had died, at war with King Philip; and his faction foresaw a bleak future, since it was evident that his brother John could never hold his own against the King of France.

These Crusaders would be a band of brothers, old friends, of the same social rank, speaking the same language. There would be none of the national and diplomatic intrigues which had wrecked the Third Crusade. The Count of Champagne would lead them, with the Count of Flanders as his lieutenant; most of the others were important French noblemen, the Counts of Blois, Perche, Montfort and others, with their kinsmen and household knights.

Pope Innocent III backed the proposal. It was a good time for a Crusade since the Papacy needed no defenders in Europe.

There was no German Emperor; though Philip of Suabia, brother to the late Emperor Henry VI, was at war with his Guelf rival Otto of Brunswick. The little King of Sicily, Frederick the son of the late Emperor, was actually the Pope's ward. The Greek Emperor, Alexius Angelus, had opened slow and reluctant negotiations about a possible religious submission to Rome.

The Crusade, managed by a committee of equal barons, was slow to get under way. The whole of the year 1200 was occupied by Parliaments of Crusaders, often held on horseback in a convenient meadow. It was remembered that King Richard, that skilful commander, had pointed out that Egypt was Saladin's weak spot, and had recommended that the next Crusade should sail direct to the Nile. The Crusaders looked round for a fleet to take them there. Venice was interested. But the Venetians were merchants, not chivalrous knights; and they made it clear that they must be paid for their services.

In the spring of 1201 Count Theobald died suddenly, in his early twenties. After various French noblemen had declined the burdensome honour Boniface, Marquis of Montferrat, agreed to lead them. He was a brother of William King of Jerusalem, and of Conrad who had saved Tyre. But he was a Ghibelline, a friend of Philip of Suabia, and Pope Innocent did not trust him.

At last the question of transport was settled. The Venetians agreed that in return for eighty-five thousand silver marks, paid in advance, they would provide shipping to carry four thousand five hundred knights, nine thousand squires, and twenty thousand foot. At their own cost the Venetians would add an escort of fifty armed galleys, on condition they shared equally in all conquests. The army would sail in June 1202.

When they arrived in Venice the Crusaders found that they could not raise the money. A camp had been prepared for them on the Lido, where they were stuck until the Venetians consented to take them away. After a most unpleasant stay they agreed to pay in kind, by capturing from the King of Hungary the disputed town of Zara. The Venetians were so pleased that their Doge, Dandolo, took the Cross, though he was blind, and very old. In November 1202 the expedition sailed for Dalmatia.

The Crusaders had been unable to pay their fare because many who had promised to join them preferred to travel independently. There was already something fishy about this General Passage. Simple enthusiasts who yearned to liberate the Holy Places could not see the point of attacking Cairo before Jerusalem. Those better informed did not believe that the Venetians would close their most valuable trade route by making war on the Sultan of Egypt; the promised fleet would in fact take them somewhere else.

These last had guessed right. While the contract was being negotiated the Venetians sent envoys to Saphadin to explain that he need not close their warehouses in Alexandria; this Crusade was politics, and in Venice politics never interfered with commerce.

When the Crusaders were encamped before Zara the abbot of Vaux got up and denounced their action, pointing out that if they fought against fellow-Christians as the mercenaries of Venice they would lose the spiritual benefits of the pilgrimage. But by this time the leaders were terrified lest the expedition should disperse, leaving them penniless and alone at the back of beyond. Only the Venetian fleet could take them anywhere, to the Levant or back to Italy. The assault proceeded, and in five days Zara was won.

Since it was already November the expedition wintered in the captured town. All went well, except for a riot between Frenchmen and Venetians which caused some casualties before the leaders could suppress it. In the new year envoys arrived from Philip of Suabia to say that Alexius Angelus, rightful Emperor of Constantinople, had interesting proposals to lay before them.

Isaac Angelus, first Emperor of his dynasty, had irritated his subjects by heavy taxation and general incompetence. By 1189 it was evident that soon he would be overthrown. To keep the Empire in the family his brother Alexius struck first. After a well-organised palace revolution Isaac was blinded and imprisoned, though from brotherly affection Alexius did not kill him; his son, young Alexius, was also imprisoned. The elder Alexius ascended the throne with the title of Alexius III. In the winter of 1201 young Alexius escaped from his dungeon and took refuge with Philip of Suabia, who had married his sister.

To French noblemen, brought up in a society where all power and property descended by strict hereditary succession, this seemed a terrible story. They could not know that in Constantinople the Empire was bestowed by the palace guards, and that the blinding of a superfluous brother was an old Greek custom. Any good knight would be justified in helping young Alexius to recover his rights.

In return for their help young Alexius offered them all they could desire. Once he was on the throne of his ancestors (he did not explain that his father had overthrown the Comneni) he would find the money still owing for the hire of the Venetian fleet; he would pay the cost of the conquest of Egypt and send ten thousand men to help them; he would endow in perpetuity five hundred knights for the defence of the Holy Sepulchre; and he would compel the Greek Church to submit to Rome. This last point must silence any objections from the Pope, who had already excommunicated the Venetians for their attack on Christian Zara.

In April young Alexius joined the Crusaders, who proceeded by way of Corfu and the Hellespont to the Sea of Marmora. In June 1203 they arrived before Constantinople.

To the surprise of most Greeks the palace guards decided to fight for Alexius III. After some skirmishing the Crusaders took the Tower of Galata, across the harbour from the city. They encamped by the gate of Blachernae, at the head of the Golden Horn. Since the land walls of Constantinople extended for more than three miles there could be no complete invest-ment of the city. The Crusaders were under the impression that they faced enormous odds; but the populace viewed with indifference this squabble between Alexius III and Alexius IV, and there were only a few thousand palace guards.

On 17 July the Crusaders assaulted the Blachernae gate. After heavy fighting they were beaten back by the Varangians, English and Danish mercenaries who formed the Emperor's personal bodyguard. At the same time Venetian galleys approached the harbour wall; but under battery from stone-throwing engines they faltered. At last Doge Dandolo, eighty years old and blind, commanded his squires to put him ashore with the Banner of St Mark clasped in his arms. When the Venetians saw their sacred Banner in danger of capture they swarmed after him; some straddled the yards of their ships to jump direct to the battlements below. Later more than forty witnesses swore that the Banner had been carried by an angel to the summit of a tower. By evening twenty-five towers of the harbour wall had fallen to the Venetians. They feared to advance farther into the great city, and the Crusaders were still held up outside Blachernae; so they set fire to the houses before them as a barrier against counter-attack.

Venetians were seldom eager to fight in the Holy War; but when they fought for their own Banner of St Mark they fought like heroes.

Next morning Alexius III fled by an unblocked gate; and his ministers took blind Isaac from his dungeon and restored him to the imperial throne. It was a simple but subtle move. Just as the Crusaders were getting ready to sack the greatest city in the world they were told that it was on their side after all and must not be harmed. After Isaac had agreed that young Alexius should share his throne they withdrew peaceably to their camp.

The Crusaders decided to remain where they were until next spring, while young Alexius collected the money he had promised them and the army which would help them to conquer Egypt. Soon it became apparent that Alexius had promised more than he could perform.

Constantinople, though stocked with ancient treasures, was no longer prosperous. Emperors did not like their merchants to go abroad, beyond the reach of imperial tax-collectors; it was better that foreigners should come to buy in the shop-window of the world. But by this time the right to export free of duty had been sold to several Italian cities for cash down; and the immensely valuable trade with the Far East had shifted to Alexandria. The promised gold bezants were just not to be had.

When commanded to submit to the Pope the clergy played for time. They did not defy the Emperor, but neither did they carry out his orders. By the spring of 1204 the Crusaders, cheated by Greek shopkeepers and in danger of being murdered when drunk, were growing very angry.

They had some excuse. The Greeks had never genuinely helped in the Holy War, since the days when Alexius I said goodbye to the First Crusade outside Nicaea. Greek diplomatic theory laid down that a wise ruler made friends with whoever lived on the far side of his enemy; since the Turks of Iconium were the most dangerous foes of Constantinople the Emperor very often sought alliance with the infidel ruler of Syria. Isaac Angelus had congratulated Saladin on his conquest of Jerusalem, because under infidel rule there would be no Latin clergy in the Holy Sepulchre. To score off the Pope the Greeks would use any weapon.

In general Greeks got on better with infidels than with Latins, perhaps because they shared a common form of government. An infidel Sultan, like a Greek Emperor, had seized power by his own efforts; he was maintained on his throne by a mercenary army; the sole duty of his subjects was to pay taxes, and in return he owed his subjects no duty at all. Every Greek was shocked by the boisterous conduct of Frankish freemen, who thought nothing of armed resistance to a lord who infringed the rights of his men.

The Crusaders burned down a mosque they found in Constantinople, maintained for the convenience of visiting infidel merchants; and with the mosque a number of Greek houses. If they had searched Venice they would have found a similar mosque; but that they did not know, for while waiting for their ships they had been shut up on the Lido.

In January 1204 the Greeks rioted against Alexius IV, whom

they regarded as a mere sponge sucking up their money to give it to Franks. In the riot the statue of Athene made by Pheidias for the Athenians was destroyed, the most famous relic of antiquity in Constantinople. But the palace guards were still loyal, and the rioters were dispersed.

In February the visit of a Frankish deputation, demanding money due to them, was the signal for another riot. This time the guards, commanded by one Murzuphlos who had married a daughter of Alexius III, joined the mob. Alexius IV was murdered; his father Isaac was so roughly handled that he died within a few days. Murzuphlos reigned as Alexius V.

The Crusaders were filled with righteous wrath. They had restored a legitimate Emperor, and been cheated of their payment. Perhaps the Doge, and the Marquis of Montferrat, knew better what they were doing. They wished to destroy a commercial rival of Venice, and an Empire which rivalled that of the Hohenstaufen. Incidentally, they would be the richer for doing it. They may have expected some such development when first they sailed for the Marmora.

On 12 April the Crusaders stormed Constantinople for the second time. Alexius V fled. While fighting raged within the city the Greeks offered the crown to Theodore Lascaris, husband of another daughter of Alexius III. As soon as he had been elected he fled to Asia, in company with the Patriarch of Constantinople.

The sack that followed was most repaying, especially as the Franks held it to be their religious duty to pillage schismatic churches. The booty was divided as had been previously agreed: three-eighths for the Venetians, three-eighths for the Franks, one-quarter for the new Latin Emperor.

The new Emperor was Baldwin, Count of Flanders; so to even things up the new Patriarch was a Venetian. The Marquis of Montferrat felt that someone had cheated him, a thing that often befell the allies of Venice; but he had to be content with the vassal Kingdom of Salonica. The Venetian share turned out to comprise all the commercially profitable harbours and islands in the Empire. The Franks got the mainland of Hellas. No one wanted Bithynia, on the Turkish border; so Theodore Lascaris remained there as Emperor in exile, with his capital at Nicaea.

Next year King Boniface of Salonica was defeated by the Bulgarians, and died in captivity. But Hellas, and the islands of the Aegean, remained in Frankish hands until taken by the Turks. Constantinople was ruled by a Frankish Emperor until 1261.

Pope Innocent was very angry when he heard what had been done, though he could not excommunicate faithful Latins who had brought the Greeks into communion with Rome. He ordered the Crusaders to leave Constantinople immediately, and complete their pilgrimage by continuing to Outremer. But he was too late. Already the papal legate with the expedition had absolved them from their vow, in consideration of the great service they had rendered to Christendom.

Now that all the islands of the Aegean were Venetian communication between Italy and Acre was safe and easy. Otherwise no advantage accrued to Outremer. In fact Outremer was weakened; since many barons of the land emigrated to Hellas, where rich fiefs were to be won. But the Franks had avenged themselves on the Greeks for their hostility to the Holy War, and they felt the better for it.

Perhaps the Latin conquest of Constantinople was a crime, but the Greeks had only themselves to blame for the hatred they had inspired in the west. Alexius Comnenus had asked for the First Crusade and then deserted it. After more than a century his betrayal had been repaid.

CHAPTER XVII

The Fifth Crusade

In the Holy Land there was peace. At last Saphadin had gathered to himself all the dominions which had been ruled by his brother Saladin. But his throne was insecure, and he had no desire for foreign war. Besides, he was intelligent enough to see that an infidel attack on Outremer might spark off another Crusade; while the petty remains of the 'Kingdom of Jerusalem' could not harm him.

In 1208, when Queen Maria was seventeen, her uncle John of Ibelin sent envoys to France to find her a husband. What he sought was a wealthy and powerful ruler who would bring reinforcements to Outremer. But great Frankish lords saw no future for 'Jerusalem', and even the honour of a crown could not persuade them to settle in Acre.

Of late years Pope Innocent III had weakened the appeal of the Crusade by dispersing it. He was not to blame for the Frankish conquest of Constantinople and Hellas, though he had recognised accomplished facts; but he gave the spiritual rewards of Crusaders also to knights who fought the Albigensian heretics. A knight who wished to fight for the Cross need only make the cheap and comfortable journey to Languedoc; if he wanted land in addition he could probably get it in Hellas; he could worship in the Holy Sepulchre only by going as an unarmed pilgrim. There was nothing to be gained by fighting in Outremer.

It was more than a year before the envoys could find a volunteer to wear the crown of Jerusalem, and he had nothing to recommend him except good birth and military experience. John of Brienne was a landless younger son, about sixty years of age, serving in the household of King Philip of France. Both the Pope and King Philip gave him money for his travelling expenses. In the autumn of 1210 he married the youthful Queen Maria and was crowned in Tyre.

The truce with Saphadin had recently expired. But there was no serious fighting, except that the infidels built a castle on Mount Tabor from which they could raid the suburbs of Acre. In 1212 King John made another truce with Saphadin, to endure for five years. He was alarmed by the military weakness of his Kingdom, and begged the Pope to gather a new Crusade which would reach Outremer about the time this truce ran out.

During the same year Queen Maria died, leaving an infant daughter who may have been christened Isabella but was usually called Yolande. John of Brienne had lost his title to 'Jerusalem', though as a crowned King he kept his royal style. The barons of the land elected him to be regent for his infant daughter; but when she should marry her husband would displace him, and in the meantime it was not impossible that the barons of the land might choose another regent.

This was also the year of the unhappy 'Children's Crusade'. In France and the Rhineland great crowds of children gathered behind boy-preachers, who declared that such innocents must liberate Jerusalem by miracle. Arrived at the coast they waited for the sea to divide before them, that they might cross it dry-shod like the Israelites of old. When the sea remained in place most of them went home. But many had died of hardship during the journey and there were persistent rumours that others were offered free passages by wicked merchants who sold them by the shipload to infidel slave-dealers. This juvenile hysteria did not affect the military situation in Outremer, but it helped to give the Holy War a bad name among the indifferent.

In 1215 the Council of the Lateran began to plan a General

Passage to reach Outremer as the truce ended. But in 1216 Pope
Innocent III died, and the urgency went out of the planning.

Every crowned head in Europe had been invited to join this
General Passage; only the King of Hungary accepted, and the
King of Norway who died while preparing to set out. It was
reported confidentially to the new Pope, Honorius III, that out
in Outremer nobody really wanted a Crusade. Saphadin kept
good peace, so that merchants both Christian and infidel were
doing very well. The infidels could capture Acre and Tyre
whenever they wished; but they preferred to buy European
goods in them. There was no danger to these remaining
Christian ports unless fanatical Crusaders started another war.

That may have been true; but in that case the myriads who
had died on the First Crusade had died in vain and the Holy
Places would remain for ever under infidel rule. Pope Honorius
decided to make one more effort to free Jerusalem. The Frisians
were gathering a great fleet, enough to transport the Hungarians and a German army led by the Duke of Austria, anxious
to make amends for his father's bad conduct. Unfortunately the
timing went awry. The Frisians stopped in Portugal to fight the
Moors, while the Hungarians and Germans waited for them in
Dalmatia until their money was gone. In the autumn of 1217
the Frisians reached Italy, too late in the year to continue to
Outremer. Rather than wait until next spring the King of
Hungary and the Duke of Austria hired a few local ships to take
them to Acre; but for lack of money they left most of their
followers behind.

Saphadin was taken by surprise. He had not expected any
Crusaders before spring, and because of a local famine he had
few troops in Palestine. Acre was also short of food, so in
November 1217 the Crusaders went raiding, in company with
King Hugh of Cyprus. No enemy opposed them. They crossed
the Jordan and marched along the eastern shore of the Sea of
Galilee. During the march King Hugh died, leaving as heir his
baby son Henry. By February 1218 the rest of them were back
in Acre, having done a lot of plundering but no fighting. The
King of Hungary, who had come chiefly to gather relics, then

went home. He marched overland by way of Antioch, Armenia, Iconium and Constantinople. The Sultan of Iconium sent him a safe-conduct and entertained him on the way; so peaceful at that time were relations with the infidel.

Since the Duke of Austria remained in Outremer Saphadin thought it wise to evacuate Mount Tabor, the only gain brought by the Crusade so far. But in the spring the Frisians arrived, with news that French Crusaders were in Sicily waiting for ships.

At a council in Acre King John reminded the Crusaders of Coeur de Lion's advice, that the weak spot of the infidel empire was Egypt. It was agreed that the Frisians should carry the whole army, including the French, to the Nile. By the end of May 1218 the Crusaders had landed before Damietta, at that time the largest port in the eastern Delta. The most eminent of their leaders was King John, but since the death of his wife he ruled no Kingdom; so the Duke of Austria and the military Orders would not obey him.

The long siege of Damietta was a series of disappointments, mishaps, and feats of arms. During the summer the heat was appalling, but the winter of 1218 was exceptionally cold and wet. The Christians could not understand the behaviour of the Nile, which rises during the dry summer and shrinks during the rainy winter; they did not know, though their opponents knew, which stretches of the flat plain would be covered by the flood, or which streams would be navigable. But they were obstinate and brave, and they sat it out.

In August, after several failures, they stormed the tower on the west bank opposite Damietta and removed the chain which blocked the advance of their ships. In the same month Saphadin died, partly of dismay at the news. His great empire was divided between two of his sons, one taking Egypt and the other Syria. But the new Sultan of Egypt did not trust his emirs; the army he gathered on the river a few miles above the Crusaders dared not break through the siege lines to relieve Damietta.

In September reinforcements reached the Christians, a considerable army of French and English led by the Count of Nevers. Unfortunately the Pope, who had paid for their ships, had appointed as legate Cardinal Pelagius. As soon as the Cardinal arrived he assumed supreme command, on the grounds that King John was no true King. He was energetic and a good quartermaster, but inexperienced as a soldier.

He explained that this did not matter, for soon a greater leader would arrive. Frederick II, German Emperor and King of Sicily, had taken the Cross and was gathering an army in Italy. Naturally, the Crusaders before Damietta were reluctant to launch an offensive before the mighty Emperor arrived.

In February 1219 the Sultan of Egypt suddenly retreated southward; not because he feared the Crusaders but because he had uncovered a conspiracy to murder him, started by his leading emirs. Then his brother joined him with an army from Syria and he felt strong enough to advance again; but the Crusaders had moved south of Damietta and were too well encamped to be dislodged. The infidels outnumbered them greatly, but during the spring they withstood many fierce assaults.

In March the Sultan of Syria ordered the destruction of the walls of Jerusalem and of his castles in Galilee. He feared that while his army was in Egypt the Franks of Acre might overrun the Holy Places, and he hoped that if they found no strong fortresses he could drive them back to the coast on his return. The infidel settlers in Jerusalem fled in panic across the Jordan. The Crusaders in Egypt were much encouraged by the news; but the summer heat brought sickness to their camp and a determined assault on Damietta was beaten off with heavy loss.

In May the Duke of Austria went home. He had fought for two years in Outremer, and amply fulfilled his Crusading vow; no one reproached him with desertion. But in his fleet many more recent arrivals fled shamefully.

In August the discouraged Christian foot mutinied; but instead of going home they rushed to attack the Sultan's camp. They got in, were driven out again, and finally fled in panic.

The English Crusaders particularly distinguished themselves in the rearguard action which just saved the Crusaders' camp.

St Francis of Assisi had recently come to Egypt to convert the Sultan. Now that the sword had failed Cardinal Pelagius gave him permission to enter the infidel lines. He was so obviously holy that the Sultan of Egypt received him in his tent. They had a friendly conversation, of course through interpreters; who may have softened the saint's blunt approach. The Sultan remained a Moslem, but he liked St Francis; who had to refuse the rich gifts pressed on him because of his vow of poverty. A Moslem guard of honour escorted the saint back to the Christian camp.

The two Sultans were growing worried. They could not drive out the Christians, and meanwhile they had other distractions. In Egypt the harvest had failed and famine threatened; in Syria there was danger of rebellion. In September a Christian prisoner was released to carry suggestions for a truce, with the startling bait that it might include the surrender of Jerusalem.

No truce was arranged, because reinforcements reached the Crusaders. Savarie of Mauleon, a great lord of Poitou, brought ten galleys filled with armed men. Probably they included some English; for Savarie had been an important servant of King John Plantagenet and one of the executors of his will. These newcomers repelled a treacherous attack on the Christian camp which ended the temporary truce.

In October the Sultan of Egypt again sought peace. His offer was most generous, for he was really afraid. He knew that soon Damietta must fall, and even treachery in time of truce had not been able to defeat the Crusaders. If the Christians would leave Egypt and make peace the infidels would hand over all the Holy Places, the True Cross, and the western half of the Kingdom of Jerusalem as far as the river Jordan. Though the Sultan would continue to hold the castles beyond Jordan he was willing to pay rent for them, in token that he was only a temporary occupier.

If the Sultan's word could be trusted there was nothing

more to fight about; the Christians had won the Holy War. King John, the barons of the land, and the Crusaders from Europe all wanted to accept this remarkable offer. But the Orders advised against it for military reasons. They pointed out that without Outrejordan Galilee and even Jerusalem would be indefensible; the Christians must have a stronger frontier, or the infidels could sweep them back to the coast whenever they mustered another great army. As the Orders saw it the Crusaders were being asked to surrender what they could hold, their fortified camp on the Nile and the strong town of Damietta which must soon be theirs, in return for a wider stretch of country where they would be merely tenants at the will of the infidel.

After some argument Cardinal Pelagius decided to refuse the terms, ostensibly on the narrow theological ground that a Christian might never make permanent peace with the infidel, though temporary truces, with a time limit, were permissible. This was sound doctrine for both Christians and Moslems. Until the Sultan of Turkey was overthrown in this century his treaties with Christian powers were labelled truces. Only with another Moslem could he make a treaty of peace, in accordance with the theory that he was perpetually at war with all Christendom.

Probably Pelagius decided rightly. The then Sultan of Egypt may have been an honest man, but sooner or later some fanatic would have led the infidels against indefensible Jerusalem.

But the real reason why Pelagius wished to continue the war was because he hoped for even greater gains. He expected to conquer all Egypt, and thus cut in half the Moslem world. After that anything might happen. South of Egypt a chain of Christian though heretical Kingdoms stretched from Ethiopia to the western Sudan; perhaps one of their Kings was the fabled Prester John, the great Christian Emperor who was believed to reign on the far side of Islam. Or perhaps Prester John reigned over a new people, the Mongols, who were streaming out of central Asia; some Mongol chiefs were known to be Christian, though heretical, and the rest seemed to follow no religion in particular. Meanwhile the late Queen Tamara had made Georgia in the Caucasus into a strong military power which threatened Mesopotamia from the north. In Spain the Christians were advancing. Perhaps within a generation Mecca would be a Christian city and there would be no Moslems anywhere. In any case the German Emperor Frederick would soon be in Egypt.

With complete victory just round the corner this was no time to end the Holy War.

In November 1219, after a siege of sixteen months, the Crusaders took Damietta by escalade, against trifling resistance. The place had not been starved out; the captors found ample provisions. But the infidel garrison had been disabled by sickness. Quarter was granted, though the town had fallen by assault; but all infidels who could not offer ransom were sold into slavery.

At once the Crusaders quarrelled over their new possession. King John, with the backing of the barons of the land and of the Orders, claimed it as a fief of the Kingdom of Jerusalem. Cardinal Pelagius said it ought to be ruled on behalf of all Christendom by the Church, that is by himself as papal legate. In the end a decision was postponed. King John might govern Damietta, but only until the Emperor came. Then Frederick might dispose of it as he would.

In February 1220 King John was called away on urgent business. After the death of Queen Maria he had married the elder daughter of the King of Armenia. King Leo had died in 1219, leaving two daughters but no son. He had named as his heir a nephew; but by feudal law, which was new to Armenia, his daughters and their husbands took precedence of a nephew. King John must visit Armenia to claim his rights.

But while King John was in Acre his wife died, and his claim to the Kingdom of Armenia died with her. However, he did not return to Damietta; partly because he was on very bad terms with Pelagius, partly because the Sultan of Syria was menacing the castles of 'Jerusalem'.

In Damietta the Crusade stood still. Reinforcements came from the German Emperor, and Pelagius was eager to advance. But the knights would not follow a Cardinal; they declared that King John was the only leader acceptable to an international army. Until he returned they would not fight.

Meanwhile Damietta was made into a Christian city. The chief mosque became the Cathedral of Our Lady, and the See was offered to Peter des Roches, the Poitevin Bishop of Winchester. He was a famous warrior who had helped to win the battle of Lincoln which saved England for King Henry III; he accepted, but took so long to arrange his affairs that he never reached Egypt.

During the summer of 1221 the Emperor sent more reinforcements but still did not come in person. The Sultan of Egypt was strengthening his fleet. When the Nile rose he sent ships down another branch of the stream, which raided Cyprus and did great damage. Pelagius was blamed for letting them past his ships. But lack of money had compelled him to lay up many ships; and anyway no foreigner could believe, until he had seen it with his own eyes, that the Nile would always flood during the rainless summer.

The Emperor sent word to forbid any advance until he had joined the army; but by July it seemed evident that he would delay for yet another year. A large force of Germans landed in Egypt, led by the Duke of Bavaria. Old King John came back from Acre, reluctant but fearing to be accused of cowardice. Against the advice of all his military experts Cardinal Pelagius led the great army, five thousand knights and forty thousand foot, southwards up the Nile.

By the middle of August the Christians were floundering among the rising waters. The Egyptian fleet slipped into the Damietta Channel downstream of them, by way of a canal that a month ago had been a mere trickle of water; the Sultan's army barred their advance, entrenched behind other flooded channels. The Crusaders tried to retreat, but in the deep mud their horses could not move. Pelagius with his ships broke through the blockade to reach Damietta; but since he took with him most of the food the knights in the front line soon began to starve. Many of the infantry had already been snapped up by bedouin light horse. At the end of the month Pelagius sent envoys to the Sultan to treat for peace.

The Fifth Crusade ended in failure, but not in tragedy. The Sultan, still nervous, wanted above all things to get rid of the Crusaders. They must evacuate Damietta, and swear a truce for eight years. In return they would be fed from Egyptian magazines until they had left Egypt. As a bonus the Sultan would return the True Cross.

Hostages were exchanged, to be returned when the evacuation was complete. King John, the most eminent Christian hostage, was feasted by the infidels who admired him as a hero. Everyone on both sides kept the terms to the letter. In September the hostages were freed, Damietta became once more an infidel town, and the Crusaders sailed for home. But they had to leave without the True Cross, which the Sultan could not find. Presumably the Greek canons of the Holy Sepulchre had hidden it.

The Fifth Crusade had been very near repeating the overwhelming success of the First. For more than three years a great army threatened Cairo from Egyptian soil. But it lacked a competent general. King John was competent, but not grand enough to get himself obeyed; Cardinal Pelagius was no soldier. Above all, everyone waited for the Emperor, and he never came. Perhaps the chief blame must be imputed to Frederick II, though it ranks among the least of his sins and crimes.

CHAPTER XVIII

Frederick II

Barbarossa's grandson, the Emperor Frederick II, was probably the wickedest monarch of his age; he was also one of the most powerful. From his mother he inherited the Kingdom of Sicily, which his father had made into a centralised autocracy; as his father's heir he had been elected German Emperor, though in Germany he was never so absolute as in Sicily. The main object of his policy was to conquer northern Italy, which divided his two realms. He saw himself as a successor of the ancient Roman Emperors, suzerain of the Pope. He had no religious belief of any kind, perhaps because he had been reared in Sicily where Moslems were still numerous. He chose to live after the fashion of a Moslem ruler; a troupe of Moslem dancing-girls accompanied his wandering court, and at Palermo he maintained a large harem, guarded by eunuchs.

In form he was a Christian, because a German Emperor could not be anything else. In his dominions he fostered the Church, provided his Bishops obeyed him rather than the Pope; and he persecuted heretics with great severity, not because he disliked their beliefs but because they had disobeyed his command to conform. He owed his imperial crown to papal support and the Popes had protected his hazardous childhood. Honorius in particular expected great things from his young ward, for Frederick was brilliantly intelligent.

Frederick had taken the Cross in 1218. During most of the Fifth Crusade he was in Italy, ostensibly preparing to sail for Outremer. He sent over substantial bodies of German troops. But he himself always found an excuse to delay, chiefly because he had promised that on his departure he would appoint different regents for Sicily and the Empire, which he wished to keep united. Even Pope Honorius was beginning to doubt his good faith.

In 1222 King John, regent of 'Jerusalem', came to Europe in search of a husband for his daughter. During a leisurely tour of France and Spain he himself married, though in his seventies, a young princess of Castile. But it was hard to find a husband for the Queen of 'Jerusalem', as it had been hard to find a husband for her mother. At length Hermann of Salza, Grand Master of the Teutonic Knights, suggested his friend the Emperor Frederick, recently widowed. It seemed a most suitable match, though the negotiations moved slowly. At last, in November 1225, Frederick married Queen Yolande, in Italy.

Immediately after the wedding Frederick shut up his Empress in the guarded harem at Palermo, where no one was allowed to see her; and he cheated old King John, that popular hero. He had told John that he might remain regent of 'Jerusalem'; now he went back on his word, and even took by force the money John had collected in France for the defence of Outremer. The Pope showed what he thought of this double-dealing by making King John governor of the papal states, until in 1228 another post was found for the aged hero. He was appointed regent of the Latin Empire of Constantinople with the title of Emperor. He married his ward, young Baldwin II, to the four-year-old daughter of his own latest marriage; and died, in his ninetieth year, in 1239, still bearing the style of Emperor of Constantinople.

In 1227 Frederick was still lingering in Italy. Pope Honorius, his old guardian, was dead, and Gregory IX told him he must fulfil his vow immediately or face excommunication. In September the great imperial army sailed from Brindisi. But

The Emperor Frederick II

almost at once the Emperor fell sick. The fleet sailed on, but Frederick's ship put back to Otranto.

The sickness may have been genuine, but Frederick still hankered after delay. He stayed at Pozzuoli taking the waters until the season was too late for voyaging. In November the Pope excommunicated him with great ceremony in St Peter's at Rome.

Frederick paid no attention. In June 1228 he set off again for Outremer, with a small following. But he was no longer King of 'Jerusalem'. His Empress had died in the harem at Palermo, leaving an infant son. By the law of Outremer baby Conrad was King, and it was for the barons of the land to choose a regent. For the husband of the late Queen had no absolute right to the regency, as Frederick himself had proved to old King John.

The barons of Outremer were proud of their free constitution. They claimed that it had been devised, on the purest feudal principles, by the heroes of the First Crusade. Its essence was that every offender must be judged by his peers, a peasant by peasants, a burgess by burgesses, a baron by barons. But since the King had no peers the High Court, composed of barons, judged disputes between a King and a baron. Without a verdict from the High Court a King might not confiscate a fief. The power of a regent was even more limited. His sole duty was to defend the Kingdom as he found it, and in no circumstances could he deprive a baron of his castle; a case of such gravity must wait until the King came of age. The barons of the land knew how Frederick had treated their cousins, the Norman barons of Sicily; they were willing to fight rather than submit to Hohenstaufen absolutism.

Frederick landed first in Cyprus. There he was undoubtedly suzerain, for his father had bestowed a crown on King Amalric. The reigning King was a child, Henry I; his mother Queen Alice was nominally regent but her uncle John of Ibelin governed as bailli in her name.

John of Ibelin, lord of Beirut, was the greatest baron of the land and a true knight; as a true knight he must face death rather than surrender what was rightfully his. When Frederick ordered him to resign his post of bailli he obeyed his suzerain; but when he was ordered to give up Beirut he defied the Emperor, though threatened by armed Germans who crowded round him; for in 'Jerusalem' Frederick was only regent, unable to dispose of fiefs.

Civil war threatened Cyprus until a treaty was made. The child-King did homage to his suzerain, Queen Alice remained regent but the suzerain appointed another bailli, and John of Ibelin sailed with Frederick to Acre.

About this time Frederick was excommunicated again, for the grave sin of going on Crusade while excommunicate. So in Acre the clergy, the Templars and the Hospitallers would have nothing to do with him. The Teutonic Knights stood by a fellow-countryman, but otherwise he commanded only the small force he had brought; for the Germans he had sent on the year before returned home rather than serve an excommunicate. He was not strong enough to face the infidels in battle.

Luckily the Sultan of Egypt also shrank from the Holy War. He was no more a believing Moslem than Frederick was a believing Christian; he was also busy fighting his brothers and nephews to unite all the dominions of his uncle Saladin. Two atheists ought to decide without rancour the custody of the Holy Places.

After a winter of negotiation peace was made in February 1229. On the face of it Frederick had gained a complete diplomatic victory. Jerusalem, Bethlehem, Nazareth and most of Galilee were returned to the Christians, with Jaffa and Lydda to form a link with the coast. All the Holy Places had been freed. The Holy War was won.

The barons of the land pointed out that it was a paper victory. Frederick's gains were held at the will of the Sultan, who could take them back as soon as he had conquered his kinsmen. The castles of Galilee were ruinous, and the fall of Lydda would cut the new Kingdom in half. Jerusalem itself was not truly liberated. The treaty laid down that the Moslems should keep the Temple, containing the mosque of Al Aksa from which Mahomet is alleged to have taken off for his flying visit to Heaven; it also contained the original headquarters of the Templars, which set them against the treaty. Moslem pilgrims must be allowed to visit this site in unlimited numbers, and no Christian might enter it; so that an army of fanatics might be assembled in secrecy within the city. Furthermore, Frederick himself might repair the ruined walls of Jerusalem, but no one else might; after he had gone back to Europe all fortification must cease.

Only the Emperor and the Sultan were pleased with their agreement. The infidels saw it as a cowardly surrender, the Christians as illusory. But Frederick, still excommunicate, decided to fulfil his Crusading vow. With his own followers and the Teutonic Knights he marched on Jerusalem, though no other Franks would accompany him. The Holy City was almost deserted, but the infidel governor duly handed over the keys. On the same day came word that the Patriarch of Jerusalem was sending an interdict which would forbid any public religious ceremony while it was in force.

To anticipate the interdict Frederick went next day, 18 March 1229, to the Holy Sepulchre to be crowned. Not a priest was to be found in the shrine, and even the Teutonic Knights threatened to desert their lord if one of his excommunicate priests offered Mass. Without any religious service Frederick placed a crown on his own head.

He then visited the mosque of Al Aksa, where his blatant atheism made a bad impression. He remarked gratuitously that though the treaty forbade Christians to trespass on Moslem shrines he had not broken it; for he was no Christian. He never understood that pious Moslems, though they may fear Christians as dangerous enemies, loathe and despise atheists.

Next day the interdict was published and Frederick fled from Jerusalem; so no more fortification might be done. At Acre the barons received him coldly. He had crowned himself and he had concluded a treaty, things which might be done by a King but never by a regent.

On 1 May the Emperor left Outremer for ever. He had hoped to embark secretly, but the secret leaked out; his subjects gathered in the street to pelt him with filth. By the time he died, in 1250, it was widely believed that he was Antichrist in person.

Jerusalem was now an open city, exposed to infidel raids. It was controlled by a small garrison of Frederick's Germans; but the Orders and the barons of the land would not concern themselves with the defence of a town held by an excommunicate. In 1230 Frederick's excommunication was lifted for the time being, and a few more Christians settled in Jerusalem. But most of the knights of Outremer were busy with the civil war in Cyprus, where the local Franks were fighting to expel Frederick's governor. In this war John of Ibelin performed prodigies of valour, and by 1233 had driven out the last of the imperialists. Frederick's representative governed Jerusalem, but on the coast his authority was confined to Tyre. The citizens of Acre had set up a Commune, though in practice they were ruled by John of Ibelin until he died in 1233. After that there was no central authority, nor was it very much missed. The barons of the land ruled their own castles, the Italian merchants were governed by their Consuls, the Orders obeyed only the Pope. In theory the King of 'Jerusalem' was Conrad, son of the Emperor and the late Queen; he was a child in Sicily, who never visited his realm so that his subjects could not even swear homage to him.

The Pope suggested that 'Jerusalem' might be united with Cyprus, but the barons would not hear of it. Administrative convenience could not outweigh the letter of hereditary right; reasonably enough, from the barons' point of view, since hereditary right had made them barons. King Henry ruled prosperously in Cyprus.

The truce with the Sultan was due to expire in 1239, so the Pope tried to organise a General Passage. It was not very popular, except among the French. About a thousand French knights and their followers reached Acre in the autumn of that year, led by King Theobald of Navarre who was also Count of Champagne.

It seemed a good moment for an offensive. Al Kamil, the Sultan of Egypt who had defeated the Fifth Crusade, had died the year before, and there was civil war as his kinsmen struggled for the succession. The Emperor Frederick, of course, did his best to hamper the campaign. He feared that the Crusaders would not recognise his authority as regent of 'Jerusalem' on behalf of little Conrad. Besides, he believed that civil war among the infidels should be exploited by diplomacy, not by arms. So the Crusaders might not pass through Italy, and no Italians or Germans joined them.

From Acre the Crusaders marched south to bar the passage from Egypt through Sinai, according to the traditional strategy of the Holy War. But at Gaza the Count of Bar advanced with nearly half the army, against the advice of every veteran and the direct orders of King Theobald. Bogged down in soft sand, his men were wiped out by Egyptian arrows. King Theobald retreated to Acre.

While the Crusaders were thus occupied the infidels raided Jerusalem. The city was indefensible. The garrison retired into the Tower of David, where they surrendered on terms after a siege of a month. The infidels destroyed the Tower and withdrew.

King Theobald stayed in Outremer until the autumn of 1240. By changing sides repeatedly in a war then raging between the Sultan of Egypt and the Sultan of Damascus he gained some strong castles for 'Jerusalem'. But his double-dealing shocked even the toughest politicians, and the barons of the land were glad to see him go.

In the same autumn another eminent visitor arrived, Richard, Earl of Cornwall, younger brother of King Henry III of England. He came as a pilgrim, not as a warrior; but he was already known as a skilled diplomatist, and his exalted birth won him the respect of class-conscious Outremer. The Emperor Frederick had recently married his sister, so that he came with the goodwill of both Guelfs and Ghibellines. He brought peace to the factions of the coast, where Templars and Hospitallers bickered in the streets and every castle was held either for

Frederick or the Ibelins. He then negotiated with the Sultan of Egypt, who ceded Tiberias and most of Galilee as the price of peace. When he left Outremer in May 1241 he had strengthened the Kingdom without ever drawing his sword.

In 1243 the Templars, by skilfully playing off against one another various infidel neighbours to Jerusalem, got back their orginal headquarters in the Temple. Perhaps a little more diplomacy would win back Outrejordan as well, and then the Kingdom would be as big and strong as before Hattin. So the whole army of Outremer mustered at Acre, prepared to march as allies of the emirs of Syria against the Sultan of Egypt.

The Sultan of Egypt also sought allies. In northern Syria were encamped some nomads from the steppe, Khwarismians who lived by plunder. When the Sultan had hired them as mercenaries they set off to join his army at Gaza. As they rode south, to the number of ten thousand, they swooped suddenly on Jerusalem. On 11 June 1244 they broke into the unfortified city.

The Khwarismians slaughtered and plundered, but in numerous walled convents the Franks held out. In answer to frantic appeals their ally the emir of Kerak arranged terms. After yielding the city the Christians might march unharmed to the coast. On 23 August six thousand of them set out, men, women, and children. But the truce bound only the Khwarismians. The bedouin of the desert gathered to rob and enslave the fugitives, so effectively that only three hundred reached Jaffa.

The Khwarismians pillaged in particular the Holy Sepulchre, where they slaughtered the priests at Mass. They set fire to its roof, and desecrated the Frankish tombs in it. When there was nothing more worth taking in Jerusalem they rode on to join their allies at Gaza.

The army gathered at Acre was the largest Christian host ever assembled in Outremer. The armies of Damascus, Homs and Kerak joined it, led by their infidel emirs. Meanwhile the Egyptians and Khwarismians waited for them. On 17 October 1244, at the village of La Forbie a few miles north of Gaza, the great battle was fought.

The terrible battle of La Forbie was the bloodiest disaster since Hattin. In particular the Orders suffered heavily. Of more than three hundred Templars present only thirty-three fought their way out, of more than three hundred Hospitallers twenty-six, of a lesser number of Teutonic Knights three. The dead numbered five thousand, the prisoners eight hundred. This huge loss fell on the permanent garrison of Outremer, for there were few Crusaders from Europe in the army that marched to Gaza. Barely enough able-bodied men were left in the country to hold castles and walled towns.

Luckily the Egyptians were too occupied with their war against Damascus to invade Outremer in earnest. But by 1247 the Sultan of Egypt had established his supremacy over his kinsmen, and the wandering Khwarismians had been wiped out in battle. In that year the infidels took Tiberias and the other inland castles of Galilee. They captured Ascalon by a sudden assault which brought many casualties to the Christian garrison. But the other coastal towns of Outremer were unmolested. The infidels no longer feared Franks, and they liked to have near them these convenient outlets for trade with the west.

CHAPTER XIX

The Crusade of St Louis

In the year 1244 Louis IX, King of France, fell ill. He vowed that if he recovered from his sickness he would lead a Crusade to Outremer. A very holy man and a stainless knight, he was canonised soon after his death and will be referred to henceforth as St Louis.

In the east a new power had appeared, the Mongols. They were an enormous horde of all the nomads living between Russia and China, gathered into one army by the great Genghis Khan. By the 1240's Genghis Khan was dead, but there was still a Great Khan of all the Mongols reigning at Karakorum in farther Asia; though most of his far-flung armies were led by semi-independent generals descended from the imperial house.

In Europe the Mongols had already defeated the armies of Russia, Poland and Hungary, and it had seemed that they must conquer all Christendom. But whenever a Great Khan died all his generals returned to Karakorum to elect his successor, as had happened in 1242. So they had retired back to the steppe, though before they vanished they had reached the shores of the Adriatic. The Pope had preached a Crusade against them, but the Emperor Frederick had simultaneously called out all his own supporters; since the two summonses cancelled out, nothing had been done. Now a quite different horde from the great Mongol Empire was threatening the Caliph of Baghdad.

231

The most exciting thing about these Mongols was that they had not yet chosen a religion. In their obscure home they had been pagans, worshipping Good Luck under the guidance of witch-doctors known as Shamans. As they came into contact with higher cultures some of them had become Buddhists, a few had become Moslems, and a number had embraced the heretical, Nestorian variant of Christianity. Soon, if they were to hold together, they must all follow the same faith; and there was a chance that it might be true, Catholic Christianity.

They were a horrid people, who massacred harmless civilians in the countries they conquered; in particular they would offer easy terms of surrender to a garrison and break their word as soon as the place yielded. But they were beginning to grow more civilised; and of course if they became true Catholic Christians they would become chivalrous at the same time. The Pope had already sent them missionaries, who had been received politely. Perhaps they could be induced to attack the Moslems from the north while St Louis attacked them from the south? There was a real opening for a new Crusade, which might not only liberate Jerusalem but destroy Islam in its birthplace at Mecca and Medina.

St Louis made thorough preparations, so that his army was not ready to start until August 1248. He was the undisputed leader, and most Crusaders were his born subjects; though volunteers came also from the Rhineland, from England, and even from Scotland. There would be no arguments about command, no government by a council of war, no international rivalries.

St Louis, always scrupulous to observe the rights of others, sent envoys to King Conrad of Jerusalem seeking permission to enter his Kingdom. The Emperor Frederick, on behalf of his son, gladly gave the required permission and then passed on what he knew of the Crusaders' plans to his old friend the Sultan of Egypt. But while St Louis was wintering in Cyprus Christian envoys arrived sent by the Mongol general in Mosul, and the alliance with the Mongols seemed just round the corner.

St Louis sent his own envoys to Mosul, bearing suitable

presents. They were forwarded to the Mongol capital of Kara-korum. There they discovered that the presents they brought were regarded as tribute from the King of France, intended to buy off a Mongol invasion. They hastened back to inform their master. St Louis, ashamed at the slight on his honour, broke off negotiations.

Nevertheless, the Mongol army at Mosul would distract the Sultan of Egypt, whose empire now included much of Meso-potamia. St Louis recalled the expert advice given by Coeur de Lion fifty years before. He determined to strike at Egypt. From Cyprus the Crusaders sailed direct to Damietta, where they arrived in June 1249.

The campaign which followed has been described in detail by a knight who took part, John de Joinville, Seneschal of Champagne and a close friend of St Louis. From his account we can see some of the difficulties of commanding knightly Crusaders.

At first all went well, chiefly because the Sultan of Egypt, Ayub son of Al-Kamil and grandson of Saphadin, lay dying in Cairo. He had left a strong garrison in Damietta; but they rashly left their walls to oppose the Christians on the beach. St Louis jumped from his galley into waves which reached his shoulders, and in full armour waded ashore on foot. After fierce fighting the dismounted Crusaders beat the mounted infidels, who fled in such dismay that they evacuated Damietta. Before they left they remembered to plunder the town, but they were in such a hurry that they neglected to burn the bridge over the Nile. The Christians of Damietta, then numerous, informed the French; who took possession of the place without further fighting.

This easy capture of a fortress which for more than a year had held up the Fifth Crusade was a splendid start. But in a few days the Nile would flood, and St Louis decided to wait until it had subsided in October. The dying Sultan moved up with his main army to Mansourah (Victory Town), recently built on the spot where King John had surrendered. He sent forward light horse to harry the invaders. St Louis fortified his camp outside Damietta, and strictly forbade his men to go out and skirmish with the enemy.

Whereupon a knight named Walter of Autreche had his destrier secretly brought into his tent, while he himself was strapped into his armour. Suddenly his men drew back the tent-flaps, shouting their warcry; while Walter, alone, charged out on the foe. On the way his stallion pecked and put him down; then it continued towards the mares ridden by the Egyptians. Four mamelukes rode out to attack the prostrate knight. A rescue-party brought him in, so gravely wounded that he died the same night. St Louis condemned his disobedience, but it is evident that Joinville admired his spirit.

When the flood had subsided the Crusaders advanced towards Cairo. About the same time Sultan Ayub died, while his son and destined heir, Turanshah, was far off in northern Syria. But until Turanshah could arrive the Sultan's widows and courtiers concealed his death by issuing orders under his seal. The Egyptian army remained in Mansourah. On 14 December 1249 the Crusaders reached the north bank of a canal running east from the Nile just to the north of Mansourah. The canal was unbridged, and its south back was lined with Egyptian siege engines.

St Louis must proceed by formal siege. He built engines to counter the Egyptian engines. But the infidels got the better of the exchange, for they threw barrels of Greek Fire which the Crusaders could neither concoct nor extinguish. Next the Crusaders tried to make a solid causeway of earth and sand across the canal, since for lack of timber they could not bridge it. But as fast as they advanced the Egyptians cut away the southern bank, so that the canal remained as wide as before. Mameluke horse had worked round to the north of the Crusaders, carried in boats across other branches of the Nile. The Christians must protect their camp from attacks from the rear. In one of these raids a brother of St Louis, the Count of Anjou who later became King of Sicily, had his leg broken.

With the invasion at a standstill morale was low. Joinville frankly thanks God that he was not on guard over the siege

engines when they were destroyed by Greek Fire; for there was
no way to prevent the burning of sentries as well as machines.

At last a local Christian told St Louis that for five hundred
bezants he would show him a ford over the canal.

On Shrove Tuesday, 8 February 1250, the Crusaders set out
to attack Mansourah. The plan was that the knights should
cross by the ford four miles to the east, which was too deep for
infantry; then they would ride west along the south bank and
halt to cover the crossing of the foot. The Count of Artois,
another brother of the King, led the van, which included the
Templars and the English Crusaders. There followed a main
battle, and the King in person led the rearguard.

With some knights drowned the Count of Artois got the van
over the ford. On the southern bank he should have waited
for the main body, as the Grand Master of the Temple reminded
him. But he answered that Templars did not want to win the
Holy War, for fear their occupation should be gone. He
charged at once, hoping to surprise the infidels in their camp.

In this he succeeded. It was early morning, and the mamelukes were still asleep. Their leader was killed in his night
clothes and they were driven from their camp with heavy loss.
They fled into the neighbouring town of Mansourah, where
they took refuge among the houses.

The Count of Artois set off in pursuit, though his comrades
advised him to wait for the King. The Earl of Salisbury in
particular suggested caution, to which Artois replied by calling
him a tailed Englishman, an ancient taunt. 'Today I shall go
where no Frenchman will dare to ride level with the tail of my
horse', said Salisbury. The whole vanguard charged into
Mansourah.

But the mamelukes had rallied. In the narrow streets knights
got lost, and they were an easy mark for arrows from the roof-
tops. Nearly all were killed, including both Artois and Salisbury; the Templars alone lost nearly three hundred mounted
men, knights or light horse.

St Louis, with the second and third divisions, had to fight
his way four miles down the south bank of the canal before he

reached the half-finished causeway by which his foot hoped to cross. It was a scattered, bloody battle. At one point the survivors of Joinville's ten knights were holding a ruined house. Joinville, who had lost his shield when his horse was killed under him, was acting as horse-holder. After four knights had been severely wounded one of the remainder, Everard of Siverey, suggested that he might seek reinforcements. This is how he put it:

'My lord, if you think that neither I nor my heirs will be blamed for it, I shall go and ask help from the Count of Anjou.'

Joinville replied that in such danger even a good knight might seek help without blame. Siverey, who had been so badly cut on the face that his nose hung down below his lips, persuaded the Count of Anjou to come to the rescue, and then died of his wound.

Later in the day, when Joinville's squire had brought him another horse, he was holding a little bridge against a crowd of infidels who shot so fiercely with arrows and javelins that he had been wounded in five places and his horse in fifteen. With his few companions he had just learned for certain that all the knights still in Mansourah were dead. The Count of Soissons turned to him, saying: 'By God's bonnet, you and I will yet talk of this day in ladies' chambers.'

Knights such as these might be killed, but they could not be routed. By nightfall St Louis held the mameluke camp and a substantial bridgehead south of the canal. But a young emir named Bibars had rallied the infidels; they had seen the Lilies on the surcoat of the dead Count of Artois and believed they had killed the King. Before the Crusaders could advance they must fight another battle, and meanwhile they had lost a third of their knights.

Only three days later the mamelukes attacked the bridgehead. The knights were still too bruised from the battle of Shrove Tuesday to put on armour, and more of them were killed before the infidels were driven off. St Louis held on, hoping for a civil war in Cairo. But by the end of February Turanshah had arrived and been recognised as Sultan. There was nothing for it but retreat, especially as the infidels had carried warships across the desert on camel-back and launched them on the Nile below Mansourah. The Crusaders did not know what had interrupted their communications until a little Flemish ship broke through the blockade and the Flemings told them that more than eighty Christian galleys had been captured upstream of Damietta.

Meanwhile corpses which had fallen into the canal during the battle were rising to the surface, so that in the Christian camp sickness was added to famine. In April St Louis withdrew north of the canal, amid heavy pressure on his rearguard. He had already proposed the bargain which had been offered to the Fifth Crusade, the surrender of Damietta in exchange for Jerusalem. But Turanshah had refused it, for he saw that the Franks were beaten.

It was planned that the Christian sick should be carried north by boat, while the army kept pace with them on the eastern bank. But the King himself was sick with dysentery, so sick that his drawers must be cut away; there were just not enough able-bodied fighters. After one day's march the army could go no farther. St Louis was carried into a cottage where he began to negotiate terms of surrender with the Sultan.

There followed a sad chapter of accidents. Agreement had just been reached in principle that the Crusaders might leave Egypt unharmed in return for the surrender of Damietta, when a rumour ran through the army, perhaps put about by bribed traitors, that the King was already a prisoner and that the only hope of saving his life was for every man to lay down his arms. Many knights had made up their minds to die fighting rather than yield; but all his followers loved St Louis and at once all surrendered. Since the treaty was not yet sealed the Sultan might claim that the Christians had surrendered unconditionally.

Among the sick all those who could not leave their boats unaided were killed immediately; partly because the Egyptians feared infection, partly because such men had no value as slaves. St Louis was fettered while lying helpless on his bed. To reduce the dangerous number of able-bodied prisoners the Sultan ordered three hundred of them to be killed every day.

St Louis, undismayed by his own grave danger, began to bargain with the Sultan for the ransom of his men; when threatened with torture he answered merely that he was their prisoner and they might do with him as they wished. He was on the point of reaching an agreement when the mamelukes of Egypt, angered by Turanshah's preference for his old companions from Syria, murdered their Sultan and set up their own commander in his place.

Bargaining must be begun again, with the disorderly committee of mamelukes who now ruled Egypt. St Louis refused steadfastly to yield any castle of Outremer in return for his own freedom; on the ground that these castles belonged to Conrad of Hohenstaufen, not to him. He also considered it beneath his royal dignity to buy himself with money. But Damietta, which he had conquered, was his to surrender. In return for Damietta he would be freed, and he would pay a million bezants for the freedom of all his followers. The King and his leading barons were put on a river-boat at once, for the infidels knew that St Louis would never abandon his followers. The lesser men were held in prison in Cairo, to be released only as the ransom came in.

There had been a danger that Damietta would be yielded before the King was released. As soon as they heard of the disaster at Mansourah the Italian sailors who formed its garrison were all for immediate flight. Queen Margaret of France, who was having a baby at the time, saved the town by her courage. When the child was born her only attendant was an eighty-year-old knight, and the boy was named Tristan, the Child of Sorrow. She persuaded the Italians to stay by paying for their food from her own purse. When the King arrived, having passed through a crowd of mamelukes who threatened him with swords wet from the massacre of other Crusaders, Damietta was still Christian.

In May 1250 Damietta was handed over to the infidels, though it still contained many Christian sick who could not be moved, and the army's emergency-reserve of salt pork. The mamelukes had promised to send these on at the first opportunity; instead they murdered the sick and burned the pork, which their religion forbade them to eat. But St Louis was scrupulous to keep his side of the bargain; partly to save the Christian foot still in Cairo, but even more because it was his custom to keep his word.

In Damietta the whole ransom was paid over, large though it was. At first the Templars would not hand over their money-chests, because the silver they held as international bankers belonged in fact to their clients. Joinville had to pick up an axe, saying that this would be the King's key, before the genuine keys were produced. But too much has been made of this, as evidence of Templar greed. There was no serious attempt at concealment or defence; Joinville saw the chests as soon as he asked for them. It was rather that individual Templars were afraid to take the responsibility of parting with money entrusted to them; most of the senior knights of the Order, including the Grand Master, had been killed at Mansourah. They only waited for Joinville to demonstrate, before witnesses, that St Louis would use force if persuasion failed. For the rest of the campaign Joinville continued to bank with the Temple, without any suggestion that the Templars had acted improperly.

By the end of May 1250 St Louis was back in Acre and the surviving prisoners had been released from Cairo. Most of the great lords, including the King's brothers, returned to France as quickly as they could. No one reproached them, for at Mansourah they had done more than their duty. But St Louis remained in Acre, at the head of a small army. He held no official position in 'Jerusalem', which was still in theory a fief of the Hohenstaufen. But most of the barons of the land were of French descent, and he was accepted tacitly as their leader.

For four years St Louis governed Outremer, protecting it rather by diplomacy than by arms. Luckily a civil war had broken out between the mamelukes of Egypt and the Syrians, still loyal to the house of Saladin; so the infidels were too busy to invade. It was also said that an important Mongol chieftain,

St Louis

Sartaq son of Batu, had become a Christian; and there were
hopes that he might campaign against the infidels in conjunc-
tion with the army of Outremer.

Sartaq's conversion may have been genuine; but he was not
important enough to conduct his own foreign policy without
reference to the Great Khan at Karakorum. The Dominicans
whom St Louis sent there soon realised that the Mongols as a
nation worshipped nothing greater than Good Luck, and that
any embassy from a Christian King was regarded as an offer
of submission. Prester John did not reign in Mongolia. Slowly
Christendom came to see that nothing good could come from
these barbarians.

In 1254 St Louis went home. His mother, who had been
regent of France during his absence, was now dead; and the
miserable King Henry III of England was menacing the realm
of an absent Crusader.

He left Outremer at peace with the neighbouring infidel
powers, Egypt and Damascus. The King of 'Jerusalem' was
now little Conradin, son of the late King Conrad. He was two
years old. His father had never seen Outremer and it was
unlikely that he would. But an acknowledged and absentee
sovereign made government by the High Court, the barons of
the land, legal and convenient. Acre and Tyre seemed safe
enough for the time being, though of course they were safe
chiefly because the infidels found it useful to have Italian
merchants living so close. The small communities of Franks
domiciled in the east could not expand the limits of Christendom
by their own efforts, and were no danger to anyone.

By 1256 all the Frankish cities of the east were the scene of
a destructive civil war between Venetians and Genoese, with
Pisans changing sides between them. As the war progressed
the Orders and the barons of the land were drawn in, and blood-
feuds began which continued after the fall of Outremer. In 1261
a papal legate made a local peace, but in the wider theatre of the
Mediterranean the war continued. In the same year the Latin
Emperor, a Fleming allied to Venice, was driven from Constantinople by the Greeks of Nicaea and the Genoese.

The Crusade of St Louis

As a reward the Greeks granted the Genoese trading stations in the Black Sea, now a more valuable market than the Levant. The great Mongol Empire had brought peace to the steppe, so that the commerce of China and India came to Europe by way of the Crimea, instead of by Acre or Alexandria. Outremer was growing poor, as well as weak in a military sense.

In 1258 the Mongol Hulagu had sacked Baghdad. He massacred the whole population, including the last of the Caliphs, and destroyed the irrigation system. Henceforth Mesopotamia was a poor and unimportant province of Islam, and the infidels had no undisputed religious head. The Mongols next took Aleppo and Damascus. Bohemond V, Prince of Antioch and Tripoli, and the King of Armenia became their clients. Then Hulagu retired eastward on the death of his Great Khan, and the Mongol advance was halted. A Christian Mongol named Kitbuqa remained in Damascus with a small army.

In 1260 the mamelukes of Egypt advanced to drive back the Mongols. They sought help from the Franks of Outremer, but the Franks could not make up their minds. Kitbuqa was a heretical Christian; but he was also a savage. The Egyptians were infidels, though civilised. In the end the Franks stood neutral, doubtless hoping that both sides would be exhausted by a long and bloody war.

But at the Pools of Goliath the mamelukes met the Mongol army, and destroyed it in a single battle. Kitbuqa was taken prisoner and then killed, because he reproached his captors for their habit of murdering their Sultans. In the battle the emir Bibars especially distinguished himself, the same who had rallied his men outside the camp at Mansourah. On the way back to Egypt he went out hunting with the Sultan. While another emir clasped the Sultan's hand in greeting, so that he could not defend himself, Bibars stabbed him in the back. Then the whole bodyguard rode home to headquarters, boasting of what had been done. The Sultan's second in command inquired which emir had struck the fatal blow. When Bibars admitted the murder he was immediately enthroned as Sultan of Egypt.

Sultan Bibars, as an enemy of the Mongols, felt an especial

hatred for their faithful allies, Bohemond of Antioch and the
King of Armenia. During his conquest of Syria he raided some
Christian castles but won no important success. In 1266 he
besieged the Templar castle of Safed in Galilee. After several
assaults had been repelled he offered the garrison their lives if
they would yield. When they had laid down their arms they
were murdered to the last man. Bibars then captured Toron and
marched through the coastal plain, killing every Christian he
met, whether Frank or Syrian peasant. But he dared not attack
either Acre or Tyre.

In May 1267 he almost took Acre, by advancing under the
banners of the Templars murdered at Safed. The deception was
discovered just in time, and his assault on the walls was beaten
off after heavy fighting.

In August of that year the Venetians and Genoese fought
two naval battles in the harbour of Acre.

In the spring of 1268 Bibars set out to clear up the outlying
Frankish castles south of Acre. He captured Jaffa at the first
assault, though hand-to-hand fighting continued for twelve
hours until the wall was carried. All the unarmed inhabitants
were killed, but the soldiers of the garrison were allowed to
retreat unmolested to Acre. In April Bibars took the Templar
castle of Beaufort. It was captured by mining rather than by
assault, and for once Bibars showed some mercy. Christian
women and children were allowed to go free; and the men were
only enslaved, not killed.

Then Bibars appeared suddenly before Tripoli; but Tripoli
was a strong fortress and all the Franks of the north hurried to
its defence. The mamelukes vanished as suddenly as they had
come. A fortnight later, in the middle of May, they were outside
Antioch. The feint had succeeded. The reinforcement of
Tripoli had weakened the garrison of Antioch.

After taking the port of St Simeon the enormous Egyptian
army was strong enough to besiege Antioch on every side, a
thing the host of the First Crusade had never been able to
accomplish. The garrison could not man every stretch of the
long walls climbing up to the summit of Mount Silpius, though

the mighty fortifications built by Justinian were still in good repair. The assault came after a few days. On 18 May 1268 the Christian city of Antioch went down fighting. The knights and clergy were killed sword in hand. The inhabitants found in the streets were killed on the spot, those who hid until resistance had ceased were enslaved. There was at least one slave for every soldier in the Egyptian Army, and the bottom dropped out of the market for young girls.

Antioch was so near the Mongol posts on the Euphrates that Bibars did not care to hold it; and he had killed or removed all its inhabitants. The walls of the great city, once the third in the Roman Empire, were deliberately destroyed. Never again has Antioch flourished.

After returning to Damascus Bibars made a truce with 'Jerusalem'. There were rumours that St Louis might come out again on Crusade, and at last Acre had a resident King with something of an army. Conradin, last heir of the Hohenstaufen and titular King of 'Jerusalem', had been defeated and killed by Charles of Anjou. With strict regard for hereditary descent the barons of the land crowned Hugh III of Cyprus, heir of Queen Maria's younger half-sister, Alice of Champagne. King Hugh restored some kind of order to the land, where no King had resided since John of Brienne left for Italy. But he could not control the Orders, who obeyed no one less than the Pope.

In 1270 St Louis set out on his second Crusade. But this time he was not trying to free the Holy Places. Charles of Anjou, now King of Sicily, reported that the emir of Tunis was inclined to become a Christian if there were a Frankish army on the spot to protect him from the anger of his infidel subjects. This was worth following up. If the line Sicily—Malta—Tunis were in Christian hands the central Mediterranean would be closed to infidel ships, and Spain and Morocco would be cut off from Mecca.

It was a sound strategic plan, but most French knights felt that they had done enough Crusading. Joinville, that good knight, was one of those who would not volunteer. Nevertheless, in July 1270 St Louis landed near Carthage with a strong army. At once the emir retired into Tunis, where he fought stubbornly for his faith. He had never intended to turn Christian; he had hinted that he might only because he feared King Charles of Sicily.

Sickness broke out in the camp of the besiegers. By the end of August St Louis and his young son Tristan were dead, and Philip his heir was dangerously ill. King Charles led back to Europe the remnant of his brother's army. Tunis continued to provide a useful base for infidel corsairs.

St Louis was the most noble knight and the most holy man ever to go on Crusade. All who knew him loved him, and posterity reveres him. But in fact he accomplished nothing to strengthen Outremer. He gained Heaven, but not Jerusalem.

CHAPTER XX

The End

In the summer of 1270 Prince Edward, son and heir of King Henry III of England, set off to join St Louis before Tunis. He brought with him his wife, his brother Edmund, and a small force of his personal followers. By the time he reached Tunis St Louis was dead, so he wintered in Sicily and in the spring continued to Outremer. He reached Acre in May 1271.

He had hoped that his followers would form the nucleus of an army made up of all the soldiers of Outremer. The barons of the land were willing to follow him, for as heir of England he enjoyed some of the prestige of Coeur de Lion; but the Venetians and Genoese refused to fight, for fear of damaging their lucrative trade with Alexandria. Since their chief exports were weapons, armour and galley-slaves Edward denounced them as traitors to Christendom; whereupon they showed him the charters, sealed by the High Court of 'Jerusalem' in return for cash down, which entitled them to trade with the enemy even in time of war. The barons of Cyprus added that for their part they need fight on the mainland only for four months in any one year, and then only if their King led them in person. On meeting this obstruction Edward gave up all hope of raising an army.

There remained diplomacy, in which he was expert. The old dream of Prester John was now discredited. But the great Mongol Empire had broken up, and the reigning Ilkhan of

Persia, Abaga, was a pagan Mongol married to a Greek princess and reputedly a friend of Christians. His most dangerous enemies in the west were the mamelukes of Egypt, so that at least in foreign policy he was hostile to Islam. But his dominions stretched from the Euphrates to Afghanistan, from the Persian Gulf to the Caucasus; so that he could not often direct his main attention to Syria.

In the autumn of 1271 Abaga sent an army of ten thousand horse, small by Mongol standards, to raid south from Aleppo. At the same time Edward marched inland by Mount Carmel with all the men he could muster. But his followers would not attack even a small castle away from the coast, since none of them would volunteer to hold it if it were taken. Sultan Bibars ignored the raid, and Edward soon retired to Acre. The Mongols also retired when the main mameluke army moved north against them.

In May 1272 'Jerusalem' and Bibars sealed a truce for ten years. But the Sultan feared Edward's ability as a diplomatist, though he did not fear his army. He arranged that an Assassin should stab Edward with a poisoned dagger. Perhaps the future Queen Eleanor sucked poison from the wound, though the story was first written down a century later. Anyway, after a severe illness Edward recovered. In September 1272 he left Outremer for ever.

When he left he intended to return, at the head of a great army; and everyone expected he would, for the whole east had been impressed by his honesty and efficiency. But when he reached home his father was dead and he was King; for the rest of his life the conquest of Wales and the attempted conquest of Scotland kept him busy.

Oddly enough, though Edward and the Ilkhan had never met they liked and trusted one another. Abaga kept the King of England informed of his plans to conquer the mamelukes, and whenever he invaded Syria looked for help from a Crusade. In 1281 he fought a great battle with the mamelukes. Among the allies of the Mongols were King Leo III of Armenia, some knights of the Hospital, and some Christian Georgians. But these Christians fought as vassals of the Ilkhan, not as Crusaders. The cities of Outremer observed a cautious neutrality, bound by a truce which still had a year to run. At the battle of Homs the Armenians in particular won great glory; but losses were so heavy on both sides that the Mongols retired and the mamelukes did not pursue them.

Abaga died in 1282. Succeeding Ilkhans sent Christian envoys to Europe, hoping to arrange a concerted attack on Egypt. But nothing every came of it, and presently they saw that the Franks were too busy fighting among themselves to spare time for a Crusade. In 1295 the Mongol-Persian Empire adopted Islam as the official state religion, though many Christians, mostly heretics, remained in the country.

In the surviving cities of Outremer no one bothered about the infidel menace; it was more amusing, and more remunerative, to fight your neighbours who came from European countries with which your own was at war. The Temple quarrelled with the Hospital, Venetians and Genoese continued their interminable naval war, among the barons of the land Ibelins were at feud with Montforts. Occasionally all would combine to defy the orders of the King of Cyprus who was also King of 'Jerusalem'; for the sacred constitution embodied in the 'Assizes of Jerusalem' was more important than any preparation to resist the mamelukes.

In 1277 Charles of Anjou, King of Sicily, added to the confusion by buying the claim to the throne of Maria of Antioch, descended from another daughter of the late Queen Isabella. She came of a junior line, but she herself was a generation nearer to the original ancestor; a point of feudal law never settled by universal consent which bedevilled also the contemporary dispute among the claimants to the crown of Scotland. Henceforth discontented vassals could appeal from the King of Cyprus to the King of Sicily. But in 1282 the 'Sicilian Vespers' destroyed the power of King Charles, and for the rest of his life he was too busy fighting in Italy to try for a crown in Outremer.

In 1286 Henry II, King of Cyprus, came to Acre to be

crowned King of 'Jerusalem'. His coronation in Tyre, the only other city of his new Kingdom, was celebrated with great rejoicing. But the Grand Masters of the three Orders had to mediate before he might enter his palace, held for the King of Sicily by an Angevin mercenary captain.

Bibars, the first mameluke Sultan of Egypt, died in 1277, to be succeeded by a line of adventurers, some claiming to be heirs of their predecessor, some prominent slave-mercenaries; until in the 16th century the Turks conquered Egypt.

In 1289 Tripoli, the last fragment of the Principality of Antioch and so not a part of the Kingdom of 'Jerusalem', was ruled by the Countess Lucy, sister of the late Count and married to an Angevin supporter of King Charles. Her rule was opposed by the Commune of Tripoli, by the eminent baronial house of Embriaco, by the Venetians, and by the Orders. So that when the Templars gave warning that the mamelukes were about to attack, their rivals suspected some political motive and would not believe them. Nevertheless, in March a great Egyptian army sat down before Tripoli.

Within the threatened town the Christians closed their ranks; everyone recognised the authority of Countess Lucy. Though the mamelukes explained that they were not breaking their truce with 'Jerusalem', since Tripoli was outside the Kingdom, the Orders and the Kingdom of Cyprus sent help. The Venetian and Genoese admirals promised to fight the infidel instead of one another.

But the mamelukes, rulers of innumerable Egyptian pioneers, excelled in siegecraft. After less than a month the walls began to crumble under the battering of great engines. In despair, the Venetian admiral ordered his ships to sail away with all the Venetian property in the place. The Genoese admiral, fearing that the Venetians might take Genoese property also, ordered his ships to follow. On the same day, 26 April 1289, while the remaining defenders were justifiably dismayed, the mamelukes began a general assault. At once there was a rush for the remaining ships in the harbour.

Several eminent fugitives got away to Cyprus, including the

Countess Lucy. Many Christians fought gallantly in the streets even after the defences had been overrun. After they had killed all the knights the infidels raged through the town. Every male Christian was cut down, and all the women and children sold into slavery. Then the Sultan of Egypt, who had no fleet, ordered the destruction of Tripoli lest one day the Christians might reoccupy it. A new town of Tripoli was built some miles inland, round the old castle of Mount Pilgrim.

The inhabitants of Acre and Tyre were shocked, but they could do nothing. They had taken it for granted that Italian markets on the coast of Syria were so useful to the mamelukes that they would be left in peace. But Tripoli had been outside the Kingdom. The truce protected them, and no Sultan of Egypt would break his word.

In the summer of 1290 there was a riot between Christians and Moslems in the streets of Acre. Apparently the Moslems provoked it by insulting a Christian lady; but it ended with a number of Moslems killed. The Sultan of Egypt claimed that such a massacre ended the truce. At the beginning of September he began to gather his army.

Within a week the Sultan was dead, probably from natural causes. Of course the inhabitants of Acre boasted that God had preserved them by miracle. They had in fact been granted a reprieve, for the ensuing war between ambitious mameluke emirs and the son of the dead Sultan postponed the invasion for a year. But in March 1291 the new Sultan Al-Ashraf was again marching against Acre, after murdering the Christian envoys sent to beg peace from him.

On 6 April 1291 the siege began. The citizens had received ample warning, and their double circuit of walls was in good repair. But in spite of appeals for help no great Crusade had come from Europe; only a company of Lombard crossbowmen and a few individual knights errant, of whom the most famous was the Burgundian Otto of Grandson. The three Orders had mustered every knight they could gather. A few English volunteers had come out at the expense of King Edward I. The Venetians and Pisans did their duty; though the Genoese, whose business in Acre had been ruined by Venice, stood neutral. King Henry lay sick in Cyprus, but he sent a Cypriot contingent and his brother Amalric commanded the defence. Many noncombatants had been ferried over to Cyprus, and there was no shortage of supplies. The whole number of defenders was about a thousand mounted men, knights and light horse, and fifteen thousand foot. Against them the mamelukes brought sixty thousand horse and a hundred and sixty thousand foot.

For a month the battering continued, and during this time the Christians won a few minor successes. Italian catapults knocked out some important Egyptian siege engines, and sallies by the knights of the Orders killed many infidels until they were discontinued as wasteful of limited man-power. On 4 May King Henry arrived from Cyprus with a hundred knights and two thousand foot, all he could raise in his island Kingdom. Everyone was glad to see King Henry, a good knight and a skilful commander; but in a sense his arrival was depressing, for now it was known that no more help would come.

King Henry sent envoys to beg peace. The Sultan very nearly murdered them with his own sword, though in the end he offered to spare the Christians if they would leave Acre at once and never come back. These terms were refused. The business men and wide boys of Acre had suddenly remembered that they were Crusaders, in the forefront of the Holy War; they would die fighting rather than surrender.

On 15 May the infidels carried the battered outer wall, so that only the Gate of St Anthony barred them from the city. On the 18th, an auspicious Friday, they mounted a general assault all the way from St Anthony's to the harbour. After the inner wall had been lost the Christians continued to fight in the streets.

The Grand Master of the Temple was killed. The Grand Master of the Hospital was carried to the rear, gravely wounded. In the evening the surviving Christian leaders tried to organise an evacuation by sea. King Henry and his brother got away, with many Cypriots; perhaps they left too soon, but Cyprus could not be left defenceless. Otto of Grandson took over the command. He rallied a rearguard, filled the Venetian ships with wounded, and was himself the last man to embark. The elderly Patriarch of Jerusalem, already wounded, was carried by his servants to a small rowing boat. He encouraged fugitives to crowd in after him, so that the boat sank and all were drowned. Presently the last ship had gone and still the quay was crowded with fugitives. The Templars retreated to their fortified headquarters, where they prolonged resistance for a few more hopeless days. In the end the infidels undermined the walls, and the fall of the whole building killed many assailants and all the defenders.

It was rumoured that Roger de Flor, later Captain of the mercenary Grand Catalan Company which ravaged Hellas, made his fortune at the sack of Acre. He had been a Templar, and now prudently deserted. He seized a Templar ship, sold passages in it to the highest bidder, and passed the rest of his life as a prominent and successful brigand.

After all resistance had ceased the infidels sacked Acre. Years later a few freed slaves drifted back to Europe, but no one ever knew how many of the inhabitants had been killed and how many enslaved. In Damascus the price of a girl fell to one drachma, but the Moslems themselves believed that the majority of the Christians had been killed.

In fear of Christian sea power the Sultan deliberately destroyed Acre. Fortifications, churches and palaces were pulled down. No more commerce came that way, and within a generation the great merchant city had become a shabby village.

On the very next day, 19 May, the infidels appeared before Tyre. The strongest city of Outremer might have endured a long siege, but why persevere in a hopeless struggle? The Cypriot garrison sailed home without striking a blow. At Sidon the Templars held out until July, when they left by sea. Beirut, protected by a private truce, was taken by treachery in the same month. In August the infidels sacked the monasteries of Mount Carmel. A few hermits escaped to England, where St Simon Stock organised them into an Order of Friars. By the end of 1291 there were no more Franks in Outremer.

Epilogue

The military Orders were left without occupation. The Templars loitered aimlessly in Cyprus and Venice while the King of France plotted to seize their extensive endowments. In 1308 they were suppressed; after their chief officers, under torture, had confessed to all the crimes alleged against them. Even in France these confessions were regarded with scepticism; in England, Spain and Portugal they were frankly disbelieved. But Templar endowments were divided between secular rulers and the Order of the Hospital, to the general satisfaction.

The Teutonic Knights transferred their energies to the coast of the Baltic, where they conquered the pagan enclave between Poland and Brandenburg. In the 16th century a majority of them turned Lutheran; and the land they ruled, under the name of Prussia, was merged with the Electorate of Brandenburg.

The Knights of the Hospital turned to naval warfare. From their base at Rhodes, and later from Malta, their galleys attacked infidel corsairs throughout the Levant. They continued to rule Malta and fight the infidel until Napoleon and the French Jacobins conquered them in 1800. As a sovereign and international Order they still persist, with their headquarters in Rome. But they have returned to their original task of the care of the sick; today they manage hospitals, but they no longer wage war on the infidel.

Since 1291 there have been many Crusades, and the movement has never been formally wound up. In theory, the Pope might preach another Crusade tomorrow. But these later Crusades were fought to push back invading Turks, or to quell the Barbary corsairs.

The hope of liberating Jerusalem lingered long in Christian minds. King Henry IV of England was comforted by a prophecy that he would die in Jerusalem (he died in the Jerusalem Chamber of the Palace of Westminster). When Christopher Columbus discovered gold in the New World his first thought was that this wealth might be used to equip an army to free Jerusalem; and Queen Isabella of Castile supported the idea. But there was always a local war to be settled before the Christians could set out again for Outremer. Never since 1291 has an army been assembled with the specific objective of freeing the Holy Places of Palestine from the infidel.

Perhaps Godfrey of Bouillon was right. The Kingdom of Jerusalem as it existed before Hattin was too weak to stand as an ordinary secular state; there was just not enough agricultural land to support the knights necessary for its defence. The barons of the land were too few; and they could not always be expected, as ordinary laymen, to put the defence of the Holy Places before their own secular interests. It was bad luck that the Orders came into existence after the Kingdom, and that there were three of them. A single Order, directly ruled by the Pope, might have kept Jerusalem a Christian city to this day.

But while Outremer existed it was a good place to live in. Feudal knights, with a clean slate to work on, founded a realm where justice and freedom flourished. As often happens, the wicked were too strong for them. But they did their best until they were beaten, and no man can do more.

Index of Principal Persons and Places

Index

Baldwin IV, King of Jerusalem, son of King Amalric, his leprosy, 136; succession, 138; character, 138; regency, 138–9; assumes power, 143; victory at Montgisard, 144–5; appoints regent, 146; campaign against Saladin, 146; revokes regency, 148; last years and succession problem, 149; death, 150

Baldwin (of Montferrat) V, King of Jerusalem, birth, 140; accession, 150; death, 150. Other references, 145, 160

Baldwin, Archbishop of Canterbury, joins Third Crusade, 174; and the marriage of Princess Isabella, 175; death, 175

Baldwin, Count of Flanders, joins Fourth Crusade, 203; becomes first Latin Emperor of Constantinople, 209

Baldwin II, Latin Emperor of Constantinople, 222

Balian, Lord of Ibelin, marriage to Maria Comnena, 140; escapes from Hattin, 159–60; holds Tyre against Saladin, 161; defends Jerusalem, 163; negotiates surrender of Jerusalem, 164–5. Other references, 148, 149, 150, 151, 158, 168, 175, 193

Balliol, Roussel de, 18, 21, 26

Bartholomew, Peter, finds Holy Lance, 64; fresh revelations, 69; death, 73

Beirut, and First Crusade, 74; Andronicus Comnenus Lord of, 133; yields to Saladin, 161; Saladin offers to cede, 192; taken by Amalric II, 201. Other references, 119, 146, 167, 195, 199, 224, 225

Berengaria of Navarre, betrothal to Richard I, 181; marriage and coronation in Cyprus, 183–4

Bertrand, Count, 118, 120

Biandrate, Count of, leads Lombard Crusade, 84

Bibars, Emir, at Mansourah, 236; murders and succeeds Sultan of Egypt, 242; campaign in Outremer, 243; captures and destroys Antioch, 243–4; truces with Kingdom of Jerusalem, 244, 247; and Prince Edward, 248; death, 249

Bohemond I, Prince of Antioch, as Count Bohemond fitzRobert, joins First Crusade, 31; passage to Asia Minor, 34–5; at Dorylaeum, 44–6; at Antioch, 55–69; becomes Prince of Antioch as Bohemond I, 70; expels Greek Patriarch and appoints Latin, 82–3; captured, 83; ransom and return to Antioch, 89; defeat at Harran, 87–90; return to Europe, 90; campaign against Alexius, 90–2; retirement, marriage and death, 92; character, 92

Bohemond II, Prince of Antioch, accession, 92; coming of age and marriage, 98; death in battle, 99

Bohemond III, Prince of Antioch, accession, 122; repels Nureddin, 129–30; defeat and capture at Artah, 130; ransomed and seeks help from Empress, 131; and Andronicus Comnenus, 133; truce with Saladin, 151; further truce, 166; helps Richard I in Cyprus, 183. Other references, 146, 199, 201

Bohemond V, Prince of Antioch and Tripoli, ally of the Mongols, 242; Bibars and, 243

Bohemond, Count of Tripoli, disputes succession of Antioch, 201. Other reference, 199

Boniface, Marquis of Montferrat, leader of Fourth Crusade, 204; King of Salonica, 209; defeat and death, 210

Byzantium. See Constantinople

Cairo, occupied by Amalric, 131–2, 134; Shirkuh in, 134; unrest in, 144; Fourth Crusade and, 233–4, 236, 239. Other references, 15, 118, 130, 135, 147, 189

Cairo, Caliphs of, Hakim, 15; armed forces, 71–2; negotiates with Crusaders, 72–3; negotiates with Alexius, 73; wars with Baldwin I, 87–9; relations with Baghdad and Damascus, 118; weakness of, 125; appeals to Nureddin, 134; extinction, 135. Other reference, 25

Caliph, the, first appointed, 13; relations with Eastern Emperor, 14; office divided, 15. See also Baghdad, Caliphs of, and Cairo, Caliphs of

Charlemagne, Western Emperor, 15

Charles, King of Sicily, as Count of Anjou, at battle of Mansourah, 227; return to France, 239; defeats Con-

Index

Index

Index

Emperor Manuel and Conrad attack, 119; William II, King of, 170, 173; Richard I in, 180–1; Frederick II and, 221, 222; Charles of Anjou and, 244, 248

Sidon, yielded to Saladin, 161; captured by King Amalric II, 201; Templars abandon, 252. Other references, 96, 174, 199

Sivas, Turks of, capture Bohemond, 83–4, 89; attack County of Edessa, 100. Other reference, 90

Stephen, Count of Blois, joins First Crusade, 30; deserts from Antioch, 62; joins Lombard Crusade, 84; death, 88. Other references, 36, 44, 67

Tancred, joins First Crusade, 31; in Cilicia, 47, 50–1; at Arqa, 72–3; at siege of Jerusalem, 75–7; Prince of Galilee, 81; regent of Antioch, 83; second regency of Antioch, 90; death, 92. Other references, 35, 70, 89

Tarsus, occupied by Crusaders, 50–1. Other references, 86, 87.

Taticius, 43–4, 47, 48, 57–8

Temple, in Jerusalem, destroyed by Romans, 11; in siege of Jerusalem, 76–7; Frederick II visits, 226; Templars return to, 229

Temple, military order of, foundation, 94–5; Louis VII and Grand Master, 115; at siege of Ascalon, 132; rivalry with hospital, 134, 139, 228, 248; disaster at Springs of Cresson, 151–2; at Hattin, 158–60; yield Gaza, 161–2; at Arsouf, 188; and Cyprus, 190, 194; and Frederick II, 225–6; regain the Temple, 229; losses at La Forbie, 230; with St Louis, 235, 239; fall of Safad and Beaufort, 243; at Acre, 250–2; abandon Sidon, 252; suppressed, 253. Other references, 110–11, 125, 135, 138, 144, 149, 150, 156, 157, 164, 173, 190, 192, 199, 217, 227, 228, 249

Teutonic Knights, military order, founded, 201; and Frederick II, 225, 226; loss at La Forbie, 230; at Acre, 250–1; move to the Baltic, 253. Other references, 222, 249

Tiberias, siege of, 156–8; surrender, 161; returned to Christians, 229; retaken by Egyptians, 230. Other reference, 151

Tripoli, city of, siege and capture, 89; absorbed by Antioch, 199; besieged by Bibars, 243; siege and fall, 249–50. Other references, 161, 170

Tripoli, County of, set up by Raymond, 82; recognises King Baldwin II, 94; invaded by Nureddin, 129–31; truce with Saladin, 151; joined to Antioch, 199. Other references, 89, 161, 242

True Cross, found 12; rescued from Persians, 13; leads army of Jerusalem, 156; captured at Hattin, 160; negotiations for return, 186–7, 190, 198. Other references, 157, 186, 187, 216, 220

Tunis, St Louis's Crusade to, 236, 244–5

Turanshah, Sultan of Egypt, Chapter XIX passim

Tyre, captured by Venetians, 94; held against Saladin, 161; saved by Conrad of Montferrat, 168; abandoned by garrison, 252. Other references, 163, 166, 171, 172, 174, 178, 179, 181, 184, 193, 199, 201, 212, 241, 250

Urban II, Pope, council at Piacenza, 20–1; council of Clermont, 21–3; death, 77. Other reference, 81

Venetians, position in Outremer, 94; quarrels with Pisans and Genoese, 202, 241, 248; Chapter XVI passim; at siege of Tripoli, 249; at fall of Acre, 252. Other references, 81, 129, 162, 246

Zengi, Chapter VIII passim